# ST.
# DE

St. Francis de Sales
1567-1622
Doctor of the Church

# ST. FRANCIS DE SALES

## A BIOGRAPHY OF
## THE GENTLE SAINT

*By*

Louise M. Stacpoole-Kenny

TAN BOOKS AND PUBLISHERS, INC.
Rockford, Illinois 61105

Nihil Obstat:      J. N. Strassmaier, S.J.
                     Censor Deputatus

Imprimatur:     Edmund Canon Surmont
                     Vicar General
                     Westminster
                     October 11, 1909

Originally published by R. & T. Washbourne, Ltd., London, and Benziger Bros., New York, in 1909, as *Francis de Sales: A Study of the Gentle Saint.*

Reprinted in 2002 by TAN Books and Publishers, Inc. Footnotes added by the Publisher, 2002.

ISBN 0-89555-709-6

Library of Congress Control No.: 2001-132397

Cover illustration: From a painting by an unknown 17th-century artist. Turin.

Printed and bound in the United States of America.

TAN BOOKS AND PUBLISHERS, INC.
P.O. Box 424
Rockford, Illinois 61105
2002

*Vive Jesus!*

## PUBLISHER'S PREFACE

IT has been said that St. Francis de Sales has no enemies. The author of this delightful little biography calls him "the Gentle Saint"; he is also commonly known as "the Gentleman Saint."

But St. Francis de Sales had brains as well as heart, and one must not allow his winning personality to obscure the fact that he was very intelligent and in fact one of the greatest men of his day. At the university he simultaneously pursued degrees in law and in theology. He was examined in both fields, yet the examiners declared they had never before met anyone so well prepared. St. Francis de Sales is in fact one of only thirty-three Doctors of the Church during nearly 2000 years.

St. Francis' reconversion of the Calvinists of the Chablais region of France is one of the great missionary stories in the history of the Church. Figures vary, but they reach as high as 72,000 Calvinists converted back to the True Faith in just 4 years—almost the entire Chablais. Yet these people and their leaders had previously been notably hostile to Catholicism, and St. Francis had been given no resources to work with, not even a roof over his head.

In addition, the Saint co-founded one of the great religious orders in the Church—the nuns of the Visitation—and he wrote a book that has become one of the three or four most popular Catholic classics: *An Introduction to the Devout Life.* One Pope expressed the hope that that volume might be read "by all." St. Francis' *Treatise on the Love of God* is also a spiritual classic and is built on the firm foundations of scholastic theology. Plus, *The Catholic Controversy* reveals on every page the author's great command of Church history, theology and biblical prophecy.

Perhaps the best assessment of our Saint comes from another Saint, his contemporary: St. Vincent de Paul stated that St. Francis de Sales was the best Christian he had ever met. This comes from a fellow Frenchman who was himself dubbed "the Father of his Country" because of his great accomplishments for war-torn 17th-century France. St. Vincent even stated that at one low point of serious illness in his own life, his most comforting thought was of how clearly God's infinite goodness was reflected in the Bishop of Geneva, St. Francis de Sales. "For if a man can be so good," he said to himself, "how good You must be, O my loving Creator, how sweet and how gracious!"* It is the story of this good man that the present little volume sets out to tell.

---

*\**St. Francis de Sales: A Testimony by St. Chantal*, newly edited in translation with an introduction by Elisabeth Stopp (Hyattsville, Maryland: Institute of Salesian Studies, 1967), p. 96.

# CONTENTS

# ST. FRANCIS DE SALES

# CHAPTER I

## *IN WILD SAVOY*

On Thursday, August 21, 1567, between nine and ten in the evening, Francis de Sales was born in the old Château de Sales, in a tiny room called "la chambre de St. François d'Assisi," on account of a picture of the seraphic Father that hung over a small altar.

Seven years previously his father, François, Seigneur de Nouvelles, had married the young daughter of Melchior de Sionnay, Seigneur de la Vallière, de la Thuile, and de Boisy. She was heiress to all these vast possessions ; consequently, on her marriage she was given the broad lands of Boisy, her husband taking the title with the estate, so they were generally known as Monsieur and Madame de Boisy.

On a glorious afternoon in August I visited the old château ; but, indeed, only the room in which our Saint was born remains—it is now a small chapel. Such a tiny room ! I thought of that other birth-chamber far away in the town on the Avon, in leafy Warwickshire, where the greatest of poets and dramatists first saw the light—he who was and is the poet of all time, and in whose marvellous plays all sorts and conditions of men can find that which best they love. Even so is Francis, the Saint of all time. Just as much can we, the children of this hurrying twentieth century, find balm and consolation in his writings as, in the sixteenth, did those zealous, ardent men and women to whom his wonderful letters were addressed, for whose instruction he penned the " Devout Life " and the " Love of God."

The brilliant August sunshine flooded the little chapel, as I pictured to myself, that day, centuries ago, when Francis de Sales, an infant only a few hours old, received the holy water of Baptism. The day was probably just as radiantly fine, and certainly the high mountains of Savoy looked as beautiful, and the trees as fresh and green as when M. de Boisy, with his first-born son in his arms, looked out through the narrow casement, and carried his precious burden carefully wrapped up down the long road to the little parish church of Thorens.

His sponsors were his grandmother, Mme. de la Flèchere—she having, on the death of Mme. de Boisy's father, married again—and her brother-in-law, Dom Francis de la Flèchere, Prior of the Benedictine Monastery of Saligny.

The child received the name of Francis Bonaventure, but he was always called Francis—not only because it was his father's name, but in honour of his great patron and favourite Saint, the gentle seraph of Assisi.

Then, the ceremony over, how joyous is the home-coming! The newly-baptized baby is placed in his young mother's arms; she, in her pride and gladness, feels a strange, overmastering presentiment that her boy will one day be a Prince of the Church, a Saint, holy and learned beyond compare :

"And thou, child, shalt be called the Prophet of the Most High. To give knowledge of salvation to His people unto the remission of their sins. To enlighten them that sit in darkness and in the shadow of death. To direct our feet unto the way of peace."

Certainly "the child grew and was strengthened in spirit." Many writers tell us little anecdotes of his childhood and early youth, illustrating his gentleness and docility, his love of prayer and solitude, the rapidity with which he learned the Catechism, taught him by his devoted mother and the good M. Déage, a holy clergyman who, when he was quite a small boy, became his adviser and tutor, a position he retained until Francis had himself become a priest.

Yet we are rather pleased to learn that he was not quite angelic—there were little faults, little vanities, even a love of goodies. He would not have been a lovable, human boy if at so early an age he had not occasionally got into mischief; and, above all things, at all times he was decidedly human. There is a distinctly interesting story about a stolen visit to the kitchen and the devouring of hot cakes. They were scaldingly hot and burned his fingers horribly, but he grasped them firmly, and ate them all up with great relish. Afterwards he honestly confessed his disobedience, for he had been strictly forbidden to go into the cook's department.

At seven years of age he was sent to the College of La Roche, and two years later, M. de Boisy having, for political reasons, to leave the Château de Sales and go to reside at the Château de Brens in the Chablais, Francis was placed at the college at Annecy, the faithful M. Déage in attendance.

Here he devoted himself to prayer and study, spending long hours over his Latin exercises, and made great progress in the " humanities "—a rather curious expression, and one we never use now, nor do most of us know its meaning. As far as I can make out, it meant a general knowledge of literature and the classics, and the cultivation of mind and body necessary to enable a man to take his place in the world as soldier, courtier, or senator.

His work finished, Francis flew off to the nearest church, gathering together as many as possible of his companions, so that the good folk of the town, gazing after the little band on their way to visit Our Lord in the Blessed Sacrament, and admiring the fair beauty of the young de Sales, would cry out: " Comme il est beau, qu'il est aimable ! Il est l'ange visible de la patrie ; et si Dieu lui conserve la vie, il sera un jour l'ornement et la gloire de sa famille " (" How beautiful and how good he is !  He is indeed the visible angel of our country ; and if God preserves his life, he will one day be the ornament and the glory of his family ").

When ten years old he had the great happiness of making his first Holy Communion.  As I knelt in that quaint old church of the Dominicans I pictured to myself the scene.  It is no longer an almost deserted church.  It is filled with an oddly attired congregation—men in hose and doublet, with clanking swords and long curling locks ; women in coif and stomacher, with curious head-gear completely hiding their hair ; peasants dressed very much as they are now in most of the Swiss Cantons.  The Holy Sacrifice is being offered at a brilliantly-lit altar ; solemnly peal the deep notes of the organ, gradually growing lower and lower, until at last they die away, and naught is heard but the tinkle of the little bell as the priest turns round with the Sacred Host—" Domine, non sum dignus "— and the faithful approach the communion rails. Amongst them is a fair, blue-eyed boy, who, devoutly kneeling before the altar, for the first time receives his Lord.  One can fancy the ecstatic joy

that filled the soul of Francis, already a child
Saint, one who had never lost, was never to
lose, his baptismal innocence, but was to pass
through life uncontaminated by the world, un-
scathed through the fires of trials and temptations.

It was in this same church, years afterwards,
that it pleased Our Lord to give a signal manifes-
tation of His love for His chosen servant.

The face of the Saint while preaching became
transfigured, shining with a heavenly light, while
burning words fell from his lips, touching even
the hardest hearts, and all recognized even in his
own country the Seer and Prophet.

From the day on which he received for the first
time the Holy Communion his desire to consecrate himself to God increased. But his father
had planned out quite a different career for him.
He wished him to become an advocate and a
member of the Senate of Savoy. However, as
receiving the tonsure meant very little in those
days—not even binding the recipient to wear
the ecclesiastical dress or put aside the sword,
and certainly in no way compelling the final
taking of Holy Orders—M. de Boisy allowed his
son to go through the ceremony at Clermont in
1578.

In actual years Francis was only just eleven,
but so wise and learned, so sedate and saintly,
that it was difficult to realize he was so very
young. Yet was the old Adam not yet quite

dead, for it cost him bitter pangs to part with his beautiful golden curls. He wept copiously, and it was only after a desperate struggle that he quietly resigned himself to lose his much-admired hair; but finally he conquered the repugnance of nature, and when the fatal moment arrived, without even a sigh, he placidly allowed the scissors to shear off his precious locks.

From her place Mme. de Boisy watched the pitiless steel as it cut off one by one those dear curls, and doubtless, the ceremony over, and the crowd dispersed, she picked them up and carried them home; and, gaining the solitude of her own room, she wept her woman's tears, prayed her woman's prayers, as she gazed on their golden splendour, so silk-like and soft—the fair hair of her own boy. She realized that he was no longer hers only. He was now consecrated to the Most High. He had taken the first step on the thorny path of sacrifice and renunciation, a path that would lead far from home and from her loving arms; for she knew, though her husband did not, that Francis was determined to become a priest, and that no obstacles would make him turn aside from the career he had chosen. She rejoiced that her son should serve the Lord of Hosts, yet was her heart torn with anguish at the thought of losing him; but she remembered that she herself had offered her unborn child to the Lord when she knelt before the holy winding-sheet at Annecy[*]a short time before

[*]At that time, the "Shroud of Turin" was at Annecy, France.

his birth. God had taken her at her word, had accepted the gift, and she would not even allow a wish to withdraw it to sully the generosity of the oblation. " Blessed be His Most Holy Name !"

# CHAPTER II

## FROM *LA VILLE LUMIÈRE* TO THE *ETERNAL CITY*

WHEN Francis was thirteen, in 1580, M. de Boisy resolved to send him to Paris to study at the University. He wished him to reside at the College of Navarre, as it was to it all the young nobles of Savoy were sent; but it had not too good a reputation, the students were a bit wild, and the discipline lax. Francis feared he would be led away by wicked companions and become depraved, so he entreated his father to let him go instead to the College of the Jesuits. Then, as always, he had a particular affection and reverence for the sons of St. Ignatius, and he had heard that at their college the spirit of piety and of holiness reigned supreme. His mother agreed with him. She, too, ardently desired to place her son with the *Saints Pères*, feeling that under their care he would be secure from danger to soul or body. With some difficulty she succeeded in persuading her husband, but finally he gave a reluctant consent.

As usual, the faithful M. Déage accompanied Francis. No sooner arrived in the gay city, instead of amusing himself, he started studying at once with his usual energy, attending lectures, reading, writing, and giving most of his spare time to prayer and works of charity. He communicated every week, heard daily Mass, frequently visited the Blessed Sacrament; but in spite of his fervour and devotion, he was for six weeks the prey of a most terrible temptation to despair. His soul was torn with anguish; he felt he was predestined to be lost for ever; but even when this horrible idea possessed his mind, it was not fear of the pains of Hell that tormented him: no, it was the appalling dread that in that place of everlasting misery he would blaspheme his God. 'O Jesus,' he would cry, 'if I am doomed never to see You in Your Heavenly Kingdom, grant at least, oh, dearest Lord, that I may love You while I remain in this world. O Mary, Mother of God, shall I then never behold you? Pray, beloved Mother, that even when burning in the fires of Hell I may never blaspheme you or your adorable Son. If it is His most holy will that I must lose Him for eternity, may His will be done; but at least grant that I may love Him and praise Him, even when damned."

So he wept and prayed, and at last that dear Mother came to his aid. Kneeling before her statue in the Church of St. Étienne des Gris, he devoutly recited the *Memorare*, and even as he prayed the evil that was like a hideous leprosy fell from his soul, the frightful torment ceased, his thoughts grew serene and tranquil, his troubled mind was at rest, and he blessed the Name of the Lord.

Thus saved through the intercession of the Blessed Virgin, his gratitude to her was unbounded; he promised to recite the Rosary every day in her honour, and frequently to repeat the *Memorare*.

He spent five years in Paris, studied theology under John Suarez, Greek under Père Sirmond, and Hebrew under Genebrard. In order to finish his education, M. de Boisy decided to send him to the University of Padua to take out his degree of jurisprudence. So in 1586 he set out, travelling through the most famous cities of France, until he reached his own home in the Chablais. He had never visited the Château de Brens in all these long years. His mother could scarcely recognize her son in this tall lad of eighteen; and he, on his side, found his three brothers tremendously grown. They were called Galloys, Jean-François, and Louis—fine boys, with a great admiration for their eldest brother, particularly Louis, who from the first reverenced him and consulted him on all points. He was a gentle boy, studious and wise beyond his years; Jean-François, on the contrary, was a bit rough, and easily lost his temper. Of Galloys we hear but little, though afterwards he succeeded his father as Seigneur de Boisy, and was known in the country as the Peace-maker. Of the other two and of himself François used to remark: "We three make a splendid salad dressing—Jean François is the vinegar: he is so strong and pungent; Louis is so wise: he is the salt; *ce bon gros* François is the oil, so much he loves gentleness and sweetness."

It was a sad day for the loving mother and the fond brothers when he had to set out on his long journey to Padua; but M. de Boisy was determined that his heir should receive the education due to his birth and rank, and he still cherished the hope that Francis, having been called to the Bar, would become a senator. So, notwithstanding the severity of the winter, he set out, accompanied, as usual, by the good M. Déage. They crossed the Alps in safety, and arrived at their destination early in 1587.

At Padua, Francis studied Roman law under Guy Panciroli, one of the most famous professors of his time. Needless to say, our Saint devoted himself with ardour to his studies, working day and night; but, knowing that the care of his soul and conscience was more important than the mere training of his mind, he sought a wise and learned director to help him in the task. He at last selected Père Possevin, S.J., a saintly and discreet man, who assisted him to decide his vocation. He had never really wavered in his intention to embrace the ecclesiastical state, but out of deference to his father's views, he once more weighed the pros and cons, entreating Père Possevin, S.J., to pray that he might know God's will.

After long meditation and mature deliberation, the prudent Jesuit told him there could be no doubt on the subject—that it was indeed his vocation to enter the priesthood. Going further even, he prophesied that his humble penitent would one day be a Prince of the Church and a bulwark of the Faith.

Francis was so gentle and sweet-tempered, so courteous and considerate, that a few of his comrades took it into their heads that all this affability and sweetness was due to weakness and timidity. They therefore resolved to make him appear as a contemptible coward, and so ruin the influence for good he was gradually obtaining over the greater number of the students.

One night they lay in wait for him, expecting that as soon as they rushed out and attacked him he would fly for his life, shouting for mercy. Exactly the opposite happened. Instead of his running away from them, it was he, one against many, who put them to flight. No sooner had he perceived their intent than, drawing his sword, with a few vigorous thrusts—he was a splendid swordsman — he not only disarmed them, but brought them to their knees, praying him to have compassion on them, as their injurious words and attempted blows had only been intended as a joke. Francis smiled grimly. He quite understood the whole affair, but, with his usual gentleness, he generously forgave them.

Francis was a very handsome and graceful, as

well as skilful and intrepid, cavalier. He could dance as well as he could fence, and was remarkable for his courtly and polished manners, his agreeable conversation and gallant demeanour.

He was so noticeable a personage that he attracted the attention of a fair but frail Princess, who fell wildly in love with him, and sent a friend to request him to visit her. But Francis was true to the one beloved mistress he had chosen as his Queen, Mary Immaculate, and no earthly loveliness could charm the eyes that revelled in her spiritual beauty. She was his Mother, his Protectress, his Queen. It was before her altar in Paris he had made a vow of chastity, and to that vow he remained faithful all his life. Not by the slightest word or deed would he sully the purity of the soul he had consecrated to her service. So he turned a deaf ear to the solicitations of the luckless ambassador, who went so far and was so foolish as to offer him jewels and gold to induce him to go and see the enamoured Princess.

"Let your Princess keep her treasures; I will none of them nor of her. Go !" he commanded.

The austerity of his life, the long hours he devoted to study and prayer, his excessive mortifications and severe fasts, at last affected his superb health. He lost his appetite, grew as thin as a skeleton; he could not sleep, and at last completely broke down, and was soon dangerously ill. For days his life hung in the balance. Poor M. Déage was in despair. He wearied Heaven and the doctors to save the life of his dear pupil; but in the end, resigning himself to the inevitable, he broke the news to Francis that there was no hope of his recovery—that, in fact, he was on his death-bed, and had better prepare to receive the Last Sacraments.

Unutterable joy filled the soul of the holy youth. He burst forth into canticles of praise and of divine love, and, selecting the most beautiful passages of Holy Scripture, he cried in a clear, melodious voice:

"How lovely are Thy tabernacles, O Lord of Hosts! My soul longeth and fainteth for the courts of the Lord.

"Blessed are they that dwell in Thy house, O Lord; they shall praise Thee for ever and ever.

"O God of Hosts, hear my prayer; give ear, O God of Jacob.

"I will praise Thee, O Lord my God, with my whole heart, and I will glorify Thy Name for ever.

"For Thou, O Lord, art my hope; Thou hast made the Most High thy refuge. I will sing unto the Lord as long as I live. I will sing praise unto my God while I have my being.

"May His holy will be done in life and in death!"

Then, turning to his good old tutor, "I wish," he tells him, "my body to be given to the dissectors. It has been useless living; dead, I hope it may be of some use, and may prevent fights and rows."

He alluded to the terrible practice, not only of the medical students, but of the surgeons, of tearing corpses from the tomb to dissect them, and the consequent quarrels between them and the relatives and friends of the dead, who tried to protect the bodies of their loved ones from desecration.

But Heaven was not yet to throw wide its portals to receive this saintly soul. Many years of life were yet before him ere, the combat over, the victory won, he was to enter into the joy of the Lord. Thus it was that when at the last gasp he most unexpectedly recovered, and very soon was once again his old bright, healthy, energetic self.

To make up for lost time, he set to work with redoubled zest, consecrating himself with fresh fervour to the service of God and of His Blessed Mother, by whose powerful intercession he had now recovered the health of the body, as in Paris he had received the health of the soul. His friend and fellow-student, M. de Challes, tells us : " Francis had more virtues than were necessary for canonization, and the proof is that he had the gift of prophecy. He foretold to me that I should marry and have children, and when I asked him, ' And you ?' he replied, ' God destines me for the altar.' "

Thus confident of his sublime vocation, he

endeavoured to prepare himself for it, not only by the sanctity of his life, but by the cultivation of his mind. He studied theology as well as jurisprudence, and excelled in both these abstruse sciences. Soon he was ready to take his degree.

In September, 1591, it was conferred on him by Panciroli at the University of Padua. As not only the professors and students, but the citizens as well, revered him as a Saint and esteemed him as a genius, the ceremony of conferring his degree was a particularly brilliant one. All wished to honour the new graduate. Nor was he wanting in gratitude to his Alma Mater. In an eloquent speech he thanked the Bishop, the Rector, the Professors, saying : " If I know anything it is to you I owe it—to you in particular, Guy Panciroli, prince of jurisprudence, and I ask you to give me with your own hand the ring, the cap, and the privileges of the University."

Panciroli then placed the crown and cap on his head, and conferred on him the degree of Doctor, remarking :

" The University finds in you, Francis de Sales, the sublimest qualities of head and heart ; and it is with the greatest pleasure it receives you among its graduates."

Francis had completed his education, but before returning to Savoy he visited Rome. We can imagine the devotion with which he prayed at the tomb of the Holy Apostles, and the ardour with which he went from shrine to shrine, from church to church; with what joy he knelt at the foot of the Crib of Bethlehem in the Church of Santa Maria Maggiore. Nor did he neglect to visit the Roman remains, the Colosseum, the ruined baths, all the wonders of ancient, of more recent—in fact, of all—ages, that make Rome the Eternal City.

Finally, having satisfied both his devotion and his curiosity, he returned home by way of Loreto and Venice. At Loreto he was filled with joy at the sight of the Holy House of Nazareth, in which Jesus, Mary, and Joseph lived and worked and prayed for so many years.

Once more he consecrated himself to God and the Blessed Virgin, renewing his vow of chastity; then, prostrate on the ground, he kissed it fervently, watering it with his tears, while burning words of divine love broke from him.

To the good M. Déage it seemed that his face became like that of an angel, shining and transformed by the fire of the Spirit; and from that time he treated his pupil with the greatest respect and veneration, probably repenting of his impetuosity in Paris, when he used to box the boy's ears without rhyme or reason, apparently only to amuse himself by giving vent to an irritable temper. Francis put up with the cuffs with good humour, for he always cherished a sincere affection for the good old man.

# CHAPTER III

## *A PRIEST OF GOD*

On a beautiful day in the spring of 1592 a gallant cavalier rode up to the old Château de Thuile, now the residence of M. and Mme. de Boisy. He was accompanied by a venerable, white-haired priest. Even before they dismounted the fond parents rushed forth to embrace the long-absent son—the mother eager, excited, breathless; the father equally excited, but slower and more dignified. Then the three brothers pressed round him, and Francis de Sales had some difficulty in recognizing in these tall, handsome lads the boys he had left some five years previously; and there was little Bernard, the youngest, shy and timid, and somewhat in awe of this stately young man.

He was now twenty-five, fair and debonair, with kind blue eyes, a winning smile, and a gentle, refined manner. He was an accomplished cavalier, could ride, fence, converse on every subject; for, knowing his father's wish that he should become *au fait* in all the accomplishments suited to his rank, he had endeavoured to perfect himself in worldly arts, believing that what is worth doing is worth doing well.

M. de Boisy was enchanted. Dreams of the future success and glory of this adored son flitted through his brain, and, as the first step in this brilliant career, he insisted on his going to Chambéry to be called to the Bar. There he met the man who was to be his lifelong friend, almost brother—Antoine Faure. He was an advocate and senator, and was distinguished for his ability and piety.

On November 24, 1592, Francis de Sales was admitted as an advocate by the Senate of Savoy.

When riding home through the forest of Sonay, a curious incident occurred. Francis was a splendid horseman, but nevertheless he was suddenly thrown to the ground. Even as he fell his sword slipped from the scabbard, and the scabbard from the baldrick, and sword and scabbard formed a cross on the ground. He remounted, but after a few moments was again thrown, apparently without any reason, for the road was a good one, and once more the cross was formed by the sword and scabbard. Again Francis sprang into the saddle, but had only gone a few paces when once more he fell to earth, his baldrick and scabbard slipping, as twice previously, and for the third time sword and scabbard formed a cross.

M. Déage, who, as usual, accompanied him, was astounded. He himself, though an infinitely less expert rider, had had no difficulty in retaining

his seat. Surely there was something supernatural in these three successive falls, and the
cross.

Yes, he and Francis felt it was a portent, and
that Our Lord thus wished to manifest to His
chosen servant that it was now time for him to
put aside not only his worldly dress, but to give
up for ever the life of a gallant and a nobleman,
to put away the sword, take up the cross, and
enlist under the standard of the Crucified.

But M. de Boisy was obdurate. Vainly did his
cousin, the Canon Louis de Sales, endeavour to
persuade him to allow his son to embrace the
ecclesiastical state; vainly did Francis plead his
ardent longing to consecrate himself completely
to the service of God, urging that it was no new
idea, but that since his childhood he had wished
and prayed to become a priest. Mme. de Boisy
added her entreaties, representing to her husband
that it was clear that their son's vocation was
inspired by Heaven, and that it would be wrong
—indeed, sinful—to oppose him; but even her
influence failed to induce the old noble to give his
consent.

He was resolved that his eldest-born should
inherit his lands and honours. He conferred on
him the title of Seigneur de Villaroget, at the
same time giving him the lands appertaining to it.
These possessions, with the title, were held by
the eldest son of the house. Not content with
thus endowing him with worldly goods and

honours, M. de Boisy now wished to marry him to Mdlle. de Suchet, the fair daughter of the Seigneur de Végy. This charming girl was young, well-dowered, pretty, and attractive. She lived with her parents at Sallanches.

Father and son visited her several times; but though Francis treated her with the greatest courtesy and deference, enjoyed her society, and admired her, yet he absolutely refused to become her husband, telling M. de Boisy that he would never marry.

Failing in his matrimonial schemes, the old man sought to persuade his son to accept the office of Senator at the Court of Savoy. This distinction was pressed on Francis by the Prince, and it required great strength of mind to refuse, especially as M. de Boisy insisted on his accepting it.

However, Christ Our Lord did not abandon His chosen servant. When things were at their darkest and Francis was almost in despair, his tender heart torn between the duty he owed his parent and the duty he owed his God, a way was found to soften and conciliate the stern father, and to enable the son to follow unopposed his sublime vocation.

The Provost of the Chapter of Geneva died, and the Canon Louis de Sales, having consulted the venerable Bishop Claude de Granier, travelled to Rome and solicited the Pope to confer this dignity upon his cousin Francis.

Returning to Annecy, he hastened to interview.

M. de Boisy, telling him that this was the highest dignity—next, in fact, to that of Bishop—and that he should no longer stand in his son's way, now that the designs of Providence were so clearly shown.

He had a tough fight, but finally triumphed. M. de Boisy consented that Francis should accept the offer and should follow his call to the sacred ministry. Giving him his blessing, the good old soldier cried: "May God for ever bless you, my son! It is He Who has inspired you, and in His Name I give you my paternal benediction."

Many months previously Mme. de Boisy had with her own hands made a soutane for her best-beloved son, and now he put away for ever the sword and the gay dress of a noble, and donned the sombre black of a priest.

On the Feast of the Ascension, May 26, 1593, he was installed by the Chapter at Annecy, all welcoming their new Provost. Only doctors or nobles were admitted to this dignity: Francis de Sales was both, having received a brilliant degree at Padua and being descended from a long line of noble ancestors. His predecessor had also held the rank of Senator, and M. de Boisy entreated him to accept that office, but Francis absolutely refused.

"I feel," he said, "that God has inspired me to devote myself entirely to His service. He is my one and only Master, and He will brook no rival."

"Well, then," cried the poor father, decidedly

23

annoyed, "I see I only lose time arguing with you. Go then and serve God only."

Delighted at this command, he immediately quitted everything that savoured of the world, resigning the lands and title of de Villaroget. He commenced a retreat under the guidance of an old priest—M. Bouvard—who taught him his new duties, but was indeed surprised to find how well Francis already knew them. He understood and used the Breviary as though accustomed to it for years.

"The fact is," Francis told him, "that while I was at Padua I used to recite the Canonical Hours with the Theatines; and while M. Déage and I travelled together we always said the Holy Office.

There was no need for delay, so on June 18, 1593, Francis de Sales received Minor Orders from the hands of the saintly Claude de Granier; and four days later, on Saturday, the eve of the Feast of the Holy Trinity, he was made sub-deacon. He said afterwards:

"I was a prelate without ever being a subject. I would rather have been a simple cleric, rather have carried the holy water than the crozier."

On September 18 following he was made deacon, and on Saturday, December 15, 1593, he was ordained priest. His soul inflamed with Divine love, he prepared himself by prayer and fasting to celebrate his first Mass.

This great event took place on December 21,

the Feast of St. Thomas the Apostle, in the Cathedral of Annecy.

"From that day," says Père la Rivière, "he gave himself up to an interior and peaceful life; he became changed into another man. One saw it in his eyes, his speech, his manner, and there seemed something so angelic and Divine in his appearance that everyone was compelled by a gentle violence to esteem and love him."

## CHAPTER IV

### *A LIGHT TO THEM THAT SIT IN DARKNESS*

In the Cathedral at Annecy, nearest to the door, is a very old confessional, hacked and cut to pieces in places, perhaps by devout pilgrims.

It is the one in which Francis de Sales listened to so many tales of sorrow and of sin, consoling and comforting so many broken-hearted, world-weary souls. We know that he selected this confessional that the halt, the blind, and the infirm might find him without difficulty.

And here is the pulpit from which, while still only a sub-deacon, he preached his first sermon, at the express wish of the Bishop of Geneva, Mgr. de Granier. He prepared it for Corpus Christi, but Père Fodiri—a famous Franciscan preacher—arriving at Annecy, Francis entreated him to give the people the consolation of hearing him.

Consequently Francis did not preach until the octave. His sermon was perfectly prepared—he had given much time and study to its composition —but when the hour came he was seized with a fit of nervousness, trembled in all his limbs, and had scarcely strength to mount the pulpit.

There a numerous crowd were eagerly awaiting him. Recommending himself to God in a short but fervent prayer, he became at once calm, and forgetting everything but the sublime subject he had selected—the Blessed Eucharist—he electrified his audience by the strength and fervour of his language and the grace and clearness of his ideas. Many shed tears, and above all, his devoted mother, who felt that her hopes were indeed realized, and that her son was likely to become a guide and a helper to many.

Not so the father. M. de Boisy did not approve of his son's sermons. For one thing, he thought he preached far too often, and, for another, that his style was far too simple and unaffected. Years later Francis confided to Mgr. de Belley:

" I had the dearest and best father in the world, but he had passed the greater part of his life at the Court and camp, and he understood the ideas of a courtier and a soldier better than those of a priest or a confessor. When I was Provost I preached constantly and everywhere. I never refused to do so, 'tant m'était chère la parole de notre Seigneur' (so dear to me was the Lord's word).

" My father, hearing the bell ring for devotions, would inquire: 'Who is going to preach?' and the reply was always: 'Who should it be but your son, the Provost.' This annoyed him greatly, so much so that he remonstrated with me. 'Look here, Provost,' he said, 'you preach much too often; you make yourself too cheap. And then your sermons !—*grand Dieu !* no Latin, no Greek, no learned quotations. Your language is so simple and unstudied, a child could understand it. *Voyez-vous*, that is not the way the great men of my day used to discourse?' And so on, and so on."

But poor M. de Boisy had soon another and more serious grievance, for Francis volunteered to go on the mission to the Chablais to convert the heretics. This really was a terrible trial for the good old man, now nearly seventy years of age, as he remarked to Mgr. le Granier with tears in his eyes :

" I permitted my eldest son, who is the hope of our house and the staff of my old age, to devote himself to the Church as a confessor, but never will I consent that he should become a martyr."

The Bishop was touched by this deep grief, but Francis was unmoved. He was resolved to set out as soon as possible on his hazardous mission, taking with him only his cousin, Louis de Sales.

The necessity for the mission was that the southern side of the Lake of Geneva, known as the Chablais, had become estranged from the Catholic Church. In 1536 the Protestants of the Canton of Berne, taking advantage of the war between Charles III., Duke of Savoy, and Francis I. of France, had taken possession of the countries of Vaud, Gex, and Ternier, soon becoming masters of the Chablais as far as Thonon, dividing the conquered country into four districts—those of Gex, Gailliard, Thonon, and Ternier—establishing there their own religion, and suppressing the Catholic Faith. After thirty years Savoy recovered it, but did not restore Catholicism. In 1589 it was again seized by the Swiss; then the Duke once more obtained possession of it, it was again retaken by the Swiss; but they had finally, in 1593, to surrender the Chablais to Charles Emmanuel, Prince of Savoy.

Charles Emmanuel resolved to undertake the conversion of his people, mainly from political motives. He feared that as long as his subjects were of the same persuasion as the Swiss, they would naturally lean towards their co-religionists and snatch at every opportunity to free themselves from his authority.

Consequently he requested the Bishop of Geneva to send missionaries into the Chablais. For years the Bishops of Geneva had been unable to reside in or even to visit that city, and had had to remove to Annecy. There Claude de Granier held a meeting of the priests of the diocese, to consult on the best means of carrying out the Duke's wishes, and the Provost was the only one who volunteered to undertake the dangerous mission.

On September 9, 1594, Francis and Louis de Sales set out from Annecy on their hazardous journey. They left a mourning town. The good folk, while lost in admiration of their heroic courage, grieved for their departure, and shuddered at the thought of the perils their loved Provost and his cousin must encounter. He was going among a rude and lawless people—a people who had so maltreated Père Bouchert, who had gone among them at the order of the Bishop to preach the Word of God, that he remained only a very short time, and fled, partly because he feared to lose his life, partly because he despaired of doing any good.

The cousins soon arrived at the dear old home —the Château de Sales—once more the residence of M. and Mme. de Boisy. Here they spent a few days in prayer and meditation, preparing themselves for their great mission. They made general confessions, received the Holy Eucharist, and were ready to set out when M. de Boisy again endeavoured to dissuade his son.

"You are mad," he told him, "to go among those savages; they will cut you to pieces, and when you are dead you will be of no use to the Church. Much better stay quietly at Annecy, preach, celebrate the Holy Sacrifice, hear confessions, take care of your flock and of your poor old father."

All his arguments, and even threats, were useless. He quite refused to help Francis—not a penny would he give him; and as the Prince, while entreating and accepting their help, gave them no pecuniary aid, they would have had to set out utterly penniless, and without even a change of raiment, if the gentle mother had not come to their assistance. Mme. de Boisy supplied them with linen, clothes, money, etc. She could not give them much; but, as Francis observed, the Apostles had nothing.

He gave his priestly benediction with grateful fervour to his dear mother, who, though probably far more broken-hearted and far more afraid than the obdurate father, was still willing—nay, glad and proud—that her boy should devote himself so nobly to the service of God.

If it was His most holy will that this adored son should give his life for the conversion of sinners, *soit;* she was perfectly resigned. Once again she said, as in the old days when she wept over his shorn golden curls: "Blessed be His Holy Name!"

It was on the Feast of the Exaltation of the Holy Cross that the Provost and the Canon set out on their journey from the Château de Sales. They went on foot, without attendants, carrying small bags containing their clothes, a Bible, a Breviary, and Bellarmine's "Controversies."

After a long day's march, they arrived towards evening at the citadel of Allinges, in the heart of the Chablais, situated about six miles from Thonon, the principal town and the stronghold of Calvinism. The Baron d'Hermance was Governor of the fortress, having in his command a troop of Catholic soldiers. He was a faithful adherent of the Duke of Savoy and an old friend of the house of de Sales; therefore he greeted the cousins with effusion and warmth. Francis handed him two letters—one from the Duke of Savoy, ordering him to care for and to protect the missionaries, and the other from the Bishop of Geneva, very much to the same effect, but mentioning them by name.

D'Hermance insisted that they should rest, but on the following morning they got up at daybreak and celebrated Mass in the little chapel. Then they were ready to set out for Thonon.

"You must first inspect our fortress," the Baron said, taking them all over the citadel and showing them the cannon, remarking: 'But we shall no longer require them, if, with the help of God, you succeed in converting the heretics. Look at this superb view! From this terrace you can see the Lake of Geneva, the snow-capped mountains, the fertile valleys. Is it not beautiful?"

Francis only sighed deeply. Leaning on the parapet, he looked sadly forth over this fair land whose glorious beauty was ravaged by the signs of persecution—ruined churches; presbyteries and castles burned to the ground; crosses overthrown; gibbets erected instead: desolation everywhere. All this he saw from the height on which he stood, and he could not restrain his tears as he thought of the millions of souls plunged in the darkness of schism, separated from the True Church.

In the Chablais there were seventy-two parishes, containing 30,000 persons, and among them there were only 100 Catholics.

The holy Apostle groaned aloud, and covering his face with his hands, wept bitterly; then, turning to his cousin Louis, he said: "Let us hope, in the goodness of God, that He will bless our work, and that we shall be able to rebuild His sanctuaries, re-erect His altars, and gather the lost sheep into the true fold." He then consulted d'Hermance about the best means to pursue.

"Two things are absolutely necessary," the Baron informed him: "you must return to the fortress every night, and you must not attempt to say Mass in a heretic town. It would be uselessly risking your life; they would probably stone you, or cut you in pieces. No, my friend; content yourself for the present with preaching the Word of God at Thonon and in the neighbourhood. Celebrate Mass here, or in the church of Marin at the other side of the Drance: that little village has always remained true to the Faith. Then there is also the little chapel of St. Bernard, on the lakeside; it is in ruins, but we will get it repaired."

The cousins followed this sage advice, saying Mass every day at daybreak at the Château d'Allinges, and then going to Thonon. There were truly but few Catholics in that town, and the Calvinists would not listen to them. Not content with ignoring, they spread all sorts of evil reports about them, saying they were magicians, sorcerers, and wicked men. Nevertheless they persevered.

Generally Francis went to Thonon and Louis to the surrounding villages. They were not discouraged by the small number of their congregations, but tried in every way to win the hearts of the people. Francis made use of his knowledge of law and medicine to help them in every way, and was always ready to come to their aid; but this kindness and good-nature only infuriated them. They even threatened to kill the priests.

These reports reached the ears of the unhappy M. de Boisy. He was in despair. Surely this reckless son of his would perish, murdered by these butchers. He could stand it no longer. Francis must return to Annecy; so he sent a trusty servant with a horse to bring back the Provost, whether he would or no. Francis refused to leave his post; but, pitying the anxiety his father felt on his account, knowing that this anxiety and distress of mind had their root in the great love he bore him, the Provost sent back Canon Louis to calm the old man's fears, and also to ask for money and clothes, for they were quite at the end of their resources.

M. de Boisy was just as determined as his son. He refused to give them the least assistance, thinking that without help from him they would be compelled, *bon gré, mal gré*, to give up the mission.

Again Mme. de Boisy came to the rescue, promising Louis to do all in her power to aid her dearest son. She immediately sent off a trustworthy messenger with money, linen, and other necessaries. She did more. Knowing how it would cheer the lonely priest in his self-imposed exile to see a member of his own family, she sent his favourite brother Louis to visit him and give him all the home news. One can picture the meeting, the joy of Francis at seeing again his favourite brother, now a gallant cavalier and a polished courtier, attending at the Court of the Duke of Nemours, then at Annecy. Yet Louis was really unchanged; he was still the same unaffected, gentle, straightforward fellow, as devoted as ever to his saintly brother, and delighted at the chance of conversing with him.

He tells him of Jean-François, he of the biting tongue and sarcastic speech, now curbing his quick temper and preparing for the priesthood. Galoys and Bernard are helping the old lord to look after his broad lands and great possessions; and James, the youngest boy, had decided to become a Knight of the Order of St. John of Jerusalem.

Then, the two sisters—Gasparde the elder, was a stately and demure maiden, and little Jeanne, the youngest child, growing every day prettier and holier. Francis had himself baptized this little sister of his, and cherished a fatherly as well as brotherly affection for his own dear little girlie. How it must have delighted the loving heart of the gentle Saint to hear the latest news of the happy home circle, and to converse *à cœur ouvert* with Louis! It greatly encouraged him to know that his mother approved of and was ready to help his work, and that her courage never failed, not even when his life was in danger. Never once did she entreat him to return home. She realized that, having once put his hand to the plough, he was in honour bound, to say nothing of higher motives, to continue his work, and she did all in her power to assist him.

"When I preached in the Chablais," Francis afterwards told a Sister of the Visitation, "I wished I could learn a trade, so that I could earn something by the work of my hands; but I was so stupid I could only mend my garments. It is true, however, that while there I cost no one a farthing, for my good mother kept me supplied with all I required, sending secretly money and linen from the Château de Sales."

# CHAPTER V

## *A SOLDIER OF THE CROSS*

TRUTH is stranger than fiction, and if the hair-breadth escapes and thrilling adventures of Francis de Sales were related in a modern novel, most readers would shrug their shoulders and mutter: "What rubbish! So far-fetched! Too absurd!"

I often wonder if in later years the holy Bishop of Geneva ever narrated his adventures to the Nuns of the Visitation. Would his modesty allow him to do so? or would he in holy simplicity refer all to the glory of God, looking upon himself as a mere instrument in the hands of Providence?

> ". . . Of most disastrous chances,
> Of moving accidents, by flood and field;
> Of hair-breadth 'scapes i' the imminent deadly breach,
> Of being taken by the insolent foe . . .
> Wherein of antres vast and deserts idle,
> Rough quarries, rocks and hills whose heads touch heaven."

And they, like Desdemona,

> ". . . these things to hear
> Would Desdemona seriously incline;
> But still the house affairs would draw her thence
> Which ever as she could with haste despatch.
> She'd come again, and with a greedy ear
> Devour up my discourse. . . ."

Then, like the disciples of Emmaus, the quiet nuns would feel their hearts burn within them at the recital, recognizing in the humble narrator the hero and the Saint. They, too, would refer all to God, and would know that it was His mercy and goodness that shielded Francis. Yet would they thoroughly appreciate the courage and perseverance of the man who so generously co-operated with Divine grace.

I will not even attempt to write of all the numerous adventures of Francis de Sales. When I think of his life in the Chablais, St. John's verse, when writing of our Blessed Lord in the Gospel, comes to my mind: "But there are also many things which Jesus did, which, if they were written every one, the world itself, I think, would not be able to contain the books that should be written." Indeed, I feel the task of giving even a short account of the mission in the Chablais overpoweringly difficult. *Mais nous verrons.*

Let us get on *doucement, sans empressement,*[*] as Francis would himself advise, for he always disliked hurry, and recommended his penitents and friends to take things quietly, to progress slowly but steadily.

This, his favourite maxim, he practised himself, for it was by means of the most gentle persuasion that he endeavoured to convert the gloomy and stubborn Calvinists. The pamphlets which he wrote during his mission and caused to be distributed among the people breathe a spirit of sweet-

_____

*gently, without haste.

ness and gentleness, at the same time clearly and decidedly expounding the truths of the Catholic Religion.* The heretics, though they would not come to listen to his sermons, read these documents through curiosity ; but many found them so convincing that they desired to learn more of a doctrine that appealed, not only to their reason, but to their hearts. Therefore, by slow degrees, by twos and threes, they went to hear the discourses of the Provost and the Canon.

When the news of this straying of their flock reached the ears of the ministers, they became, if possible, more infuriated against the priests, and resolved to have them assassinated.

Several times they hired ruffians to attempt their lives, but particularly the life of Francis, believing that if he were once removed Louis would return to Annecy.

Many and miraculous were the escapes the de Sales had from these assassins, but on July 18 two bravos were employed more desperate and determined than their predecessors. These wretches lay in wait for Francis in the forest. His friends heard a report that his life was in danger, and entreated him to spend the night at Thonon ; but the Provost, remembering that he had an important letter to write, and that the papers relating to it were at the citadel, insisted on returning there. " He that dwelleth in the help of the Most High shall abide under the protection of the God of Heaven," he said to them.

39

*These pamphlets were later published together as a book entitled *The Catholic Controversy* (also known simply as *Controversies*).

Therefore, accompanied by two Catholics and by his devoted servant, George Rolland, he set out. Arrived at the foot of the Montagne des Allinges, the ruffians rushed on him, sword in hand. His followers threw themselves before him, drawing their weapons. But Francis, imitating the example of his Divine Master, cried : " Put up your swords ; I alone will go to these men who desire to take my life."

Advancing towards them, he looked them straight in the face, smiling a little and speaking gently to them ; and so noble was his expression, so calm and kind his manner, that these rough men fell at his feet, imploring him to pardon them, excusing themselves, saying it was the fault of the Calvinist ministers, who had bribed them to murder him, but that in future, not only would they refrain from attacking him, but would devote themselves to his service.

Francis forgave them readily, promising to remember their offer and to avail himself of it. Then he and his companions proceeded on their way to the Château d'Allinges.

No sooner had they arrived there than George Rolland rushed off to the Governor and related to him their perilous adventures. D'Hermance was much alarmed. He entreated Francis to take with him in future an escort of soldiers when going to Thonon—even five or six would be a protection— but the Saint resolutely refused.

" St. Paul and the Apostles," he said, " did not

employ soldiers to protect them. They used only the sword of the Divine Word against enemies far more formidable. With this weapon they overcame the demon and successfully combated the power of the Roman Emperors. They triumphed over the vanity of philosophers and the pride of the world, and established the religion of Jesus Christ on the ruins of paganism. I wish to follow their example. Confidence in God is worth more than a legion of soldiers, and if our dear Lord gives me the grace to shed my blood in His service, certes it would be a glorious end, but one I am all unworthy of."

The Governor did not know what to reply to this discourse. At the same time, he was determined to watch over the safety of the man who had been committed to his care ; so he secretly ordered five or six soldiers to follow Francis at a distance, but to keep him in view, and be ready to defend him if he were attacked.

George Rolland was not pleased with this arrangement, so he set off for the Château de Sales to give an account of the latest attack made on his son to M. de Boisy, and of the recklessness of Francis in continuing to risk his life. The good old seigneur was more terrified than ever. He was convinced that his son would be murdered if he remained any longer in the country of the heretics, who were evidently his sworn foes. He peremptorily ordered Francis to return at once to Annecy.

Francis replied, by the same courier, as follows:

"DEAR AND MOST HONOURED FATHER,

"If Rolland was your son instead of your valet, he would not have the cowardice to retreat; nor would he have made such a fuss over such a trifle, turning a slight encounter into a battle. The heretics certainly detest us, and would like to get rid of us, but they who doubt our courage wrong us even more. I entreat you, then, my father, not to attribute my perseverance to disobedience, but to believe me ever and always

"Your most respectful and dutiful son,

"FRANCIS."

This straightforward and courageous letter appealed to the old warrior. He appreciated his son's heroic courage. He himself had faced danger and death with a brave front and a dauntless heart in the service of an earthly Prince. The intrepidity and steadfastness of Francis de Sales triumphed over his father's fears. M. de Boisy was at last willing that his son should risk his life under the standard of the Cross.

From this time the old soldier no longer grumbled, no longer endeavoured to make Francis give up his sublime mission. On the contrary, he aided and encouraged him, even giving shelter at the château to homeless converts.

Mme. de Boisy rejoiced with a great joy at this change in her husband's opinions, and he and she and the brothers and sisters now united in giving every assistance to the soldier of the Cross.

## CHAPTER VI

### *THE APOSTLE OF THE CHABLAIS*

IN 1595 Francis de Sales resolved to take up his abode at Thonon. So few conversions had taken place, and so barren, apparently, were his labours, he thought it time to adopt a more vigorous plan, and, by being in the very stronghold of Calvinism, attack it root and branch. The Governor and the garrison were deeply grieved when they heard his decision.

"They will cut you to pieces *là-bas*," d'Hermance told him. "Much better remain on here, where we are all your friends. Think of my poor soldiers, too. They will relapse into their former bad habits if you are not here to look after them."

Francis smiled, but persevered in his resolution.

"As for the soldiers," he replied, "they are now good Christians. God will protect and guide them."

Francis had not only won the hearts of these rough warriors: he had also saved their souls alive. They who had formerly been renowned throughout the country as blasphemers, drunkards, duellists, and profligates, were now pious, quiet, God-fearing men, living together in peace, love, and harmony, frequenting the Sacraments regularly—models of temperance and virtue.

This transformation was due to our Saint. His sweetness and charity had touched their hearts. In particular one hardened old veteran was so moved by one of his most beautiful discourses that when it was finished he sought out Francis, and, entreating him to hear him, threw himself at the Saint's feet, crying out in his anguish :

"God will never pardon so great a sinner. There is no hope for me : my crimes are too many and too terrible."

Francis consoled and soothed him, and persuaded him to make a general confession.

With sobs and groans the poor man went through a long catalogue of sins. He had not approached the Sacrament of Penance since he was a boy, and now he was grey-haired. He had the numerous sins of a lifetime spent in dissipation to confess. Francis absolved him, and gave him for his penance one Pater and one Ave.

"What, my Father!" cried the astonished soldier, "do you wish me to be damned that you give me so light a penance? Think of the awful crimes I have just confessed to you; how can I atone?"

"My son," replied the gentle Saint, "confide in the mercy of God. His Precious Blood was shed for you and for all of us for the remission of our sins. His mercy is greater than all your iniquities. I will perform the rest of your penance myself."

" But that would not be fair, Father," the honest fellow said, "for you are innocent; I am the culprit."

Indeed, so penetrated was this brave soldier with the sense of his guilt, and so touched by the gentle kindness of his spiritual Father, that in a few weeks he came to Francis to tell him he had left the service, and intended to become a Carthusian monk. He was convinced that it was necessary for him to devote the rest of his life to prayer and penance to atone for his manifold transgressions.

Thus it was with lamentations and mourning that the gallant soldiers saw their beloved Father depart from the Citadelle d'Allinges to take up his abode in the midst of his enemies.

He found a home with an old and respected lady —Mme. du Fong—widow of a former Procurator of the Chablais and an old friend of the house of de Sales. While still at d'Allinges he used to take his meals at her house, and used to retire there to study and prepare his sermons. Naturally she was charmed to welcome him. The Calvinists were furious when they heard that this detested papist priest had actually come to live in their own town, the stronghold of their religion. Such audacity! But they would rid themselves once and for all of the pernicious fellow. This time there should be no mistake; sorcerer though he was, he should not escape them.

That night a band of fanatics entered Mme. du Fong's house. They searched it from cellar to garret for Francis de Sales, in order to assassinate him. He was praying in his own room when he heard them break in, whispering together and growling maledictions in low tones. He continued quietly at his devotions, and though they entered his room and ransacked it, they did not perceive him. Some writers say that God made him invisible to the eyes of his enemies. Others aver that he was hidden in a secret nook, prepared for him by the pious widow.

At any rate, they did not find him, and they went off, cursing and swearing and declaring that he was a magician and in league with the devil. But the devout Catholics of Thonon thanked God, saying: "We need no longer fear the fury of the wolves, now that our good Pastor is among us. God will preserve him from the snares of the heretics."

Now that he was settled among his flock, Francis resolved to celebrate Holy Mass every day. As he could not yet say it at Thonon, he crossed the Drance every morning in order to offer the Holy Sacrifice in the Church of St. Étienne, near the little village of Marin.

In January, 1596, the bridge spanning the river was carried away by a terrific flood, and the only way to get over was to crawl across a plank. Soon this became so slippery that it was at the risk of his life that he got over it, dragging himself on his hands and knees, suspended over bottomless precipices, the roar of the torrent deafening him. Yet he went daily, determined that no obstacle, however appalling, should prevent his celebrating Mass.

He continued going to Marin until the little chapel of St. Bernard de Montjoy, on the lake just below Thonon, was ready. It was with joy and gratitude he took possession of this little sanctuary, delighted to be able to visit the Blessed Sacrament frequently during the day, to preach, hear confessions, and give Holy Communion.

The zeal and intrepidity of Francis de Sales, his unselfishness and charity, began to touch the obdurate Calvinists. Contrasting his untiring patience, his unflagging energy, his utter disinterestedness, with the carelessness, callousness, and cupidity of their own ministers, they came at last to listen to his sermons; then, telling their friends and neighbours of these learned and eloquent discourses, they persuaded them to join them, and soon a few conversions took place. Francis had been more than two years in the Chablais, and the Duke of Savoy had sent him neither money nor helpers. But for his mother's donations and the assistance of his cousin, Canon Louis de Sales, he would have been penniless and alone.

Now that more people were willing to embrace the Catholic Faith, he wrote an urgent letter to the Prince asking him to send him priests and money. He also begged him to endow a college for the Jesuits, or some other Religious Order at Thonon, and to take the civil power from the hands of the Calvinists and give it to the Catholics.

God encouraged him greatly at this time, granting him wonderful graces in prayer. His soul was consumed with love for His Divine Master, and he felt an ardent and imperious desire to immolate himself in the service of Jesus Christ, and to give his life for the conversion of sinners. A violent passion possessed him, exalting him above the earth, consuming his soul in the fire of Divine Love, and a sort of holy frenzy to do all for God.

"It seemed to me," he wrote on a scrap of paper that was found after his death, "that my zeal was changed into fury for my Beloved—*Amor meus, furor meus.*"

> " Est ce l'amour ou la fureur
> Qui me presse, O Dieu de mon cœur.
> Oui, mon Dieu, ce sont tous les deux :
> Car je brûle, quand je vous veux." *

These verses, burning with the fire of Divine Love, remind me of the beautiful poem of St. Francis of Assisi :

> " Love sets my heart on fire,
> Love of my Bridegroom new,
> Love's lamb my thoughts inspire,
> As on the ring he drew.
> Then in a prison dire,
> Sore wounded, he me threw,
> My heart breaks with desire,
> Love sets my heart on fire.

---

*"Is it love or madness
Which presses against me, O God of my heart.
Yes, my God, it is both:
For I am on fire whenever I desire Thee."

My heart is cleft in twain,
 On earth my body lies,
The arrow of this pain
 From Love's own crossbow flies,
Piercing my heart in twain,
 Of sweetness my soul dies,
For peace, comes war again,
 Love sets my heart on fire.
I die of sweetest woe;
 Wonder not at my fate:
The lance which gives the blow
 Is Love immaculate.
A hundred arm's-length; know,
 So long and wide the blade,
Has pierced me at a blow.
 Love sets my heart on fire."

Both these poems breathe a spirit of adoration, the expression of a soul wrapped in the ecstasy of Love. Nothing can compare with their beauty and grace, except, perhaps, the aspirations of the loving soul of St. Francis Xavier.

" O God! I love Thee, not that I
May reign with Thee eternally,
Nor that I may escape the lot
Of those, O God! who love Thee not.
Thou, Thou, my Jesus, Thou for me
Didst agonize on Calvary.
Didst bear the Cross, the nails, the lance,
The rabble's ignominous glance,
Unnumbered griefs, unnumbered woes,
Faintings and agonizing throes,
And death itself, and all for me,
A sinner and Thy enemy!
Ah! shall not, then, Thy love cause me,
Most loving Jesus, to love Thee?
Not that in Heaven I may reign,
Not to escape eternal pain,
Nor in the hope of any gain;
But as Thou, Jesus, didst love me,
So do I love, and will love Thee,

Because Thou art my King, my Lord,
Because, O Jesus, Thou art God."

Evidently the three great Saints who bore the name of Francis were equally inspired, all three possessing the souls of poets as well as of Apostles.

About this time a famous Advocate—Pierre Poucet—abjured Calvinism and was reconciled to the Church of Rome, and later, on October 4, 1595, the Baron d'Avrilly solemnly recanted, and was received by Francis into the Church. This conversion was one he had long desired.

The Baron was a man of great influence, and many waverers were likely to be led by him, and follow his example. It was on the feast of his beloved patron St. Francis of Assisi that this great favour was granted to Francis de Sales. During the rest of his life, on that day, he always made a special commemoration of the event.

The fervour of our Saint was increased by a letter he received from his old director, Père Possevin, S.J. This celebrated Jesuit had just arrived at Chambéry, and he wrote to congratulate Francis on the success that he had heard at last crowned his efforts, offering to join the Provost if his Superiors would give him leave.

De Sales was no less comforted and cheered by presents sent him by the Bishop of Geneva. Writing to his Provost, he tells him how pleased and satisfied he is, calling him his beloved son, the support of his old age, exhorting him to persevere with redoubled courage in his glorious enterprise, and always remember these words of Holy Scripture:

"The just cried, and the Lord heard them, and delivered them out of all their troubles. Many are the afflictions of the just : but the Lord will deliver them out of them all."

Francis hastened to answer this benevolent epistle.

"If you wish to know, Monseigneur," he writes, "all the obstacles and persecutions we have met with, and are certain still to meet, you will find them described in the Epistle of St. Paul. I know I am unworthy to compare myself with that great Apostle, but Our Lord knows how to make useful the weakest of His servants. We are getting along, but slowly, like an invalid who can hardly walk. Yes, Monseigneur, this province is paralytic, and it is only your pious prayers that can obtain its cure. I am but a miserable sinner, and quite unworthy of the graces God has granted me."

When the news of the recantation of the Baron d'Avrilly reached Rome, the Pope, Clement VIII., sent a special envoy to congratulate Francis, and shortly afterwards conveyed to him his wish that he should attempt the conversion of Théodore de Bèze, the oracle of Calvinism, who resided in Geneva, and there exercised a baneful influence over the whole population.

Clement VIII. had long at heart the hope of persuading de Bèze to abjure the errors of Calvinism, knowing that his so doing would cause thousands to follow his example. Père Esprit de Baume, a Capuchin friar, implored the Pope to charge Francis with this difficult mission. Père Esprit arrived at Thonon with the Papal Decree.

"We were overwhelmed with joy," writes Clement VIII., "to hear of the great success of your mission in the Chablais, and we now ask you to execute with your usual zeal and diligence the task Père Esprit will confide to you. It is a project we have much at heart, and we know you will undertake it with your wonted devotion to us and to the Holy See."

Francis agreed. He was ready to set out for Geneva to interview the famous heresiarch, when he received a letter from the Duke of Savoy, ordering him to come at once to Turin to discuss the various articles mentioned in the letter he had written some months previously.

Francis considered that, now that Charles Emmanuel was at last showing signs of taking an interest in the spiritual and temporal welfare of the Chablais, he should promote it by all the means in his power, and certainly not throw any obstacles in the way. The conversion of a whole people he thought of more importance than one man, no matter how powerful and distinguished that man was.

He consulted the Bishop of Geneva, and that wise and saintly prelate agreed with him that it was his duty to go at once to the Court of Turin, and to put off his conference with de Bèze.

# CHAPTER VII

### *THE TRIUMPH OF THE CROSS*

On a bitterly cold day in November, in the year of Our Lord, 1596, two belated travellers were slowly climbing the heights of the Mont St. Bernard. Snow was falling fast and furious, the north wind was piercing and violent. Still they went on, upward, upward! At last, their strength almost failing them, they could no longer see where they were going. Blinded by the snow, deafened by the storm, they could only pray for help and guidance. Suddenly a light dazzled them. Yes, it shone from the Monastery of St. Bernard. Having knocked at the door, they are at once admitted. The pious monks gave them a cordial welcome. A warm fire, a plentiful repast, a cosy room, and a comfortable bed were placed at their service. The next morning they had quite recovered. The monks wished to keep them until the storm had quite abated, but Francis de Sales insisted on continuing his journey to the Court of the Duke of Savoy at Turin.

The faithful Rolland remonstrated: the monks pointed out the dangers he would surely encounter.

He was quite determined. After celebrating Holy Mass and partaking of a substantial breakfast, he and his servant set forth once more on their perilous journey. They arrived safely at Turin. Charles Emmanuel received the Provost most graciously. He convoked the Privy Council; the Papal Nuncio attended the meeting, and they discussed the various points regarding the government of the Chablais.

After several conferences, much talk, and many arguments, the Duke at last agreed to allow the re-establishment of the old parishes, the restitution of Church property, the founding of a college of Jesuits at Thonon, a printing-press for Catholic books at Annecy. It was also decided that eight Catholic priests should travel through the Duchy, preaching and teaching the truths of faith, celebrating Holy Mass, administering the Sacraments, and receiving converts into the Church. The salaries previously paid to the Calvinist ministers were to be given to them. The Church of St. Hippolytus at Thonon was to be renovated and restored to the Catholics, to be used in future only by them for public worship.

The Duke absolutely refused to countenance the expulsion of the Protestants and the complete transference of State patronage from them to the Catholics. Francis was well pleased with the concessions granted to him. He returned home by the route over the Petit St. Bernard, and reached the Château de Sales without any misadventure. He spent a few days with his family, but he was longing to join his flock, so, as soon as he was a little rested, he wished them good-bye and hurried on to Thonon. There he was received with affection and delight by the Catholics. When they heard the glad tidings he brought them, their joy and gratitude were unbounded. They were especially pleased that the Church of St. Hippolytus was to be handed over to them for their own and only use and benefit. Francis told them he intended celebrating Mass in it on Christmas Day, and that he intended getting it repaired at once.

He lost no time, and soon had a band of workmen ready to commence operations, but at this the smouldering passion of the heretics burst forth. Their fury was unbounded. They attacked him in the streets, threatening to burn him alive if he persisted. To all their invectives and insults the Saint returned most affable replies. He paid not the slightest attention to their menaces, but quietly got his men to commence work. At the sight the Calvinists rushed forth armed with sticks and other weapons, the Catholics were quite prepared to defend their beloved pastor, and a sanguinary fight was imminent, but Francis intervened.

In his usual calm, clear tones he harangued the excited populace. At the sound of that gentle, yet firm voice, at the sight of his serene and dignified countenance, the steady gaze of his kind eyes dominated them, the tumult subsided, the people returned to their homes, and the workmen were allowed to continue their task.

On Christmas Day, 1596, midnight Mass was celebrated in the Church of St. Hippolytus. It was the first time for more than sixty years that the Holy Sacrifice had been offered up there. Great was the enthusiasm of the faithful. They trooped in from all the surrounding villages. Eight hundred people received Holy Communion from the hands of Francis de Sales. The inhabitants of three villages abjured heresy.

The inhabitants of Thonon were not the only folk who profited by the zeal and charity of the Holy Apostle. The soldiers of the regiment of the Comte de Martiniques, then stationed at Thonon, were all Catholics, but, like the garrison at d'Allinges before the coming of Francis, they had grown cold and careless in the practice of their religion.

He preached the Lenten sermons in 1597 at St. Hippolytus. The soldiers attended, and on Spy Wednesday came to the Saint *en masse*, imploring him to hear their confessions. He did so, and had the consolation of giving to all of them the Bread of Life on Holy Thursday, Holy Saturday, and Easter Sunday. From that time they were changed men, and were models to all the other battalions. Francis composed a rule of life suitable for soldiers; they faithfully adhered to its precepts, and it was soon adopted by both officers and men in other regiments.

In the midst of these arduous labours Francis remembered the mission the Pope had confided to him, to attempt the conversion of Théodore de Bèze. He considered the time had now arrived. He went to Geneva, and succeeded on Easter Tuesday in interviewing the famous heresiarch. The Pope of Geneva—as Théodore was styled—received him courteously, listened to his arguments, appeared more or less convinced, discussed several knotty points, and finally agreed to see him again.

Two more conferences took place between the Apostle of the Chablais and the successor of Calvin. The heart of de Bèze was touched, his conscience awakened—for in his youth he had been a member of the true Church—almost it seemed as though the burning eloquence, the clear reasoning of St. Francis de Sales had prevailed. But the Pope of Geneva loved power and place too well to sacrifice his position as head of the Calvinists to become a mere subject of the Pope of Rome. He could not humble himself; he would not confess his errors; and so, a few years later, on October 22, 1605, he died, as he had lived, in the darkness of unbelief. It is said that in his agony he cried aloud for a Catholic priest, and cursed his friends and co-religionists who refused to bring him one, accusing them of causing his damnation.

Francis had now as assistants not only his cousin, Louis de Sales, but also Père Esprit de

Baume, Père Cherubin de Maurienne, and Père Saunier, S.J. At last the harvest was coming in : many conversions took place daily, and in order to strengthen the Faith and increase the fervour of his flock he resolved, with the consent of the Bishop, to hold the devotion of Forty Hours' Adoration at Annemasse.

Claude de Granier was charmed. It was just the thing. He would do all in his power to make it a success, promising to open the ceremonies by himself celebrating the Pontifical High Mass. The Papal Nuncio and the Duke of Savoy also gave their approval. They did more; they most generously gave large sums to defray the expenses.

It was decided that the devotions of the *Quarant' Ores*[*] should commence on September 7. When the Calvinists heard the news, they did all in their power to oppose the project; several hostile demonstrations took place, and a tumult was feared.

Francis de Sales, nothing daunted, resolved to give the utmost publicity to the proceedings. He decided to walk in the procession all the way from Thonon to Annemasse, a distance of about twelve miles; the crucifix was to be carried in front.

When the day arrived, he offered up the Holy Sacrifice at the beautiful new altar in the Church of St. Hippolytus, gave Holy Communion to many people, and then formed the procession. But some difficulty was experienced in finding anyone brave enough to lead the way carrying

---

[*] The "Forty Hours" devotion.

the cross, so great was the dread inspired by the heretics. At this critical moment Francis turned to George Rolland, and ordered him to act as leader.

" Do not fear," he said, smiling encouragingly ; " I will be near you all the way. If they do you any harm they will do it to me ; and we will die together."

Matters thus satisfactorily arranged, they started on their long march, chanting litanies and hymns. Francis, in surplice and stole, brought up the rear, but as they advanced, they were joined by such crowds of devout Savoyards that soon the Provost was in the centre, and before they reached their destination he was much nearer the front, so many thousands flocked in from the adjoining country.

They arrived late at night at Annemasse, and having visited the church and partaken of a light supper, they retired for the night. On the following morning the venerable Bishop of Geneva celebrated High Mass ; many received Holy Communion ; the Blessed Sacrament was carried in procession through the town, and then brought to the Altar of Repose, exposed to the adoration of the vast multitude of devout souls. Francis preached several times, and Pères Cherubin and Esprit also animated and increased the universal fervour by eloquent discourses.

In the afternoon our Saint blessed a beautiful cross, which was then erected on the Geneva road, on the exact spot where one had formerly stood, but had been knocked down and destroyed by the heretics.

It was with unutterable joy that the saintly Prelate, his Provost, and all the priests and people carried the crucifix in procession from Annemasse and set it up in the place prepared for it. Francis attached to it the following verses, composed by himself:

> " Ce n'est la pierre ni le bois
>    Que le Catholique adore ;
> Mais le Roi qui, mort en croix,
>    De son sang la croix honore." *

This exquisite inscription had a marvellous effect on the Calvinists.

" Our ministers have grossly deceived us," they cried. " They declared to us that the Catholics adored wood and stone ; on the contrary, it is Our Lord Jesus Christ Whom they adore." A great number of conversions took place in consequence, for many came to receive instructions, and, convinced of the errors of Calvinism, embraced the True Faith.

Once again the Standard of the Cross was triumphant in the Chablais ; the Holy Images were replaced at the cross-roads and at street-corners, and Jesus Christ and His Blessed Mother once more reigned paramount over the land and in the hearts of the people.

---

*It is not the stone or the wood    **61**
    Which Catholics adore;
  Rather, it is the King, lifeless on the cross,
    Who honors the cross with His blood.

# CHAPTER VIII

## *THE WHITE CROSS OF SAVOY*

Francis de Sales, on his return to Thonon, occupied himself in strengthening the faith of the converts ; in seeking to enlighten those who were still in the darkness of unbelief, and in leading devout souls heavenward.

Though he hated and abhorred heresy, he loved and cherished the heretics; he always treated them with the greatest courtesy and kindness, serving them in every way, calling them his dear brothers, his beloved fellow-countrymen. Some of the other missionaries reproached him with this gentleness, telling him he was too meek and mild, and that he would never persuade such obstinate fellows to change their opinions unless he adopted severe measures. " Pitch into them ; give it them strong—hell-fire and eternal damnation "—was practically their advice. Francis re-replied : " Never have I been too severe and rigorous with heretics that I have not had reason to regret my austerity. Instead of doing good, bitter words and invectives only infuriate and make them more obstinate. I have had the happiness of converting a few heretics, but I have done so by kindness and gentleness. Love and affection have a greater empire over souls than harshness and severity. Love is more powerful than the strongest arguments, the most convincing reasons."

On one occasion he took for his text the words of St. Matthew: "But I say unto you not to resist evil; but if one strike thee on the right cheek, turn to him also the other." When the sermon was over, a Calvinist approached him, and remarked to him before all the congregation:

"Doubtless it is in order that one cheek may not be paler than the other that you have just told us to turn the left cheek to the person who has struck the right one? If I strike you now, will you practise what you preach? Bah! you are of those who say and who do not."

"My friend," replied Francis gently, "I know perfectly what I ought to do, but I know not if I should have courage and strength to do it, for I am but a poor creature. Yet I have confidence in the grace of God, for it gives strength to the weakest. Yet even if I did not calmly submit to your insults the Gospel tells you in the same verse: 'All things whatsoever they shall *say* to you, observe and do, but according to their works do ye not.'"

"But," replied the surly Calvinist, "Christ did not turn His other cheek to the servant of the high-priest when he gave Him a blow."

"You wish, then, to put Our Lord among those who say, and do not," retorted Francis, burning with just indignation. "But it is easy to understand why He did not turn His other cheek. He wished to convert the man by showing him his fault. Later on in His Passion He followed this counsel by submitting to the buffets and blows of the rude soldiers, by giving His body to the whips and lashes of the executioners."

The Calvinist retired; the courteous and clear replies of the gentle Saint had touched his heart. Many of the listeners were so impressed that they implored Francis to instruct them in the tenets of so sublime a Faith, and afterwards they were received by him into the Church.

A miracle which the Apostle of the Chablais performed about this time also helped to bring many souls into the True Fold. A woman who lived in the Faubourg St. Bon at Thonon absolutely refused to abjure heresy, though she constantly attended devotions, listened attentively to the sermons, and reverenced and esteemed Francis. Yet all his arguments and prayers were apparently wasted; she continued obdurate. A son was born to her; she deferred his baptism from day to day. The infant died. Wild with despair and sorrow, she herself carried the little corpse to the cemetery. On the way thither she met the Provost. Throwing herself at his feet, she implored him to restore her son to her, if only for a few moments, long enough to pour over him the saving waters of baptism. She promised to embrace the Catholic religion.

Francis was deeply moved. He mingled his tears with hers; then, kneeling on the ground, he prayed over the little body. His prayer was no sooner finished, scarcely had he risen from his knees, when the boy opened his eyes and moaned. He was baptized on the spot. The happy mother then carried him home in the midst of universal joy. He lived for two days, and all who doubted could verify the miracle by seeing and touching the living child. Indeed, several heretics were invited by Père Cherubin to do so, and they and many more were received into the Church.

The harvest was now indeed plentiful. Success at last crowned the labours of the saintly Apostle. In 1598 a Jesuit college was established at Thonon. The various parishes were attended to by zealous priests. Many of the ministers had fled to Berne and Geneva. These men had frequently challenged the Provost and the missionaries to controversial discussions, but they nearly always retreated at the last moment, shielding their cowardice behind some trifling pretext, and when, driven to desperation, they did appear, they were always defeated.

The majority of the people had ceased to believe in them or their doctrines—in fact, most of the inhabitants of the Chablais were no longer aliens from the fold, but good, practical Catholics.

On May 2, 1598, the Treaty of Vervins, giving

peace to Europe, was ratified. By it France assured to Savoy the undisputed possession of the Chablais and of Ternier.

Once more the banner of the White Cross waved triumphant and unchallenged over the fair lands bordering the southern shore of Lake Leman. There was no longer any danger that the Protestants of Berne would wrest them from their rightful sovereign.

To celebrate this glorious event, the Duke of Savoy and the Bishop of Geneva decided to offer up in thankfulness the Devotions of the Forty Hours at Thonon. They were desirous that the function should be a magnificent one, and were anxious it should take place without delay.

The opening day was appointed, everyone was in expectation, everything was ready, when at the last moment Charles Emmanuel sent word that it was impossible for him to be present. The Papal Legate—Cardinal Alexander de Medici, afterwards Pope Leo XI.—was unable to attend. He was travelling from France into Italy, and intended passing through Thonon *en route*.

Another day was named, and again neither Prince nor Cardinal came. Finally, Claude de Granier decided that it would be better no longer to postpone the celebration of the *Quarant' Ore* and that, later on, it could be again held when the Duke and the Legate were free.

Sunday, September 20, was the opening day. On the previous Saturday, September 19, the venerable Bishop of Geneva administered the Sacrament of Confirmation and Holy Orders to a number of persons at Thonon, in the Church of St. Augustine, of which he took formal possession. It was sixty-three years since these Sacraments had been conferred in the Chablais. Claude de Granier also consecrated numerous altars, blessed sacred vestments, and a number of crosses, intended to be erected on the highways and in the streets.

Although the Church of St. Augustine was much larger than that of St. Hippolytus, yet was it too small to accommodate the thousands who would flock in to adore their Saviour. Consequently it was arranged that the Blessed Sacrament should be carried to the large square in front of the church, and an oratory was there erected for its reception. In the midst of a tremendous congress of people, on September 20, 1598, the holy Bishop celebrated the Pontifical High Mass, and then carried the Blessed Sacrament through the streets, and brought it to the Altar of Repose, where it remained for three days exposed to the adoration of the faithful.

Francis and Louis de Sales, Père Cherubin and the Jesuit Fathers in turn preached such beautiful and convincing sermons that many of the Calvinists were converted, and devout souls were consoled and encouraged. Tremendous crowds came from the villages, and the peasants thronged in from all parts. Never was there such a spectacle of pious devotion.

The "Forty Hours" was terminated by another solemn procession, the Bishop carrying back the Sacred Host to the Church of St. Augustine. Fatigued and weary though he was, Francis instructed and received into the Church forty converts, and persuaded Claude de Granier to confirm them on the following day.

Charles Emmanuel was now free to repair to Thonon. He wrote telling the mayor he would arrive on September 29, that the Cardinal de Medici would arrive on September 30, and that the *Quarant' Ore* could open on October 1.

The courier only reached the town with this message on the morning of the 28th; nevertheless everyone was ready to welcome the Prince on his arrival.

Surrounded by nobles and courtiers, and by the citizens of Thonon, he went forth, accompanied by Claude de Granier, Francis de Sales, and the other priests, to meet the Cardinal.

Alexander de Medici went immediately to the Church of St. Hippolytus to visit the Blessed Sacrament. Later in the day he 'and the Duke held a levée. The Bishop and the Provost of Geneva and several gentlemen were present. The Legate expressed surprise and pleasure at the number of conversions, and the marvellous progress of religion and piety in the diocese. He promised to make a faithful report to the Sovereign Pontiff.

"Yes," remarked Charles Emmanuel, "this

noble prelate is the Father of the province. I
have endeavoured to second his efforts with my
authority, and I would gladly give my life, if
necessary; but here," he continued, leading forward Francis de Sales and presenting him to
Cardinal de Medici, "Monseigneur, you see before
you the true Apostle of the Chablais. This priest
is a Saint sent to us by God. He penetrated alone
into this country at the peril of his life. It is he
who has preached the Gospel, erected the Cross,
and sown the good seed. He has exterminated
heresy in this country, where it reigned supreme
for more than sixty years. He has re-established
the Faith, and now most of my subjects are sons
of Holy Church."

At this panegyric Francis was overwhelmed
with confusion. He fell at the Cardinal's feet,
humbly kissing the hem of his garment. Alexander de Medici raised him graciously, and, embracing him tenderly, said with enthusiasm:

"I thank you, Monsieur, for your energy and
zeal in the good cause. Continue to act with the
same diligence and fervour. I will make known
to His Holiness what you have done and are
doing for the salvation of souls."

At this speech Francis became even more
troubled. Hastily retiring, he implored Père
Cherubin to preach the opening sermon on the
following day. It had been arranged that Francis
himself should do so.

"All this praise has so disconcerted me," he

told his friend, "that I should never have the courage to be the first to appear before this august company."

Early on Thursday, October 1, the Cardinal and the Duke were at the Church of St. Hippolytus. The Legate received hundreds into the Church. At their head was the Minister Petit, who, burning with all the fervour of a convert, explained in a beautiful discourse the three principal reasons that had caused him t6 recognize the Church of Rome as the one established by Jesus Christ.

At the completion of the ceremony a *Te Deum* was sung, and then Claude de Granier sang the Pontifical High Mass. The music was heavenly. The chanting of the choirs of the Cardinal and the Prince was like the singing of angels. The Bishop of Geneva then carried the Blessed Sacrament through the streets ; the canopy covering the Sacred Host was borne by the Duke, his brother, and two citizens of Fribourg ; the Cardinal followed, and then came the nobles and the courtiers, the citizens, and immense crowds from the surrounding country.

Thonon was *en fête ;* the narrow streets of the grey old town were profusely decorated with flowers and foliage ; rich draperies hung from the windows ; arches of evergreens spanned the roads. The procession stopped for a few minutes at the corner of the street, where the Bishop of St. Paul de Trois Châteaux lodged. A magnificent triumphal arch was erected there. Then, as they proceeded on their way, and at the precise moment when the Cardinal passed under it, a cloud opened, and a snow-white dove flew out and alighted on His Eminence's shoulder, presenting him with a letter in Latin full of compliments; then it passed on to the Prince, to whom it conveyed another epistle. In this the greeting was in French.

The procession advanced on its way until it arrived at St. Augustine's, where was the Altar of Repose. There hour after hour processions of devout Catholics and of fervent converts succeeded each other. The Cardinal received the recantation of many heretics; indeed, it is said that more than a thousand abjured their errors during the *Quarant' Ore*. On the second day the Prince, his brother, Don Amé de Savoie, the Marquis de Lullin approached the altar-rails, and were given the Bread of Life by Père Cherubin.

Then Charles Emmanuel went to the Church of St. Augustine to spend an hour in adoration. In the evening he took part in a distinctly interesting ceremony. There stood in the Rue de la Croix in bygone years a beautifully carved crucifix which the Calvinists had destroyed. Francis de Sales had procured a new one, equally beautiful and exquisitely fashioned; he wished to erect it with all possible solemnity. In the midst of the joy of the vast multitude, and the sound of music and of song, the pealing of bells, the blowing of trumpets, the beating of drums, and the firing of artillery, the heavy Cross was borne on the shoulders of members of the Confraternity, and by them placed firmly on the spot prepared for it, the Prince lending a helping hand. The *Te Deum* was sung; hearty cheers and joyful cries arose from the people. They shouted: "Vive la Croix!" "Vive son Altesse Royale!" "Vive le Pape!" "Vive Savoie!" "Vive l'Église Romaine!"

This devotion to the Church of Rome and to the House of Savoy greatly touched Charles Emmanuel. "We have to thank God," he said, "for the badge of our house, the White Cross. My ancestors won the right to wear it on their shields when they fought against the infidel. To me the exaltation of the Holy Cross is particularly dear, and I truly rejoice that the emblem of our holy religion, the Cross of our Crucified Saviour, is once more exposed to the veneration of the faithful within my dominions. I wish that in all the towns, at the cross-roads, and on the highways crosses were erected."

His desire was soon gratified. Francis de Sales, standing on the ramparts of the Château d'Allinges and looking forth over that fair land down to the blue waters of Lake Leman and up to the everlasting hills, could see the Cross triumphant. Above him from the flagstaff waved the banner of the White Cross of Savoy, and beneath him in the valleys, in the highways and byways, numerous crucifixes stood clearly outlined; the churches were rebuilt; the presbyteries were inhabited by zealous priests ; monasteries and convents were restored. He could hear the pealing of the bells, ringing the *Angelus* and summoning the people to Divine worship. The ruin and desolation over which he had wept four years previously had vanished. The inhabitants of the Chablais were no longer aliens from the True Fold, and he, under Providence, had been the means of converting them. In this land, where, on his arrival in 1594, there had been only a hundred Catholics, there were now scarcely a hundred Calvinists. It is estimated that about seventy - two thousand people were received by Francis de Sales and his fellow-missionaries into the Church.

# CHAPTER IX

## *ROME REVISITED*

Claude de Granier had a strange and fearsome
dream. It seemed to him that he and his flock
were surrounded by wolves. He was quite alone,
and could scarcely defend them, and, in spite of
all his efforts, a few of the lambs were seized and
devoured by the fierce beasts. Shrieking in terror
"Au secours! au secours!"*he awoke. His chaplain, who slept in the adjoining room, rushed in.
The trembling Prelate related this dreadful night-
mare.

"Oh, what can I do?" he moaned. "I am old
and feeble; I am unable to look after my diocese.
Would to God that I could persuade Francis de
Sales to aid me and accept the coadjutorship."

"And why not?" inquired the chaplain. "It
has been the desire of your heart for a long time.
We all wish it. Why not send to him and ask
him to accept the office?"

The Bishop spent the remainder of the night
in prayer and meditation. In the morning he
received a visit from his nephew, the Vicar-
General, M. l'Abbé de Cissé, and explained to
him his views. This generous and unselfish priest

---

*"Help! Help!"

quite agreed with him, though he might have expected that he himself would have been appointed; yet he strongly approved, and, indeed, recommended, that Francis de Sales should be chosen.

The Provost was sent for, and the Bishop, tenderly embracing him, begged his help.

"Ah, with all my heart!" cried Francis, who had not the faintest idea what was required of him. "You know, Monseigneur, that it is always a supreme delight to me to be of use to you."

"My dear son," replied Claude de Granier, "I wish you to be my coadjutor, with right of succession to the See of Geneva."

At these words the Provost flushed, cast down his eyes, and was much troubled.

"Monseigneur," he said, "it is not the work I object to. You know I am willing to devote my life to you, and to do all in my power to assist you. But the dignity! No, I cannot accept it; I am too unworthy." He persisted in his refusal, notwithstanding the prayers and supplications of the venerable Prelate, and in the evening he returned to the Château de Sales.

Claude de Granier had set his heart on the project. He sent repeatedly to Francis, even going in person, and enlisting the co-operation of M. and Mme. de Boisy and of the relatives and friends of our Saint. In vain they pleaded. Francis was adamant. Claude de Granier was just as determined. The nobility and clergy of

the diocese entreated the Provost to accept.
Over and over again His Lordship pleaded with
his Provost, dwelling on his own great age and infirmities, and the extreme need he had of a young
and vigorous assistant.

Francis sighed profoundly. "You wish to do
me an injury," he told de Granier, "in exposing
me to the dangers of a high position. You do
not know me, Monseigneur. I am full of vanity
and conceit; I have not the necessary humility
to save my soul in so exalted a station. Pride
would ruin me."

The Bishop did not despair; though discouraged,
he yet persevered. He sent the Abbé Critain to
the Château de Sales with instructions to bring
the matter to a conclusion. Early in the morning
this good priest sought an interview with Francis.

"You must know," he told him, "that our
beloved Bishop has sent me to you to insist on
your becoming his coadjutor. He has frequently
spoken to you on the subject; he has got the
most distinguished people of the diocese to entreat
you to agree to his wishes, but you continue obstinate. Beware! You are resisting the will of
God. Not only does the Lord Bishop order you
to accept the coadjutorship, but the clergy, the
nobility, the people, all wish you to do so; they
unanimously agree that you are the right man.
They have chosen you, and the voice of the people
is the voice of God. What is more, here are the
letters patent from the Duke of Savoy, graciously

confirming your election, and a letter from the Cardinal de Medici announcing that it will give him great pleasure to solicit your nomination from His Holiness. What more can you want? Are not all these so many signs of the Divine will in your regard?"

Francis was troubled and touched by this speech. He reflected. On the one side, the thought of the episcopate appalled him; but, on the other hand, he would not oppose the designs of Providence.

He was silent for a short time, lost in thought. Then, turning to the Abbé Critain, he said :

" Let us go to the church at Thorens, and we will each in turn offer up the Mass of the Holy Ghost, and beg the Divine Spirit to enlighten us. We will pray our dear Lord to inspire me. Come, we will serve one another."

Both priests offered up the Holy Sacrifice with unwonted fervour, particularly Francis, who seemed in an ecstasy. His eyes were fixed on the Tabernacle, his face radiant with the fire of Divine Love.

On their return to the Château: "Well, Monsieur," asked the Abbé, "what reply has God given to your prayers?'

" Tell Monseigneur," replied Francis, that I still dread the responsibilities of the exalted rank to which he wishes to raise me, but, since he commands, I obey. If I am of any use, if I do any good, it will be due to his prayers."

Needless to dwell on the joy and gratitude of the venerable Prelate and of all the people when the good news was known. It was arranged that Francis was to set out for Rome immediately, but on the very eve of his departure he fell suddenly ill.

For days his life was despaired of. Added to physical suffering, he had the far greater torture of mental pain. Once more his soul was plunged in the deepest depths of agony and despair. A horrible temptation seized him, doubts of the most distressing kind overwhelmed him. The nature of this temptation he afterwards confided to Canon Louis de Sales under a promise of the strictest secrecy. It was against Faith, particularly an extraordinary repugnance to believe in the Real Presence.

This excruciating torture of soul and body wore him out. The doctors declared his recovery hopeless. They requested Madame de Boisy to make known to her son his imminent danger, and to advise him to prepare to die. The loving mother was heart-broken. Yet, in the midst of distress, there was a gleam of sunshine. She had a presentiment that Francis had not yet run his course, that he was to do even greater things for the honour and glory of God before entering into rest eternal. Nevertheless, she told her son the doctor's verdict.

Francis was plunged into an ocean of bitterness and remorse. He considered he had not done sufficient penance for the sins *he* thought so heinous and so grave. Never more in this life would he be able to atone for his transgressions. He cried aloud in the distress of his heart with penitent David, bemoaning his faults:

"Have mercy on me, O Lord, for I am weak. Heal me, O Lord, for my bones are troubled.

"Turn Thee, O Lord, and deliver my soul. Save me, for Thy mercy's sake.

"For in death there is no one that is mindful of Thee, and who will give Thee thanks in Hell?

"I have laboured in my groanings. Every night will I wash my bed and water my couch with my tears."

But after a short time these sentiments of misery and contrition gave place to confidence in God. Again making use of the words of the holy King, he cried:

"The Lord hath heard and hath had mercy upon me. The Lord is become my helper.

"That my glory may sing unto Thee, and that I be not sorrowful. O Lord my God, I will give praise unto Thee for ever."

Peace, perfect peace, came to his troubled soul. He frequently repeated the holy names of Jesus and Mary. His mind was once more at rest, the temptation vanished; but it was not until he had regained his strength that he found the solution of his difficulty.

His mother redoubled her care and tenderness. All the attention that the most experienced nurse could lavish on an invalid she gave to her dearest son, accompanied by the most devoted love. Francis, following his usual practice of asking for nothing, refusing nothing, allowed her to tend and cherish him to her heart's content. Day and night she prayed for his recovery. No less unceasingly did the Bishop and the people besiege Heaven with supplications. Suddenly the fever left Francis. He slept peacefully, and in a remarkably short time he had regained health and strength.

Claude de Granier had been so grieved at the illness of his "dear son" that he, too, had fallen sick, but when Francis recovered he recovered.

In February, 1599, Francis de Sales, the Abbé de Cissé, and the faithful George Rolland started on their journey to Rome.

They crossed the Alps to Turin, where they conferred with the Papal Nuncio on the affairs of the Diocese of Geneva. They expected to meet Louis de Sales and President Favre, but the latter had already passed through the city southwards.

After several days travelling, one afternoon Francis was thrown from his horse. It fell upon him. Fortunately, he was not hurt, but he was in a pitiable condition, covered with mud. He rushed into the nearest hotel to have a brush up and tidy himself, went to a room, and started drying his clothes at a good fire and warming himself, for he was frozen.

Suddenly a beautiful woman dashed into the room, and, approaching him, her eyes blazing with passion, her arms stretched towards him, cried:

" Oh, monsieur, no one can see you without loving you."

Francis blushed crimson, and cast down his eyes.

" Do not lower your eyes," she besought him, " but look at me, and respond to my passion."

" Leave the room!" Francis commanded, his eyes now raised, and aflame with virtuous indignation. " Go, wretched woman!"

Nothing daunted, she continued to express her love and admiration in the most ardent language, devouring him with eyes burning with unholy desire.

Francis raised his hand as though he would strike her, but she only laughed and came closer to him. There was nothing for it but flight, so, quickly gaining the door, he rushed downstairs and into the street, where he luckily met George Rolland, who had his valise, so that at another inn he was able to complete his interrupted toilet.

At last they reached the Eternal City. He found his friend President Favre awaiting him ; they put up at the same hotel, one situated near the Church of St. Sauveur in Lauro. Together they visited St. Peter's, prostrating themselves at the tomb of the holy Apostle. On March 13 he and his friends went to the Catacombs. Abbé Cissé relates that he there found Francis on his knees, bathed in tears. Surprised to find him in so melancholy and deplorable a state, he inquired if he had had bad news from home.

"No," replied Francis ; " but why do you wonder

that I shed tears? Here, in the midst of the tombs of the martyrs, who have had the happiness of shedding their blood for the Faith, the least I can do is to weep over my unworthiness. O happy martyrs! how I envy you your fate! Sinner that I am, I do not deserve to receive the martyr's crown. I do not deserve the favour of God; I can only humble myself in the Divine Presence and weep over my transgressions."

The following day Francis de Sales and Abbé de Cissé were presented to the Pope by Cardinal de Medici. His Eminence remarked that Francis was known as the Apostle of the Chablais, and that the Duke of Savoy loved to call him by that name.

Clement VIII. received them with the utmost benevolence, and listened, well pleased, to the account Francis gave of the progress of Catholicity in the Chablais.

Francis presented to His Holiness the petitions of the Bishop of Geneva. One of the most important was a request for the separation of the benefices from the Order of St. Maurice and Lazarus; another that he might devote a portion of the tithes and revenues to make up for the smallness of the stipends of the clergy and to enable him to support a number of priests to be named Canon-Theologians, whose duty it would be to travel about the country and instruct the people.

He asked for several dispensations in consideration of the distances to be traversed, and the poverty of the inhabitants. He also stipulated for the reform of the monasteries, that the different Orders should return to the strict observance of their rules, and that certain prelates should be authorized to inquire into the abuses that had arisen, correct them, and bring back the communities to their former fervour.

The Pope listened with kindness and attention, promising to consider the various articles. Abbé de Cissé then asked the Sovereign Pontiff to appoint Francis de Sales coadjutor with right of succession to the See of Geneva. Clement VIII. received this request graciously, and, turning to Francis, said: "We rejoice, my son, and we give thanks to Almighty God, that He calls you to the Episcopate. Be ready to be examined on next Monday, March 22."

Francis pleaded the Savoyard privilege of exemption from examination. The Pope admitted it, but told him that he wished not to test but to make manifest his learning. Francis prepared himself for the ordeal by prayer and fasting, and on the appointed day appeared at the Vatican.

Clement VIII. was seated on his throne, surrounded by Cardinals, Prelates, and a brilliant and numerous Court. He questioned Francis on several difficult and abstruse questions. Cardinals Borromeo and Borgia and Père Bellarmine then examined him on the most subtle and delicate points.

The Pope was so pleased with his answers, and with his charming and unassuming manner, that, descending from his throne, he approached and warmly embraced the humble candidate, crying in a loud voice: "Drink, my son, water out of thy own cistern, and the streams of thy own well; let thy fountains be conveyed abroad, and let the streets divide thy waters" (Prov. v. 15, 16). All those present joined their congratulations to the Holy Father's.

During his visit to Rome, Francis contracted lifelong friendships with some of the most distinguished men of their time—amongst others with Cardinal Borgia, afterwards Paul V.; with Cardinal Baronius, the friend and companion of St. Philip Neri; with Bellarmine, whose learned "Controversies" he always carried about with him; but his chosen friend was the saintly Ancina. He was also an Oratorian, and he loved Francis almost as another Philip, seeing points of resemblance between them: the same burning love of God, the same intense zeal for the salvation of souls. Even in expression and in manner there was a great resemblance. Both possessed that gentle and sweet kindness and considerateness which does so much to win love and confidence, and which is the perfection of strength; both had a winning smile, a soft and pleasant voice, and the spiritual beauty of feature which is the result of unsullied purity of soul. No wonder, then, that those two devoted sons of St. Philip—Baronius and Ancina—admired and loved his living counter-part. Ancina, visiting Francis one day, remarked to him with charming frankness: "I am more rejoiced to-day, my friend, to see how truly humble you are, than I was at your examination to see you so truly learned ."

Ancina afterwards became Bishop of Saluzzo. He was poisoned, and died in the flower of his age, and was deeply and sincerely regretted, not only by his own people, but by all Christendom.

Francis wrote to St. Jane Frances de Chantal : "Mgr. de Saluzzo one of my dearest friends, and one of the greatest servants of God and His Church the world has ever seen, passed a short time ago to a better life, to the incredible sorrow of his flock."

Another extract from a letter, written by the Prior of Belleville to Ancina, will show how true was the friendship between the two saintly Prelates.

"The greatness of the love Francis de Sales bears towards your most reverend lordship is shown in this, that he speaks of you with tender and even passionate affection, and cannot restrain his gladness of heart at the prospect of seeing you, and embracing you in peace and charity."

Francis was named Bishop of Nicopolis ; he now only required the Bull of his appointment as Coadjutor of Geneva. He forgot to ask for it ; he also forgot to give the money to pay for it.

When he was reproached for not doing so, he

replied with a sunny smile : " I have the best reason in the world for not giving it. I have not a sou left."

" But," they told him, "your friends are not paupers, and will be only too delighted to finance you." He retorted, laughing : "I will not be Bishop at the expense of my friends. If God wishes me to be a Prince of His Church, the Bulls will be issued without any money."

He was right. The Bulls appointing him Bishop of Nicopolis, and Coadjutor of Geneva were expedited.

On March 25 he received Holy Communion from the hands of the Sovereign Pontiff. His soul was illumined with supernatural light, and overflowed with love and ardour. He only remained a few days longer in Rome. He offered up the Holy Sacrifice at St. Peter's, and then had a last interview with the Pope. Clement VIII. received him graciously, telling him that he gave his sanction and willing consent to all the petitions of the Bishop of Geneva. Francis, falling on his knees, asked his benediction, and the Pope, with tears of tenderness and love, gave his blessing to his beloved son, Francis de Sales, promising ever to remember him in his prayers, and exhorting him to continue his career in the same spirit of zeal and self-sacrifice.

On March 31, 1599, the Bishop of Nicopolis and Abbé de Cissé left the Eternal City and set out on their long journey northwards.

# CHAPTER X

## *THE HOLY HOUSE*

FRANCIS DE SALES had received so many graces, and enjoyed such unalloyed happiness at the Holy House of Nazareth when he had visited it in 1591, that he felt an irresistible desire to kneel once more before the shrine of his Queen. He accordingly spent a few days at Loreto, hospitably entertained by the Jesuits, who had a house there.

Francis celebrated Holy Mass in the *Santa Casa.* He renewed the consecration of his soul and body to the service of Jesus and Mary. He fervently thanked them for the graces they had conferred upon him, and in particular for having been the means under Providence of converting the Chablais, a favour he owed to the intercession of the Blessed Virgin.

He spent hours before the Tabernacle shedding tears of holy joy, and wrapt in an ecstasy of Divine love. Abbé de Cissé wished to draw him away, but he entreated: "O my dear brother, I beg of you to leave me yet another hour, while I renew all the promises I made to the Mother of God in the days of my youth."

When at last he tore himself away, his soul was

filled with heavenly rapture, and his face was as the face of an angel.

They proceeded on their journey. At Milan they spent a few days, and Francis succeeded in obtaining the new " Life of St. Charles Borromeo." He had a great reverence and esteem for the devoted Bishop, and he perused the Life with the liveliest satisfaction. Arrived at Turin, Abbé de Cissé went on to Annecy, but Francis waited to confer with the Duke of Savoy on the affairs of the diocese. Charles Emmanuel received him with cordiality, quite agreeing with the contents of the Apostolic Letters. He promised to do all in his power to hasten the fulfilment of the various clauses. He particularly assisted in wresting the endowments of the benefices from the Knights of SS. Maurice and Lazarus. This Order was exceedingly loath to part with the property it had acquired, though it was most clearly proved that the country was now all Catholic, and that consequently there was no need to maintain an arrangement based on the assumption that some districts were Calvinist. They had really only been given the endowments in trust, to hold until the Faith was once more restored. Yet were they so determined to hold on to this Church property, notwithstanding the decrees of the Holy See, and the edicts of the Duke, that it was nearly two years before the affair was finally wound up.

Having finished his business with the Prince, Francis was ready to set out for Annecy. On the point of starting, he sent the following charming letter to Mme. de Boisy:

"I write you these few lines, dearest and best of mothers, just before mounting my horse to ride to Chambéry. You need not hide this note. I do not mind in the least if my Father sees it. Thank God the time is gone by, when he would not allow you to correspond with me, and we had to conceal the fact that we wrote each other letters of consolation and encouragement. *Vive Dieu!* my good mother, yet do I always remember that time with pleasure and gratitude, for you then showed me how dearly you loved me.

Be happy, and full of holy joy, my dear mother. Rest assured your poor son is in the best of health, and is looking forward very soon to seeing and embracing you. I will stay with you as long as I can, for I am yours, as you well know,

"Ever and always,

"Francis."

Arrived at Annecy, Bishop and people greeted the returned traveller with warmth and enthusiasm, delighted not only to have their beloved friend once more amongst them, but enchanted with the glad tidings he brought from Rome. Claude de Granier wished to share with him the revenues of the diocese, but Francis refused, saying he only intended to partake of the duties and responsibilities of the Bishopric, but not of the emoluments.

It had long been a favourite plan of his to get the seat of the Bishopric removed from Annecy to Thonon, in order to have it in the midst of the converts; but even he found it impossible to surmount all the difficulties in the way of carrying out this design.

Another plan of his was more successful; indeed, it was a complete success. This was to found a Congregation of the Oratory of St. Philip Neri at Thonon. When in the Eternal City in 1591 he met the Apostle of Rome. One interview they had, these two saintly souls, the one only twenty-four, beginning life, still a cavalier, and intended for the Bar, the other seventy-six, his wonderful career nearly at an end. The Saint embraced the young Savoyard with great tenderness and affection; kissing him on the forehead, he told him that he was destined to become a great servant of God and a Prince of the Church. When Francis revisited Rome he was even more deeply impressed by the sublime spirit that inspired the sons of St. Philip Neri to perform deeds of heroic charity, and to practise the greatest virtue. He felt that a community of secular priests living together, and following the rule of the Oratorians, would be of inestimable service in confirming in the Faith the large number of converts in the Chablais, and in drawing into the True Church those who were still aliens.

Francis petitioned the Pope to give his sanction to a foundation of the Oratory at Thonon.

Clement VIII. cordially approved, and in September, 1597, issued the Bull, *Redemptoris et Salvatoris nostri*, by which the house and Church of Our Lady of Compassion at Thonon were constituted a house and church of the Oratory, according to the constitution of the Congregation at Rome.

"Our beloved son in Christ, Francis de Sales, we appoint the first Superior, and Cardinal Baronius the first Protector."

It was, however, generally known and spoken of as the "Holy House," Francis having unofficially called it by that name in memory of his visits to Loreto. It was divided into four parts. The first was an ecclesiastical seminary, and was composed of a Prefect and seven priests. They lived in community, said Mass every morning, chanted the Divine Office on festivals of the first class and of the Blessed Virgin. On other days they chanted the three last Little Hours, Vespers and Compline. They rose at four in the morning during summer, and every Monday attended a conference on cases of conscience and ceremonies; on Tuesday one on the spiritual and temporal administration of the house. They dined together, and, in fact, followed the rule of the Oratorians.

The second part of the Holy House was devoted to preachers, and was composed principally of Capuchin Friars, who went into the country preaching and teaching the Word of God.

The third part was on the plan of a University,

and was copied from those of Bologna and Perugia. It was at first under the direction of the Jesuits. Later on it was managed by seculars, but finally it was given to the Barnabites, who worked it most successfully.

The fourth department was a combination of a mechanics' institute and technical school. Artisans were there taught a trade, and help and assistance were given to the poor. Those converts who were friendless and homeless were taken in, sheltered, and protected.

In order to strengthen the Faith of the newly converted, Francis de Sales published a book entitled "The Standard of the Cross." It was a reply to a pamphlet issued in 1593 by the minister La Faye. In this pamphlet the author covered with abuse and infamy the sacred emblem of our salvation. He used the most scurrilous and abominable language, hoping thus to cause the converts to renounce the Catholic Religion.

Early in 1600 Francis's book appeared. It was a full and complete refutation of La Faye's charges. According to the author's own expression, its purpose was *defaire les dires**of his opponent, and obliged him *ou à ruiner la raison et lui jurer inimitié* ** or else to acknowledge the truth of the numerous proofs and demonstrations in support of the veneration of the Holy Cross.

This work, the first-fruit of his pen, Francis dedicated to his beloved Sovereign, Charles Emmanuel, Duke of Savoy.

*"to tear down the words"
**"either to overthrow reason and swear enmity to him" . . .

# CHAPTER XI

## *HENRY OF NAVARRE*

CHARLES EMMANUEL, when in Paris, concluded a treaty with Henry IV. In it he agreed to cede to the King the Marquisate of Saluzzo, a district the then head of the House of Savoy had seized during the wars of the League. On his side the King of France gave him the province of La Bresse and other disputed territory. Henry loyally carried out his part of the contract, but at the last moment the Duke of Savoy refused to surrender Saluzzo.

He expected that Spain would support him, as he had joined in a conspiracy with Philip II. that had for its object the dismemberment of France into independent feudal states, under the protection of the King of Spain. He pleaded as a reason for his refusal that he had only consented to the treaty through fear, expecting arrest and imprisonment if he did not give his consent. The result was an immediate declaration of war.

The King put himself at the head of his army, and the Duke de Lesdiguères, with his troops, was sent into Savoy. They rapidly overran the province, and soon conquered the greater part of the country.  Other troops under Maréchal de Biron attacked La Bresse, which was soon reduced to submission.

On August 21, 1600, the King of France and of Navarre entered Chambéry in triumph.  The inhabitants of Geneva and Berne were rejoiced at his victories.  They sent a deputation to him, offering to join their troops to his to enable him to conquer the Ternier and the Chablais.

Their offer was accepted.  They then petitioned the King to proclaim the Edict of Nantes throughout the conquered country.  But Henry, careless and *débonnaire* though he was, was also keen-witted and intelligent ; he could read men, and he quite understood their motives.  He knew that they hoped to ruin the Catholics by restoring the free exercise of the Calvinist religion.  They thought the converts would easily be perverted, and would help them to destroy the churches and seize the Church property.  Consequently the King only replied that he would consider the matter.

The Bishop of Geneva, hearing of these *pourparlers**between the enemies of his flock and the victorious monarch, was much troubled and disquieted.  He wrote to the Duc de Joyeuse, who was on His Majesty's staff, entreating him to use his influence with Henry to prevent his agreeing to the petition.

Nothing definite was decided on, and affairs

*parley, negotiations

were apparently at a standstill, when Francis de Sales resolved to visit the King, who was then at the Château d'Annecy.

Henri de Bourbon received the humble Apostle of the Chablais with the utmost respect and veneration. He held his hat in his hand during the whole interview, a mark of esteem rarely shown by monarchs even to the most distinguished men. Francis presented his request. In it he implored His Majesty to leave intact all that had been done for the Catholic Faith in the Chablais and in the Ternier. Henry carefully read the petition, and then replied :

" For the love of God and of our Holy Father the Pope, and out of consideration for you, monsieur, who have so nobly fulfilled your mission, nothing shall be changed. The result of your labours shall not be destroyed. What you have done for the Catholic Faith no one shall undo. I promise you this on my honour. Foi de roi et j'y serai fidèle au péril de mon sang." *

He then signed the document. The people of Geneva, disappointed at this result, now turned to the Governor of the province. He was a Calvinist, and resided at the Château d'Allinges. They persuaded him to seize the benefices belonging to the Order of SS. Maurice and Lazarus, in order to add them to the royal revenues, representing to him that they were the private property of the Duke of Savoy.

When Francis heard of this unjust and false

---

*"On my honor as king, and I shall be faithful to it at the peril of my blood."

pretext, he set out at once for Allinges. He intended to tell the Governor the wishes of the King, and to show him the document bearing the royal signature. He could at the same time show how untrue were the statements of the Genevese.

He had only gone a short distance when he fell into the hands of a troop of soldiers, and was taken prisoner. He was brought before the Marquis de Vitry, the Captain of the King's Guard. No sooner was the identity of his captive made known to the Marquis than he released him at once, treated him with the greatest consideration, and even wished to take him to Chambéry to present him formally to the King.

" It would give me great pleasure to accept your offer," replied Francis, " for it would indeed be great honour for me to be presented to so renowned a monarch ; but as long as your Sovereign is at war with mine, I cannot do homage to him or appear at his Court."

The Marquis was charmed at this answer.

" I like you all the better for your loyalty," he told Francis candidly, "and I will be only too pleased to serve you in any way. Pray command me."

De Vitry would have retained him at the camp, so impressed was he by the gentle dignity of Francis, and so fascinated by his courteous and winning manner ; but the Coadjutor was anxious to proceed on his way, and would not tarry, so the Marquis gave him a letter of recommendation to M. de Monglan, and he resumed his journey.

Arrived at Allinges, Francis presented to the Governor the letters of the Bishop of Geneva and of the Captain of the King's Guard, and the petition Henry had given his consent to at Annecy. M. de Monglan received him with much cordiality, promised to carry out the King's wishes, and remarked that, Calvinist though he was, yet he found nothing to grumble at in them, but considered them perfectly just and right.

Francis fervently returned thanks to God and Our Lady for the favourable result of his embassy. He then carried the glad tidings to Thonon. He was welcomed with an ovation. His friends and penitents were delighted to have their *bon père* once more in their midst. The members of the Holy House greeted him as a dear and loving Father. They were getting along splendidly, doing good work nobly, but the reports they had heard had made them a little uneasy. Francis reassured them and the priests of the colleges and of the various parishes, who had feared lest they might be compelled to leave their people.

The Genevese had asked the King to banish the Jesuits. This he absolutely refused to do. In fact, he took the Order under his special protection, and, thanks to his favour, they were left unmolested. Indeed, the whole country benefited by the zeal Henry displayed in protecting the clergy, in maintaining the Faith, and in keeping

the army so well disciplined that no outrages
were committed, and private property was respected.

Through the mediation of the Pope and of
Cardinal Aldobrandini, another treaty was signed
at Lyons between France and Savoy. In this
the King gave up his claim to the Marquisate of
Saluzzo, and the Duke agreed to pay 10,000
*écus*, and to give to France La Bresse, Le Bugey,
Le Valromay, the bailiwick of Gex, and seven
villages on the banks of the Rhone. From this
date the Catholics were allowed to practise their
religion in peace.

Affairs were now in a flourishing condition at
Thonon, so that when Claude de Granier invited
Francis to preach during the Lent of 1601 at
Annecy, the Prefect of the Holy House felt he
could safely leave it and Thonon; therefore he
accepted gladly. He was preparing his discourses
when the news reached him that his father was
dangerously ill. M. de Boisy was a very old
man, having attained his seventy-ninth year; he
was, therefore, scarcely likely to recover from a
serious malady. Francis hastened to the Château
de Sales, where he found the family plunged in
grief. M. de Boisy was suffering greatly, but
was cheerful and resigned. He made a general
confession to his beloved son Francis. He was
able to receive Holy Communion three times, and
he manifested great fervour in so doing, and was
particularly pleased it was from the hands of his

son that he partook of the Holy Eucharist. He listened attentively and with much content to the exhortations and counsels of the Saint.

Francis could not remain long at home, for he had promised to commence his lectures at Annecy, and he would not disappoint the people. M. de Boisy willingly consented. As a man of honour he quite understood that Francis should keep his word, so he urged him to set out without delay. Francis took a fond farewell of this dear parent, kneeling to receive his blessing, and in return giving to the dying man his priestly benediction. The doctors said there was no immediate danger, and that in all probability M. de Boisy would live until after Easter. Therefore Francis hoped to see his father once again. When Lent was over, he would be free to return home.

Unfortunately, the medical men were wrong; M. de Boisy got steadily worse. He received the Last Sacraments, got better, and for a few days seemed likely to recover; he relapsed; once more Extreme Unction was administered, and he was warned that his end was approaching. At the news his old military ardour blazed up. It also distressed him greatly to see his wife and daughters, and the maids weeping round his bed. Calling his second son, Galloys, he said:

" My dear son, you who are my heir and also the inheritor of my courage, bring me my arms, and help me to rise, so that I may die standing, sword in hand. It is unworthy of a soldier, accus-

tomed to face death on the battle-field, to die tamely
in his bed, surrounded by weeping women."

Soon, however, his mind reverted to thoughts
of Our Lord and the life to come, and, taking the
crucifix in his hands, he kissed it devoutly, then,
raising his eyes heavenwards, he prayed fervently.
Turning to his wife and children, he gave them
his blessing, recommending them to look upon
Francis as their father, yielding him obedience
and reverence. He most earnestly besought his
boys and girls to console their mother, and to
love, respect, and cherish her. Then, quietly and
without a struggle, his soul passed away.

A messenger was immediately sent to Annecy
to relate the sad tidings to his son. He found
Francis in the sacristy, about to mount the pulpit.
On hearing the news Francis fell on his knees,
buried his face in his hands, and communed
silently with God. Then, strengthened and
calmed, he went forth into the cathedral, and
preached with even more than his usual eloquence
and unction. Taking for his text the Gospel of
the day—the death and resurrection of Lazarus—
he spoke in a clear, firm voice, with great distinct-
ness and without hurry. The sermon over, he
said to the congregation :

" My friends, I have just learned that my
beloved father is no more. He died but a few
hours since. You all, I well know, loved and
honoured him in life : do not forget him in death.
I entreat you to pray for the repose of his soul

and to allow me to leave you for a few days in order to attend his funeral."

He could no longer restrain his emotion. He wept bitterly—indeed, the assembled people united their tears to his, for the old Seigneur was much loved and respected.

In the midst of his grief Francis had the consolation of learning that the Catholic Religion had been completely re-established in the bailiwick of Gaillard, a small district close to Thonon. But there were still obstacles in the way at Gex. The people of Geneva hoped that the Calvinist Faith only would be tolerated, and that Henry IV. would forbid the free practice of the Catholic Religion. They had many reasons wherewith to persuade him to this course of action. Affairs were in such a tangle, and it seemed so probable that the Genevese would succeed in carrying their point, that Francis decided to go himself to Paris to explain matters to the King and to beg of him to allow the same liberty of conscience to his subjects in Gex as, by the proclamation of the Edict of Nantes, he had assured to the rest of his dominions.

# CHAPTER XII

## *AT THE COURT OF THE KING OF FRANCE*

AT the beginning of the seventeenth century the French Court was one of the gayest and most brilliant in Europe.

Beautiful, wicked Paris was then, as now, *La Ville Lumière*—splendid, laughter-loving, radiant, but with dark corners, and squalid alleys, where vice reigned supreme, the misery and wretchedness of the people contrasting with the wealth and grandeur of the nobles. Henri de Bourbon, King of France and of Navarre, undoubtedly did his utmost to improve the condition of the proletariate. He was truly and really the friend of the poor. "Le seul roi dont le pauvre ait gardé la mémoire" (The only King whose memory is cherished by the poor). When he cried out in generous anger, "S'en prendre à mon peuple, c'est s'en prendre à moi" (Who takes from my people, takes from me), he meant it; and he also thoroughly meant that *mot* of his: "Si Dieu me donne de la vie, je ferai qu'il n'y aura pas de laboureur en mon royaume qui n'ait moyen d'avoir une poule dans son pot" (If God preserves my life, I will see that every workman in my kingdom is able to have a fowl in his pot).

He was a wise and just ruler, a victorious general, a great statesman. With his devoted and lifelong friend, the Duc de Sully—who loved him with the love passing the love of women, even as Jonathan loved David—to advise, counsel and often to restrain, he was one of the greatest and most beneficent Sovereigns who ever reigned. With his genial, devil-may-care manner, his rollicking air, yet keen, alert brain and quick intelligence, he possessed in a marked degree the royal prerogative, the gift of discerning the characters of men.

When he first met Francis de Sales at Annecy, he felt singularly drawn towards the gentle priest. Now that Francis was at his own Court, and they met constantly, they soon became fast friends.

One day the King said to his secretary—M. Deshayes: "I see that you and M. de Genève are great friends." For although Francis was still only Coadjutor, the King and all the Court gave him the title that properly belonged only to the Bishop of Geneva.

"Which of us two do you love best—the priest or the monarch?"

"Sire!" replied the embarrassed secretary, "you must pardon me. You are my King and my lord; as such it is my duty to love and esteem you more than anyone else."

"Leave duty out of the question," retorted Henry; "tell me honestly, faith of a gentleman, which of us two you really love best."

"Sire," answered M. Deshayes, "I must acknowledge that I love and esteem M. de Genève beyond all measure; so that it would be impossible for me to care more for anyone else."

The King laughed good-naturedly. "I am not hurt, my good Deshayes," he said genially, "only tell him that I wish to be the third in this great friendship."

And in many ways Henry proved himself the friend and admirer of Francis de Sales. Yet he could not hasten on the affair at Gex, about which our Saint had come to Paris.

Henry placed the matter in the hands of his Minister Villeroi, who threw every obstacle in the way of a favourable settlement.

Nevertheless, the time Francis spent in Paris was not wasted. During the six months he was compelled to remain in the French capital he exercised so powerful an influence over all who came in contact with him that they never forgot him. For the remainder of their lives they cherished his memory, and they thanked God daily for the spiritual benefits they had received by following his counsels.

He converted numbers of all classes. Those who led worldly and tepid lives he exhorted to reform. He hardly allowed himself time for rest and refreshment. Constantly preaching, giving instructions, visiting the sick, his zeal enabled him, in the course of six months, to do work it would have taken an ordinary man a lifetime to accomplish.

At the request of Marie de Luxembourg, Duchesse de Mercœurs, he preached the Lenten Sermons at the Court. He began on Ash Wednesday. In a day or two the chapel was not large enough to contain the audience. All sorts and conditions of men and women came to listen to the eloquent preacher. Numerous conversions rewarded his efforts. One of the most obdurate and stiff-necked of the Huguenots—the Comtesse de Verdreauville—embraced the Catholic Faith. She was well known, and her abjuration caused a considerable stir not only in Court circles, but throughout the kingdom. Many who were undecided, and had for a long time hesitated to take the final step, followed her example. Cardinal de Perron sagely remarked : "God has given to M. de Genève the key that unlocks all hearts. If it were only necessary to convince the heretics, I myself could convince as many as you please. But convert them! For that send them to M. de Genève."

Francis de Sales who was so successful in leading souls from the darkness of error into the full light of faith, was, it is needless to remark, just as successful in comforting and encouraging holy souls who wished to attain to the heights of perfection.

One of his greatest friends was Mme. Acarie; she confessed frequently to him, and found in his discourses the light and grace she needed to follow her sublime vocation.

Later on she became a nun of the Reformed Order of Mount Carmel, under the name of Sister Mary of the Incarnation, and was beatified by Pius VII. in 1791.

Francis entertained a great esteem and affection for her. Eighteen years afterwards he said to a Carmelite: "Whenever I think of your Venerable Mother, I receive spiritual consolation. I always felt a great respect for her wonderful virtues. Nor did I look upon her simply as my penitent, but rather as a vessel of election, consecrated to the Holy Spirit."

Another lifelong friendship was cemented at this time between Francis de Sales and M. de Berulle. Of him, Francis often said that "he was one of the purest, and most straightforward souls he had ever met." On his side the holy founder of the Congregation of the Oratory felt great admiration for our Saint, whose evenness of temper and sweetness of disposition astonished him.

Indeed, to know Francis was to love and reverence him. At this time—1600—he was in the prime of life, full of vitality and energy. Dressed in the black robe of the priest, with close-cropped fair hair, kind blue eyes, and a sunny smile, his beard cut round—a most unfashionable style—he passed from the palace to the garret, from the castles of the great to the hovels of the poor.

Wherever he went, his gentle yet dignified manner, his courtesy and suavity, won for him golden opinions. He sowed the good seed with generous hand, and it brought forth fruit a hundredfold.

The King said of him: "If I had not been already converted, M. de Genève most certainly would have persuaded me to become a Catholic;' and he continued:

"M. de Genève is decidedly the phœnix of prelates. The rest have all a weak side. With one it is low birth; another is not overburdened with learning; another is wanting in piety; but M. de Genève has all three qualities in the highest degree. He is of illustrious birth, rare learning, and eminent piety."

Henry was eager to keep this paragon of perfection in France. At least five times he entreated Francis to remain, promising him splendid appointments.

"Stay with us, M. de Genève," he begged. "I will give you a wealthier see, and a much better position than the one you hold under the Duke of Savoy."

"Sire," replied Francis, "I implore your Majesty's forgiveness, for I must refuse your generous offer. I have married a poor wife, and I cannot desert her for a rich one. But if your Majesty has any regard for me, I entreat you to re-establish our Faith and our churches in Gex."

Henry was quite willing to grant this request, but Villeroi still threw obstacles in the way. Unable to accord at once the favour asked by Francis de Sales, the King sent him a present. This was a brevet, conferring upon him a considerable pension.

Our Saint found himself in a most embarrassing position. He did not wish to hurt the King by a refusal, nor could he accept the gift, but with his usual adroitness he hit upon an expedient.

"Sire," he wrote, "I thank you with all my heart for the great kindness you have shown my unworthy self. Yes, I accept with pleasure your Majesty's munificence, but you will allow me to tell you that at present I should not know what to do with a pension; consequently I entreat you to let your treasurer keep it for me until I require it."

Henry was charmed with this reply. More delighted than ever with this "phœnix of prelates," he did all in his power to hurry up the Gex affair. In the meantime Francis was accused of taking part in a conspiracy against the monarch. Henry only laughed good-naturedly when he heard of the accusation. Sending for Francis, he told him:

"M. de Genève, you need not go to the trouble of defending yourself. I never suspected you, but I cannot prevent stupid people spreading absurd reports and coming to me with silly stories."

While in Paris, Francis preached, at Notre Dame, the funeral oration of Philip-Emmanuel of Lorraine, Duc de Mercœur.

It was a rather difficult undertaking, as in the old days the Duke had been not only a strong partisan, but one of the Chiefs of the League, and a formidable enemy of Henri de Bourbon. Tactful as usual, Francis steered clear of dangerous ground, and managed to preach an effective panegyric on Philip-Emmanuel, without touching on politics.

Disquieting news came from Savoy. Claude de Granier was dangerously ill, and it was imperative that his Coadjutor should hasten back, in order to be consecrated Bishop. In this predicament Francis had again recourse to the King, begging of him to grant his request. "Sire," he said, " you have often told us that you are more Catholic than even your most Catholic subjects, that you love our religion even more than we do, who have been born in the Faith. You say you will have no distinctions made between Huguenots and Catholics ; your wish is that all should be good Frenchmen and fellow-citizens. Why, then, will you not give to Gex the liberty of conscience enjoyed throughout the rest of your kingdom?"

Henry quite agreed, promised he would insist on an immediate and favourable report from Villeroi, and at last succeeded in overcoming the Minister's opposition, for he alone had caused the long delay.

The Baron de Luz former Governor of Burgundy,

and consequently of Gex, had been accused of taking part in the conspiracy of Maréchal de Biron—the same conspiracy in which they had endeavoured to implicate Francis. De Luz had been thrown into prison.

He solicited an interview with Henry, and honestly confessed his fault.

The King, who loved truthful and candid people, generously forgave him. He not only pardoned him freely, but reinstated him in his former office.

Sending him back to Burgundy as Governor, he ordered him to re-establish the Catholic Religion in Gex. He also took under his protection the Catholic priests of the various districts, and gave permission to Francis de Sales to select pastors for the reconstituted parishes. He only stipulated that they should act prudently and quietly, in order not to cause dissatisfaction among the Protestants. This was not quite all that Francis had asked for, but it was a good deal, and he was well pleased.

The Coadjutor bade farewell to his many friends in the gay capital, and had a touching interview with the King.

Henry grieved greatly over his departure, remarking afterwards to his courtiers:

" I have the greatest esteem and affection for M. de Genève. He possesses every virtue, and has not a single fault. I have never met anyone so capable of restoring to the ecclesiastical state its former splendour. He is gentle, sweet-tempered, humble of heart, and of an equable disposition. He is fervently pious, but without affectation, conscientious, but not scrupulous. In one word, he is the man best suited to root out heresy and restore the Catholic Faith."

Francis set out for Savoy, and had got as far as Lyons when he heard of the death of Claude de Granier. The venerable Bishop of Geneva died on September 17, 1602. Having received the Last Sacraments with great fervour, he passed quietly away.

It was quite unnecessary for him to make a will. At his death he only owned six sous, and the sale of his goods and chattels barely sufficed to pay his debts. He was a good and generous man, a wise prelate, and a kind friend. Francis had loved him for many years. He felt his death greatly, and was for a long time plunged in grief. But he had much to do. Travelling rapidly, he soon reached Gex, where he spent a short time. He succeeded in re-establishing five parishes, appointing Canon Louis de Sales parish priest of the town of Gex. Louis, who was as disinterested as his saintly cousin, quietly but resolutely refused to accept a salary.

Matters thus fairly arranged at Gex, Francis proceeded to the Château de Sales to prepare for his consecration.

# CHAPTER XIII

## *A PRINCE OF THE CHURCH*

FRANCIS DE SALES, arrived at the Château de Sales, devoted a few days to his family before commencing his retreat—days of much-needed rest to him, and days of unutterable joy to his loving mother and the home circle. It was more than six months since they had all met together, and they had much to discuss and talk over. One can picture to oneself how, each night, Mme. de Boisy longed for the morrow.

> " In a wakeful doze I sorrow
>     For the hands, the lips, the eyes,
> For the meeting of the morrow,
> The delight of happy laughter,
>     The delight of low replies."

For Francis was not an austere and melancholy Saint; he had a sunny smile, a merry laugh, a pleasant manner, and he possessed in the fullest degree a keen sense of humour. Looking at his picture in the " Berceau de la Visitation," one can realize how his own people, and especially his mother, must have loved him.

There, in the gloom of that little chapel, hangs his portrait. As I try to get a good view of it, a welcome gleam of sunshine lights it up. I see a bearded face smiling down on me, the blue eyes seeming to read my inmost thoughts.

"What are you doing here?" they seem to ask. "Is it devotion or curiosity brings you so far from home? Are you on a pilgrimage to my shrine, or have you come to have a look at the mountains and the lake, to study the people of this old-world town, to gratify your artistic tastes, or to try and attain a greater degree of Christian perfection by the contemplation of the scenes of my labours? A little of both, *n'est-ce pas, mon enfant?*"

With his grave, sweet expression, his rather full lips, that seem inclined to smile in a humorous way at most things, and the slight soupçon of sarcasm in the curved brows, one could easily imagine how quickly he would understand our mixed motives, and, while he smiled at our follies, would yet have a tender feeling of sympathy for us.

Francis went through life in a glad and joyful spirit believing that God loves not only the cheerful giver, but the cheerful liver, for is He not the God of love? He thoroughly agreed with Thomas à Kempis:

"Nothing is sweeter than love, nothing more courageous, nothing higher, nothing wider, nothing more pleasant, nothing fuller nor better in Heaven and earth, because love is born of God, and cannot rest but in God, above all created things. Love feels no burden, thinks nothing of trouble, attempts what is above its strength, pleads no excuse of impossibility, for it thinks all things lawful for itself and all things possible."

The Gospel of Francis de Sales, as of the Beloved Disciple, was the Gospel of Love. Indeed, so sweet was his disposition, so tender-hearted and compassionate was he, that he used to say, " If God had told us to hate our enemies, I do not know how I could have obeyed Him, it is so sweet to love them."

And if he found it so easy—nay, delightful—to love his enemies, how deeply and truly must he have loved his friends, and how warm and ardent must have been his affection for his own people ! But when we think of what must have been his love of God, we can only sigh over our incapacity to form the faintest idea of the burning and consuming fire that filled his heart, and impelled him to do great things for his Beloved.

" For it is a loud cry in the ears of God, this ardent affection of the soul which saith, ' My God, my Love, Thou art all mine, and I am all Thine.' "

Having given these few days to affection, Francis went, all refreshed by his long interviews with his dear ones, and physically strengthened by the pure air of his native mountains, and was ready to go into the desert to prepare, by prayer, fasting, and meditation, to receive in fullest measure the blessings and graces he hoped Our Lord would vouchsafe to him at his consecration.

He sent to Thonon for Père Forrier, S.J., who was to guide and direct him during his long retreat of twenty days.

He started it by making a general confession. During it he devoted hours to prayer and meditation, fasted rigorously, and practised the severest corporal penances. He writes:

"I resolved to love and serve God with all the ardour and energy of which I was capable, to devote my whole life to His service. I only know one desire: it is this holy passion which causes so many works of piety to be written, so many churches, altars, and convents to be erected—in a word, which causes so many of God's servants to die amid the flames of love which consume them. It is the love of God above all things. Therefore will I always keep myself in His Divine Presence, that I may love Him more and more. I long for the happy day when I shall be eternally united to Him, and, in order to help myself on my way, and enable me to attain this longed-for end, I make the following resolutions:

"1. *Dress, Toilet.*—I will not wear rich garments, costly silks or perfumed gloves, but will have my clothes well-cut, neat, and without ostentation, suitable-to my position. In public I will wear a mantle, and rochet, and the biretta. My girdle may be of silk, but not of an expensive quality, and I will wear my rosary attached to it. I will have a well-defined tonsure, wear a round, not pointed, beard, and no moustache.

"2. *Household*.—I will not have a suite of attendants. Two priests, one to assist me in the divine office, the other to act as secretary. They must wear the Roman dress, or else that worn by the priests of the seminary at Milan, because it is cheap. I will have a *valet de chambre*, a butler, a cook, a kitchen-boy, and a lackey. I will have no women-servants. The meals will be frugal—dinner at 10 a.m., supper at 6 p.m. During the first part of the meals a holy book will be read, then conversation.

"3. *Alms*.—I will give public alms on the same days as the late Bishop, in order to set a good example; private alms I will give as God inspires me.

"4. *Devotions*.—I will assist at all the ceremonies at the Cathedral on Sundays and holidays, and I will attend as often as possible at the meetings of the Confraternities of the Holy Cross, of the Blessed Sacrament, of the Rosary and Cord, and I will endeavour myself to give Holy Communion to the members. I will celebrate Holy Mass every day at 9 a.m., devoting the time between seven and nine to reading and study, having previously spent an hour in meditation. I will read a religious book for an hour every evening after supper, and I will hear confessions several times during the week. Every year I will make an eight-day retreat.

"*Fasts*.—Besides the usual days of fasting ordained by the Church, I will fast every Friday and Saturday, and on all the vigils of the Feasts of Our Lady."

Writing some time later to the Archbishop of Bourges, he tells him: "In drawing up a rule of life I wished to arrange my time more or less precisely, but I never have the least hesitation in changing my hours to suit the convenience of others. The affairs of this diocese flow not in waves, but in torrents. I have but little leisure, crowds come to me for advice. I have to keep up an extensive correspondence on spiritual matters. I cannot neglect the souls who appeal to me to aid them, so I have often to give up study and meditation and alter the hours of meals, but it is best so. A holy liberty is what Our Lord desires: He wishes us to love Him without constraint. *Amor meus, pondus meum.**

The Château de Sales was an ideal place in which to make a retreat. It was more like a monastery than the castle of a great noble, it was so calm, so peaceful."

All the members of this happy family lived together in love and harmony. The mother-in-law with her daughters-in-law, the sisters-in-law and brothers-in-law, were all united together, sympathizing with each other, and always ready to please and to help. In fact, it was an abode of sweetness and of kindliness, where religion and virtue reigned supreme.

Later, Francis de Sales wrote to Mme. de Chantal: "Here, with my good mother and our

*"My love, my burden."

family, I enjoy the greatest happiness. It would charm you to see us all so united. Thank God, we have here, as it were, only one heart and one soul, for all seek only the glory of God."

Mme. de Boisy was the mainspring, the soul of the household. This admirable mother neglected nothing to introduce the practice of virtue into her house, and in order to succeed she consulted her son on every subject. He was her confessor and director; she looked upon him as the guardian angel of the House of Sales. She religiously followed his advice, frequently wrote to consult him, and, indeed, it was for her he wrote most of the instructions contained in " Introduction à la Vie Dévote."

Thus, calmly, in the midst of his own people, Francis spent his days of preparation. Far from the madding crowd, he was able to lift up his heart to God, and to listen to the inspirations of the Holy Spirit. Mme. de Boisy also went into retreat, praying that God would shed His choicest blessings on her dear son. She and her daughters went to infinite trouble to decorate the parish church at Thorens; beautiful tapestries covered the walls, rare and exotic plants and flowers were grouped round the altar. The armorial bearings of the House of Sales were placed in front of the choir, surmounted by a mitre, a gold cross, and a green hat with this inscription, " Après de longues années, le ciel." *

*"After the long years, Heaven."

On December 8, 1602, Francis de Sales was consecrated Prince Bishop of Geneva in the grey old church of Thorens. In that same church, on August 22, 1567, an infant only a day old, he had received Holy Baptism. The officiating Prelate was Vespasian Grimaldi, Archbishop of Vienne in Dauphiny. This venerable priest had lived in retirement for fifteen years at Evian on the lake of Geneva, devoting himself to works of charity and to study. He was assisted by Thomas Popel, Bishop of St. Paul, de Trois Châteaux, and Jacques Maistret, Bishop of Damascus.

During the ceremony the face of Francis glowed with the fire of Divine Love; indeed, so overwhelming were the emotions he experienced that he became unconscious, unable to support the devouring fire which consumed his soul. He related afterwards that he felt clearly and distinctly the Holy Trinity operating in his soul by the outward sign of his consecration. At the imposition of hands he received the gifts of the Holy Ghost; at the anointing of the head, the dignity of representing Jesus Christ on earth. When the Testament was placed on his shoulders, he was given the mission to preach the Word of God; at the consecration of hands, the power to ordain priests, to bless the faithful, and to use the keys of the Kingdom of Heaven, to bind and to loose.

When the mitre was placed on his head, he felt that he should watch over his senses with the utmost care, and that he was bound to explain and expound the Old and New Testaments. The gloves showed the obligation of good works; the ring signified his engagement to be faithful to his See, and finally, the cross impressed on him that it was his duty to sustain the weak, to admonish sinners, and to convert heretics. He said that he saw, or dreamed that he saw, as in a vision, mystic, wonderful, Our Lady, and St. Peter and St. Paul, assisting him at each step of the ceremony.

Francis spent a few more days at the Château de Sales before going to Annecy to take possession of his See. His entry was—without his desiring it—a triumphal one. The nobility of the surrounding country and four of the Counsellors met him outside the walls and accompanied him to the Church of Notre Dame de Compassion, where priests and people awaited him. There, clad in the episcopal robes, he prayed for some time before the altar.

Presently the procession started; the religious Orders and the secular clergy walked in front; then came Francis de Sales, followed by an immense throng of people of all classes. Arrived at the Cathedral, the saintly Bishop entered, prostrated himself before the Tabernacle, kissed the altar, and then sitting on the episcopal throne, had to listen to a panegyric on his own virtues preached by Dr. Nouvellet. Finally, the *Te Deum* was sung, Benediction given, and priests and people returned to their homes in the narrow medieval streets, or into the queer dark passages that run through or under the houses.

Annecy must have been very much the same then as now, though the intensely modern Rue Royale was not in existence, nor yet the handsome Hôtel de Ville. I do not think that the nasty, tall, useful factory chimneys and the long, grey, many-windowed stores, which spoil the beauty, but help towards the prosperity of the town, were there. But the quaint old arcades were, and very likely the saleswomen cried their wares just as they do now—carrots, wool, turnips, stockings, braces, baskets—everything all mingled together in "most admired confusion."

The lake and the everlasting hills were as beautiful then as now, though I do not know if the pretty gardens of the Paquier and the Champs de Mars bordered one side of it, but certainly Francis could see as we can the graceful many-coloured mountains, with white villages and slim church spires rising beneath them. There in the distance lies Talloires, where there is an old Benedictine abbey, and Menthon, where St. Bernard of Menthon was born. There also lived his tutor, St. Germain, in a hermitage perched almost on the summit of the Deuts de Lafont. Francis de Sales caused the relics of St. Germain to be removed from the nave and placed under the high altar of the church, which our Saint had repaired and richly decorated in honour of the holy abbot.

After preaching to a numerous audience and devoutly venerating the relics of the hermit of the eleventh century, the Bishop of the seventeenth, feeling himself inspired by the same spirit of contemplation, the same love of solitude and silence, cried to those near him, "Here, indeed, I should like to rest! If it were pleasing to God, willingly would I leave the heat and burden of the day to my Coadjutor, and in this retreat serve God and His Church with my rosary, my Breviary, and my pen." Then, opening a window, from which he could see the lake and town of Annecy, and admiring the beauty of the surrounding country, he continued: "What a splendid prospect! Here grand and beautiful thoughts would fall on the soul, as abundantly as snow falls on the earth in winter."

On this fourteenth day of the darkest and gloomiest month in the year of Our Lord, 1602, let us hope that the snow did not fall; and it probably did not, for the old chroniclers do not mention it.

It was a Saturday, for Francis had wished to begin his new life on the day devoted to the Blessed Virgin. So, as towards evening he entered his new home, let us fancy that the setting sun threw a mystic golden light over the translucent waters of the lake, fading gradually into softer shades, until at last it disappeared, leaving the beauty of a cloudless night. Round him the hills would grow darker and darker, seeming to come nearer and nearer, the lights in the town would gleam and twinkle, and Francis de Sales, in his own little oratory, " the world forgetting, by the world forgot," would give himself up to prayer and contemplation, letting his soul rest in the loving Heart of the Saviour.

# CHAPTER XIV

## *THE ROOM OF FRANCIS*

FRANCIS DE SALES lost no time in setting his house in order. Following the rules he had drawn up for his guidance during his retreat, he arranged his household somewhat like a monastery, with fixed hours and regulations.

Though his income was small, only about £150 per annum, he endeavoured to make a certain show as far as outward appearances went, for he wished to uphold the dignity of the Prince-Bishop of Geneva. His lackey wore a simple livery of light brown bordered with violet. The rooms allotted to the reception of visitors were handsomely furnished and beautifully decorated. These he called the apartments of the Prince-Bishop. His own room, on the contrary, was small, and was furnished in the simplest manner —a bed, a table, a couple of chairs, no carpet, a writing-desk, and a few of his favourite books. " I must be the Bishop of Geneva in public," he said, " but in private I will be Francis de Sales."

Among his books were Scupoli's " Spiritual Combat," an old friend, for in former days at

Paris and Padua he had always carried it about with him ; Bellarmine's " Controversies," another of his special favourites, and from which he had gained both knowledge and strength during his mission in the Chablais ; the " Confessions of St. Augustine "; the " Spiritual Letters of John of Avila," that wonderful book so full of mystic theology ; the " Life of St. Charles Borromeo," one of his special patrons, and whose sublime example he set himself to imitate ; the " Epistles of St. Jerome "; the " Spiritual Exercises of St. Ignatius." Early in his life at Padua, in 1587, his director, Père Possevin, S.J., had taught him the Jesuit method of meditation. He always adhered to that practical and beautiful form of mental prayer, though slightly altering it to suit his own character and the needs of his penitents, as we see in " La Vie Dévote."[*] Of course he also treasured the Old and New Testaments, and the " Imitation of Christ " ; indeed, he knew them by heart, so often had he read and pondered over them.

It is in this little room, then, that we must picture him to ourselves, praying, meditating, reading, writing. He called it "the room of Francis." In it he wrote his charming and instructive letters to his many friends — those " Letters " that are so delightful, so full of ardent piety, of grace, of cordiality ; yet often he brings in a little gossip, a witty sally, a sarcastic remark, and these, showing as they do his un-

125

---

[*] St. Francis de Sales' book, *An Introduction to the Devout Life* (also known as *Philothea*).

affected simplicity, add to the charm of the correspondence.

He says : " Through a great part of my soul I am poor and weak, but I have a boundless and lasting affection for my friends. Whoever challenges me in the contest of friendship must be very determined, for I spare no effort. No one has a heart more affectionate and tender towards his friends than I, or which so acutely feels being separated from them. It has pleased Our Lord to make me so. I love my neighbours so much, and I wish to love them even more. Oh! when shall we all be full of meekness and charity towards our neighbours ? I have given them my whole person, my means, my affections, that these may serve them in all their wants."

In it he wrote the notes and instructions to Mme. de Charmoisy. They afterwards developed into his masterpiece " La Vie Dévote," that marvellous work in which he makes himself all things to all men. He stands, as it were, on the high-road to point out to all passers-by the way to Heaven. He smooths the roughness that frightens the timid, and he tells us to have patience, particularly with ourselves and our own defects. When we read it we feel that Francis de Sales is talking to us, counselling and helping us. So simple and energetic is the language, so clear and beautiful the style, it goes straight to our hearts, helping us in our difficulties, making the hard ways smooth, penetrating to the very depths of our souls, and giving to each and all just the very advice and solace suited to our peculiar temperaments. "Lord, Thou knowest the clay of which we are formed," and surely the saintly Bishop of Geneva, like his Divine Master, knows the doubts and perplexities, the troubles and temptations, that rend our hearts and tear our souls, dimming the beauty of the Divine Presence, and leaving us a prey to the assaults of the world, the flesh, and the devil. Like his Divine Master, the Bishop of Geneva dearly loved the little ones. One of his first acts was to start Sunday-schools in Annecy. He generally taught the little people. They loved and reverenced him, following him wherever he went, just as in the old days their parents had followed him when he was a boy and their comrade. Now a younger generation ran after him, treating their Prince-Bishop with scant ceremony. People remonstrated with them, and he replied in the words of Our Lord, "Suffer the little ones to come unto Me, for of such is the Kingdom of Heaven."

So successful were these catechism classes at Annecy that he soon established them throughout the diocese.

He went to infinite trouble to select holy and zealous priests for the various parishes, never appointing one until he had passed a stiff examination by erudite ecclesiastics. He drew up a ritual for the use of his diocese based on the Roman liturgy. He also composed a book of instructions for the use of his clergy, entitled "Avertissement aux Confesseurs." This little book was much thought of and widely read both in France and in Italy.

He had some trouble in endeavouring to reform the Abbey of Sixt, an Augustinian monastery at Faucingy. This house had fallen into such a state of relaxation that the Abbot actually did not know whether he was or was not obliged to keep the rules of his Order—that is, whether he was titular or commendatory. One can fancy that, under the government of such a man, the poor monks had no clear idea of their obligations; in fact, disorder reigned.

With much difficulty Francis at length succeeded in introducing order into this chaos. For a time discipline was re-established, and the monastic rules observed, but after a while relaxations again crept in, and years later Francis had again to endeavour to reform Sixt.

Another part of his diocese now claimed his attention—namely, Gex. Unfortunate Gex, again disturbed by the Calvinists persecuting the Catholics, and seizing on their revenues. Gex was all through his life a thorn in the side of Francis, giving him more trouble than all the rest of his See.

Hearing that the Duc de Bellegarde, Governor of the province, and Baron de Luz, Lieutenant of the King, were at Belley, the Bishop of Geneva arranged to meet them there to confer on the affairs of Gex.

The Duke agreed to use his utmost authority to re-establish the Catholic Religion, and he and the Bishop journeyed together to the town of Gex. However, Bellegarde did more by his own example to convert heretics and to insure peace and concord among the members of the rival religions than his authority, backed as it was by the decrees of the King, could ever have effected. He made a general confession to Francis, entreating him to give him a rule of life, promising to follow it faithfully; and he kept his word. Occupying a high position, living in the midst of the world, he led so pure, so holy, so virtuous a life that his example caused many conversions.

While the Church rejoiced over the increasing number of converts, the rage of the heretics was unbounded. They tried to poison Francis, causing arsenic to be mixed with his food. He was seized with the most frightful spasms, writhing in agony; he thought his last hour had come. Resigned to die, he yet felt it his duty to use all means to preserve his life; therefore he had recourse to our Blessed Lady, invoking her intercession, and promising, when cured, to go on foot on a pilgrimage to Notre Dame de Compassion at Thonon. But while imploring heavenly aid, he did not neglect to seek for earthly help. Sending for a doctor, he got him to administer an antidote, and he soon recovered. Thus was he cured—by faith say some, by science say others, probably by both. With his usual generosity, he absolutely refused to allow the wretches who had endeavoured to kill him to be prosecuted, and they escaped scot-free.

There was some rumour at this time that France would cede Gex to Savoy ; but, in the end, Henry refused to give up the province, much to the grief of Francis, who felt that, under the rule of his own Sovereign, Charles Emmanuel, a devout and zealous Catholic, the True Faith would have a better chance of being firmly implanted in the hearts of the people.

The Bishop of Geneva went on to visit his dear town of Thonon, and while looking after the spiritual welfare of all classes, he gave special care to the priests of the Community of the Holy House. He confirmed their institution by a fresh decree, and wrote the following testimonial to show the great love and esteem he felt for them :

"Pope Clement VIII. made Francis de Sales, then Provost of the Cathedral of Geneva, Prefect of this House. Some time later, the same Francis was consecrated Bishop and Prince of Geneva, and was thus freed from the duties of Prefect ; but now, of his own free will, he consecrates himself completely to the service of this Congregation, with the most sincere and ardent wish that the devotion to the Holy Names of Jesus and Mary may spread from Thonon over all the diocese, and particularly to the city of Geneva, and that these Holy Names may exhale an odour of sanctity like a precious perfume, even as cinnamon and myrrh."

The Bishop of Geneva conferred Holy Orders at Thonon on Saturday, September 20, and then proceeded to Viuz-en-Salaz, one of the few lordships left by the heretics to the See of Geneva. Here he had the happiness of receiving into the Church the Baron d'Yvoire. He had had many long interviews with this nobleman, who was a stanch Protestant, and not at all inclined to change his opinions; but the arguments of the invincible champion of the Catholic Faith finally prevailed, grace conquered, and as he was a man of high position, there was great excitement in the neighbourhood. When it was known he had renounced his errors, many followed his example.

Up to this time Francis had had no communication with the greater number of the priests of his diocese, and as he was most anxious to meet all of them, he arranged to hold a Synod at Annecy on October 2, 1603. At this Convocation he made known to them his views and his wishes regarding the diocese. He divided it into twenty districts, over each of which he placed a superintendent styled an archpriest, who was bound every six months to visit the clergy of his district at their own homes, then hold a general meeting, at which all were expected to attend, and, finally, send to the Bishop a detailed account of it and of his visitation. He insisted on the strict observance of the regulations of the Council of Trent regarding dress, services, registers, etc., and impressed upon them the necessity of always carrying about with them the Catechism of the Council of Trent. He further wished them to follow the ritual he had drawn up for their use, to be zealous and diligent in instructing their parishioners, holding Catechism classes, Sunday-schools, and constantly preaching the Word of God. He desired special acts of reparation to be made on Thursday to expiate the insults offered by heretics to the Blessed Sacrament.

It was settled that every year a Synod should be held at Annecy. Having thus devoted considerable time and infinite pains to the outward affairs of his diocese, having been for so long Bishop of Geneva, he thought he might be for a short space Francis de Sales. He retired to his own room—the " room of Francis "—and sought strength and solace in prayer. But even there in his seclusion he was not free from intruders. He literally could not call his soul his own, much less a single moment of his time. Someone always required either spiritual or temporal assistance from him. He never refused the humblest or the most importunate; anything in his power to grant he gave generously and ungrudgingly.

He had given a home to his old tutor, M. Déage. This worthy priest, like many other tutors, seemed to think his old pupil was still a boy. Accordingly, M. Déage treated the august and dignified Prince-Bishop of Geneva as though he were a schoolboy—and a pickle at that—scolding him, finding fault, never pleased. Every day this very tiresome and querulous old man grew more irritable and hard to get on with ; but Francis never lost his temper, was always patient and good-humoured, submitting with a smile to the constant rebukes of his old tutor, and treating him always with unfailing gentleness and kindness. As a matter of fact, M. Déage really worshipped the very ground his beloved pupil walked on, but like many people, ready to die for those they love, he tantalized and tormented with constant pin-pricks, growls and grumbles, the man he loved most on earth ; indeed, his affection and his temper would have made life unbearable to anyone less sweet-tempered and kind-hearted than the gentle Bishop of Geneva.

> " People have teased and vex'd me,
>    Worried me early and late :
> Some with the love they bore me,
>    Other some with their hate.
> They drugged my glass with poison,
>    They poison'd the bread I ate,
> Some with the love they bore me,
>    Other some with their hate."

## CHAPTER XV

### *THROUGH THE GATE OF ST. CLAUDE*

IN 1604, while preaching the Lenten sermons at Dijon, Francis de Sales noticed amongst his numerous audience a lady who, while listening to his words with the greatest attention, earnestly studied his appearance. She was dressed in deep mourning, and was tall and stately, with a pale, calm face and a somewhat austere expression. He immediately recognized her as the widow he had seen in a vision a few months previously, when God had revealed to him that he and she would be the founders of a new religious Order. Anxious to know her name, he asked one of his most attentive auditors, André Fremiot. "She is my sister, Mme. de Chantal," he replied.

Jeanne Francoise, Baronne de Chantal, was the daughter of President Frémiot, President of the Parliament of Dijon. His was one of the most distinguished families belonging to the *noblesse de la robe*. His daughter was born in 1572, and when in her teens married the Baron de Chantal. They lived happily for many years, when a dreadful accident happened. The Baron was out shooting with his cousin, M. d'Alzury, when, creeping through underwood in pursuit of game, M. d'Alzury, imagining he was a deer, fired, and the Baron fell, mortally wounded. He died after a few days of terrible suffering, which he bore with Christian fortitude, freely forgiving his friend, and insisting that his wife should also do so.

Jeanne was devoted to her husband, and broken-hearted at his sudden death. Her five children helped to console and distract her, for, naturally, as they were very young, they took up a good deal of her time; the rest she devoted to prayer and works of charity.

In 1603 she had a vision, in which she saw the Bishop of Geneva, and God made known to her that he was to be her spiritual guide, and that she would find rest for her soul through the gate of St. Claude. But she had six long years to wait before she entered, under his guidance, on the life for which God had destined her.

During the greater part of those years she lived with her father-in-law, the Baron de Chantal, an imperious, disagreeable, sinful old man, in whose house she led a life of constant self-denial. She contrived, even in those difficult circumstances, to preserve as constant a union with her Saviour as she did afterwards, when protected from worldly cares and anxieties by the sheltering walls of a convent.

We have gained through this long probation. She was often for months unable to commune with her saintly guide. During these long absences he wrote her those beautiful letters which seem suited to the needs of every soul, from the perusal of which the most different characters can draw support and guidance. They are so simple, so natural, so affectionate, and at the same time breathe a spirit of sublime sanctity, of thorough self-renunciation, of generous, ardent love of God, with complete confidence in Him, and a perfect conformity to His adorable will.

Unfortunately, Jeanne destroyed her own letters to the Bishop. After his death, in looking over his papers, she discovered them, carefully arranged, and with marginal notes added by him. She immediately threw them into the fire, utterly regardless of the value to posterity of such an interesting record of spiritual experience.

A nun who was present succeeded with great difficulty in rescuing a few of them. They are of intense interest. Reading them, one regrets more than ever the hasty action of Mme. de Chantal, while at the same time admiring the humility that dictated it.

The first meeting between the two who were to be joint founders of a great religious Order took place at a dinner given by André Frémiot. They were placed next each other at table, and even at that first interview Francis showed a deep interest in Mme. de Chantal.

"Madame," he asked, in a slightly sarcastic tone, but with a sweet smile, "do you intend to marry again?"

"Certainly not!" answered the Baroness, surprised and a little annoyed at the question.

"Then," he said to her, pointing to the ornaments and jewels she wore, "you must lower your flag."

After this they met frequently. Besides preaching the Lenten sermons in the Cathedral at Dijon, Francis gave special instructions at the Ursuline Convent to women living in the world who desired to lead a holy and devout life. Jeanne never missed one of these lectures. She longed intensely to place herself under the direction of the saintly Bishop, but she was bound by vows she had made to her then director never to leave him.

Fortunately, he was then away, and during his absence she was free to select any confessor she pleased, though not to open her heart to him. She usually went to a Jesuit, Père de Villars. She asked his advice. He quite approved of her going to Francis de Sales.

They had a long conversation, and then Mme. de Chantal, kneeling down, made a humble but timid confession. "For," she afterwards said, "the thought of my vow prevented me from speaking freely, yet my soul was filled with joy, and I felt as though I had been listening to an angel."

André Frémiot was at this time appointed Archbishop of Bourges, and as he had never offered up the Holy Sacrifice, it was arranged that he should celebrate his first Mass on Holy Thursday. He was assisted by Francis de Sales. A vast congregation assembled, for the Frémiots were people of distinction, and had many friends and well-wishers at Dijon.

Charles Auguste de Sales, son of Louis de Sales, the favourite brother of Francis, relates the following incident in his "Vie du Bienheureux François de Sales"[*]: "My venerable uncle, Francis de Sales, knelt on the lower part of the altar-steps and advanced on his knees to receive Holy Communion. As he did so his head was encircled with rays of light, particularly at the moment the Sacred Host was placed on his tongue. It was so brilliant an aureole that it dazzled the spectators."

Mme. de Chantal, who was present, was so impressed by this marvel that she longed more and more to place herself under the direction of so holy a man.

That same day the Archbishop of Bourges gave a dinner, inviting most of the leading citizens. The Bishop of Geneva was again seated beside the Baronne de Chantal. She mentioned to him that she intended making a pilgrimage to St. Claude.

"Is that indeed so, madame?" he answered in a pleased voice. "My mother some time ago made a vow to visit that shrine, but has not been strong enough to fulfil it. I intend to go with her myself. Need I say how delighted

_____
*Life of Blessed Francis de Sales

I shall be to meet you there, madame? and as for my good mother, she will be charmed to make your acquaintance."

On Low Monday Francis bade farewell to Mme. de Chantal. "God wishes me to speak to you in all confidence and sincerity," he told her. "He has given me the grace to say Mass without distractions, but lately, when I offer the Divine Sacrifice, I constantly think of you; but the thought of you is not a distraction—no, my dear child, it only helps to unite me closer to our dear Lord. I do not know what He wishes me to understand by this."

The Bishop of Geneva left Dijon the following day, but at his first halting-place he scribbled the following lines to her:

"It seems to me that God has given me to you. I feel more certain of it every day. I frequently entreat Our Lord to place us together in His Sacred Wounds, and to give us the grace to give back therein the life we have received from Him. I commend you to your good angel. Do the same for me, who am yours devotedly in Jesus Christ,

"✠ FRANÇOIS, *Bishop of Geneva.*"

Arrived at Annecy, he again writes to her:

"Praise God a hundred times a day for having made you a child of the Church, in imitation of Mother * Theresa, who, when dying, frequently

*St. Teresa of Avila, who had not yet been canonized.

said: 'Thank God I am a daughter of the Church!' This devout practice is not always understood by Christians, but it has ever been a great devotion of the Saints. Have great feeling for all the pastors and priests of the Church. Pray God that, while working for the salvation of souls, they may save themselves; and I beg you not to forget me, since God has given me the will never to forget you. Recommend me to Our Lord, for I have more need of prayer than anyone. I beseech Him to give you His Holy Love abundantly."

This letter greatly consoled her, but the fear of having violated her vow by opening her heart to him so freely terrified her. On the Eve of Pentecost she endured a mental martyrdom which lasted thirty-six hours. She could not sleep or eat; her soul was a prey to doubt and remorse; she was torn asunder by her desire to place herself under the direction of the Bishop of Geneva and the fear of breaking her vows.

Worn out and exhausted, she visited Père de Villars, S.J., and begged him to tell her what to do. This distinguished Jesuit was remarkable for his eminent piety and profound learning. He carefully considered her case, and then told her decidedly: "It is undoubtedly the will of God that you should place yourself under the direction of the Bishop of Geneva. His direction, and not that which you are following, suits you. He has the Spirit of God and of the Church. In giving you this Saint as a director, God shows that He expects great things from you."

This advice quieted her troubled mind. She felt as though a weight were lifted from her heart, and she returned home happy and pleased. But, alas! her peace was of short duration. Her director returned to Dijon, had an interview with her, and refused to release her from her vows. He, however, allowed her to write to Francis de Sales, and their correspondence is one of engrossing interest, there is so much in it that is human and tender, united to such sublime sanctity.

Nevertheless, Jeanne's troubles only increased; for the beautiful and consoling letters she received from the Bishop of Geneva only made her long the more ardently to place herself under his direction. Père de Villars, S.J., encouraged this desire, telling her it was her duty to follow it.

"I tell you," he said, "that you must leave this director, and place yourself entirely under the direction of the Bishop of Geneva. It is God's will, and if you do not do so you will resist the Holy Ghost."

Consequently, she wrote letter after letter to Francis; but he was reluctant to accept the responsibility of causing her to break her vows. He would not annul them without feeling absolutely certain that God willed it. At last he wrote, telling her he would meet her at St. Claude.

On the eve of her departure, Jeanne went to Fontaine-les-Dijon, the birthplace of St. Bernard, to beg the blessing of God and of His Saint on her journey. She had no sooner entered the church than she was rapt in an ecstasy, and she remembered a former vision. One morning, while half asleep, it seemed to her that she was in a coach with a number of other travellers; it passed by a church, where were many worshippers. She wished to get out and join them, but she distinctly heard a voice say: "You must continue your journey. You will enter into the sacred rest of the children of God only through the gate of St. Claude." This vision again coming to her, just before starting for St. Claude, filled her with hope and confidence.

She arrived on the morning of August 21, 1605; shortly afterwards Mme. de Boisy and her son joined her there.

In the evening she had a long conversation with the Bishop of Geneva. He listened attentively to all she told him, and then, recommending her to leave all to God, wished her good-night. He visited her early the following morning; he looked exhausted, and was very pale.

"Madame," he told her, "I have spent the night thinking over your case, and begging Our Lord to direct me, and I have come to the conclusion that it is indeed His holy will that I take upon myself your direction." He was silent for a few moments, then he resumed: "Madame, shall I tell you ? But, yes, I must, for it is the will of God. The four vows you have made are good for nothing except to destroy your interior peace. I delayed for a long time before giving you my decision, because I wished to be sure of doing the will of God."

Next morning he told her to renew her vows of poverty, chastity, and obedience at the Elevation of the Mass he was about to offer up for her. On his part, he renewed his vow of chastity, and solemnly promised God " to assist, guide, serve, and advance his dear daughter in Christ, Jeanne Francoise Frémiot de Chantal, most diligently, holily, and faithfully in the love of God, looking upon her soul as his own, to answer for it before Our Lord."

After Mass he drew up the following act, and gave it to Jeanne, who always wore it round her neck in a small bag : " Omnipotent and Eternal Lord, I, Jeanne Francoise Frémiot, although most unworthy to appear in Thy Divine Presence, confiding in Thy infinite goodness and mercy, make to Thy Divine Majesty, in presence of the glorious Virgin Mary, and of all Thy heavenly and triumphant court, the vow of perpetual chastity. I vow also obedience to his lordship the Bishop of Geneva without prejudice to the authority of lawful superiors, most humbly entreating Thy infinite goodness and clemency by the Precious Blood of Jesus Christ, to receive this act as a sweet - smelling holocaust ; and

since it has been Thy good pleasure to give
me the grace to desire and offer it, deign also
to give me abundant grace to accomplish it.
Amen."

The Bishop of Geneva on the same day,
August 22, 1605, made the following act: "I,
François de Sales, Bishop of Geneva, accept in
the name of God the vows of chastity, obedience,
and poverty, now renewed by my very dear
spiritual daughter, Jeanne Françoise Frémiot, and
after having myself repeated the solemn vow of
perpetual chastity made by me on the reception of
Holy Orders, which I confirm with all my heart,
I protest and promise to guide, assist, serve, and
advance the said Jeanne Françoise Frémiot, my
daughter, as carefully, faithfully, and holily as I
can in the love of God and the perfection of her
soul, which from this day I take and look upon
as my own, in order to answer for it before God
our Saviour; and thus I vow to the Father, Son,
and Holy Ghost, one only true God, to Whom be
honour, glory, and benediction for ever and ever.
Amen.

"Made whilst elevating the Most Blessed
Sacrament of the Altar, during Holy Mass, in
presence of the Divine Majesty, of the most holy
Virgin Our Lady, of my good angel, and of the
angel of the said Jeanne Francoise Frémiot, my
very dear daughter, and of the whole heavenly
court, this twenty-second day of August, octave
of the Assumption of the glorious Virgin, to

whose protection, with all my heart, I commend this my vow, that it may ever be firm, stable, and inviolable.  Amen.

"FRANÇOIS DE SALES, *Bishop of Geneva.*"

Thus did Mme. de Chantal find rest and peace for her troubled soul through the Gate of St. Claude ; and though many years were yet to elapse before she left the world and entered religion, through these long years the wisdom, prudence, and penetration of her saintly guide led her gently along, day by day, step by step :

> " Lead Thou me on.
> Keep Thou my feet ; I do not ask to see
> The distant scene ; one step enough for me."

> " O Lord my God, do Thou Thy holy will ;
> I will be still :
> I will not stir, lest I forsake Thine arm
> And break the charm
> Which lulls me, clinging to my Father's breast,
> In perfect rest."

# CHAPTER XVI

## *THE BURDEN OF THE DAY AND THE HEATS*

In 1605 Francis de Sales preached the Lenten sermons at the little town of La Roche. He had a particular affection for it, for it was at the college there that he had spent his early childhood, and had learned to read and write. He was delighted with the fervour and devotion of the towns-people and the humble peasants, who flocked in from the neighbourhood. He spared neither time nor trouble to increase their faith and strengthen them in the practice of virtue.

It was while in the midst of this work, so dear to his heart, that he heard of the death of Clement VIII. He was deeply grieved, for he loved and reverenced him, admiring him both as a great Saint and a great Pope. Clement was undoubtedly a great Saint. He was gentle, generous, charitable; he fasted often, practised the severest corporal mortifications, gave several hours every day to prayer, confessed every evening to Cardinal Baronius, celebrated Mass every morning with extraordinary fervour, and was always ready to hear confessions. He was just as certainly a great Pope. He propagated the Faith in many lands; he quietly but resolutely upheld the rights of the Holy See; and he had the glory of reconciling Henry IV. of France to the Church in so delicate a manner that he gained the love of the monarch and the esteem of the whole nation. He assured the peace of Europe by the Treaty of Vervins, and had succeeded in restoring to the Holy See part of the patrimony of St. Peter, after the death of Duke Alphonsus II.

After his death Alexander de Medici was elected Pope, and took the name of Leo XI. He and the Bishop of Geneva were old friends; they had known each other at Thonon, when de Medici was Papal Legate, and afterwards in Rome, where they often met in 1605, and the more they saw of each other, the more their mutual esteem and affection increased. Indeed, Leo XI. had so high an opinion of the Bishop of Geneva that he wished to confer upon him the Red Hat, and had his name placed amongst those soon to be nominated as Cardinals.

When Francis was officially notified of the dignity in store for him, he was dreadfully upset. The Chaplain of the Château de Sales was with him at the time, but was on the point of returning to Sales, when Francis, showing him the letter, exclaimed with great earnestness:

"Beg of my good mother to pray with all her heart and soul and strength that I may not be raised to so high a rank—my present one is quite enough for me. For my part I will fervently beseech Our Lord that He will not permit this exalted dignity to be conferred on so unworthy a man, for I certainly do not merit it. If His Holiness commands, I must obey; but I assure you that if it rested with me, and I had only to take three steps to receive the Cardinal's hat, I would not take them."

But Leo XI. died before he was able to carry out his intention, for he only lived a month after his election, and he was succeeded by Cardinal Borghese as Paul V. He also was an old friend of Francis de Sales, having aided him to the utmost of his power to obtain the intervention of Clement VIII. in the matter of the re-establishment of the churches and monasteries in the Chablais. Francis wrote to congratulate him on his elevation to the Pontifical throne.

" You are the heart and the soul of the ecclesiastical state," he writes; " that is why I am so certain that this diocese, so exposed to the persecutions of the heretics, will receive your special care and attention. I rejoice with all my heart that you have been raised to this supreme dignity. With downcast eyes I throw myself humbly at Your Holiness's feet, and I cry aloud with all my strength, ' Vive Paul V.! Vive le Souverain Pontife !' "

The Bishop of Geneva returned to Annecy to hold his second Synod. This took place in Easter week. His next great undertaking was the visitation of his widespread diocese. He penetrated into every nook and corner, and, as Mont Blanc and the surrounding mountains formed a part, it was a very difficult—nay, dangerous—task. He climbed the mountain heights, though almost dying from cold and exhaustion, going on energetically with bleeding feet and aching limbs. No fatigue, no peril daunted him. He sowed the good seed in the most remote districts, corrected abuses, reconciled enemies, and visited the sick and dying. He was really in his splendid manhood "L'Ange visible de la Patrie "*—the name the people had loved to call him by when he was a golden-haired, blue-eyed boy.

He writes to Mme. de Chantal : " I have just received your letter of June 6, and am about to mount my horse, to start on the visitation of my diocese. It will last about five months ; therefore I cannot go to Burgundy just yet, for, my dear child, this visitation is necessary, and is, indeed, one of my principal duties. I set out with great courage, and feel a particular consolation in undertaking it, though until now I felt rather sad about it."

He returned to preach the Jubilee. Again he writes to Jeanne :

" I must tell you something about myself, for you love me as yourself. We have had for the past fortnight a very great Jubilee. . . . Hearing many general confessions, and settling cases of conscience, has kept me busy and consoled ; then

*"The visible angel of our country." (See page 5.)

there is the sea of my ordinary occupations, amid which I live in full repose, resolved to employ myself now and ever in the service and for the greater glory of God, first in myself, then in all that are under my care. My people begin to love me tenderly, and this consoles me."

The Jubilee over, he set out to visit Gex. As usual, it was in a disturbed state, and he had to devote more time to it than to any other part of his vast diocese. He never spared himself, and in the end his health gave way, and he had to go to the Château de Sales to recover. Mme. de Boisy insisted on his taking a thorough rest. It was the greatest joy to her to have her beloved son under her roof, and to be able to lavish care and affection upon him.

However, as soon as he felt a little stronger he returned to Annecy, and there drew up a report to send to the Pope, recording his apostolic work, and going into the minutest business details, and giving a full account of the state of the diocese. He mentioned the necessity of reforming many of the monasteries, and showed the expediency of increasing the number of parishes. The congregations were very widespread, and a number of the people lived at great distances from the churches. In fact, in many cases the churches were inaccessible to quite a large number of the peasants, owing to the high mountains and difficult passes they had to traverse.

Francis entrusted his brother, Jean-François,

with this document. He, the "vinegar" of their boyish days, was now a Canon of the Cathedral, and a very zealous and hard-working priest; but he was still remarkable for his caustic wit, his pungent speeches, and was rather austere and a trifle narrow-minded.

The Bishop gave him two confidential letters—one to the Pope, in which he asked His Holiness to forgive his inability to deliver his bulletin in person, as he was unfortunately compelled to remain at Annecy, owing to pressure of work and various business matters; much, therefore, as he longed once again to meet the Holy Father, he was obliged to forgo the pleasure. The second letter was to his great friend, Cardinal Baronius. Jean-François was received very graciously by Paul V., and, indeed, during his stay in Rome he was quite fêted by his brother's many friends in the Eternal City.

The requests of the Bishop of Geneva were all granted, so Jean-Francois returned to Savoy, the bearer of letters and presents from very distinguished people to Francis de Sales.

In 1607 the Bishop of Geneva founded the Florimontane Academy, with the help of his life-long friend, President Favre. Later on, President Favre insisted that Francis should accept his beautiful mansion, and make it the Bishop's palace, telling him that it was not seemly that a Prince of the Church should dwell in a small rented house. Francis most reluctantly accepted this generous offer, for he loved a poor and abject dwelling, and had meant thus to imitate his Divine Master, Who had not whereon to lay His head.

However, Francis was decidedly reasonable— the French word *raisonnable* expresses what I mean better than the English words "sensible" or "reasonable"—and he yielded to his friend's arguments; besides, he always considered it a duty to uphold to the utmost the dignity of a Prince of the Church. Knowing how men are impressed by outward pomp and show, and inclined to jeer and scoff at the semblance of poverty.

One of the most beautiful of his letters to Mme. de Chantal treats of abjection, and, though it is probably a digression, I cannot refrain from giving a few extracts from it.

"Love your abjection. But you will ask what I mean. My child, in Latin, humility is called lowliness, and lowliness humility, so that when Our Lady says, 'Because He hath regarded the humility of his handmaid,' she means because He hath regarded her lowliness. Still, there is a difference between the two, in that humility is the acknowledgment of one's lowliness. Now, the highest point of humility is not only to know one's lowliness, but to love it, and it is to this I have exhorted you. Amongst the ills we suffer from there are abject sufferings and honourable ones; many accept the honourable ones, few the abject. For example, look at that Capuchin, hungry and in rags—everyone respects his torn habit, and pities him; but look at a poor artisan, a poor student, a poor widow: people laugh at them, and their poverty is abject. A religious suffers a rebuke from his Superior; everyone admires his humility and obedience. A gentleman suffers as much for the love of God, and he is called a coward—here is a lowly virtue. One man has a cancer on his arm, another on his face; the one hides it, the other cannot do so: the one has only the cancer, but the other suffers contempt and scorn as well. That is abjection, and what I wish to say is that we must not love only the evil, but the abjection.

"There are abject virtues and honourable virtues. Patience, gentleness, mortification, simplicity, are abject virtues; to give alms, to be courteous and prudent, are honourable virtues. I commit a folly, it makes me abject; good! I slip and get into a violent passion; I am grieved at the offence to God, but very glad that it shows me how vile, abject, and wretched I am.

"At the same time, though we may love the abjection that follows an evil or a fault, yet we must not neglect to remedy it. I will do all I can to cure the cancer on my face, but I cannot succeed. I will love the abjection of it. And in the same way, in the matter of sin, we must keep to this rule. I commit a fault; I regret having done so with all my heart, but I also embrace

with all my heart the abjection that follows. But
we must have regard also to charity, which requires that we should remove the abjection for
the edification of our neighbour. In that case we
must remove it from before the eyes of our neighbour, who would take scandal from it. Fear is a
greater evil than the evil itself. O daughter of
little faith, what do you fear? Fear not! You
walk on the sea, amid the winds and the waves,
but it is with Jesus. If fear seizes on you, cry,
'O Lord, save me!' He will give you His hand;
clasp it, and go on joyously. Do not philoso-
phize over your trouble, do not analyze your feelings too closely. No: God will not lose you so
long as you are resolved not to lose Him. *Vive
Dieu!* My dear child, live all in God. Our dear
Jesus is all ours: let us be all His. Our most
honoured Lady, our Abbess, has given Him to
us; let us keep Him always in our hearts. Courage,
my child!

> "I am, yours devotedly,
> "Francis."

In his new and lordly dwelling-house, Francis
reserved for himself the smallest and poorest of
the apartments. "The room of Francis" was
unchanged. It was an exact copy of the original
—the same furniture and books, the same want of
all the comforts, nay, almost of the necessaries of
life—but from the window he had a magnificent
view of the lake and mountains. His eyes revelled

in the contemplation of the beauties of nature, and he drew from it many of those quaint and charming similes that help to make his writings so attractive.

The Florimontane Academy was a sort of literary club. Only good Catholics were received as members, and on their admission they had to make a speech either in verse or prose. At the general meetings, lectures were given by distinguished men on philosophy, mathematics, rhetoric, and on languages and literature, particularly on French literature and the cultivation of that language. Outsiders were invited to be present at these gatherings, and men of high rank had specially reserved seats. The president was elected by the members, and it was necessary that he should be a man of great virtue as well as of profound learning. The secretary was "to be of acute, clear, and ready wit, and versed in literature"; the censors were also to be literary men, and, finally, there was to be a treasurer and an attendant.

Francis had barely finished the establishment of this Academy when he started for Thonon, to celebrate a Jubilee there. Père Cherubin had obtained permission from the Pope to hold a Jubilee there for two months, and the Bishop of Geneva hastened to do his part, preaching, hearing confessions, and encouraging by every means the devotion and piety of the citizens. He re-established there the Confraternity of the Blessed Sacrament and of the Blessed Virgin. He arranged pilgrimages to the various shrines, particularly a large one to the St. Claude. It was a tremendous success, for the people of the Chablais held that Saint in great veneration.

Thus Francis went through the country doing good, from town to town, from village to village, in the valleys and on the mountains, always gentle, patient, long-suffering, glad when even the smallest good resulted from his unceasing labours, never discouraged by failure, always serene and hopeful, knowing that all things are ordained by the great Giver, and trusting in His promise, that those who believe in Him shall never be confounded.

> " Some murmur, when their sky is clear,
>     And wholly bright to view,
> If one small speck of dark appear
>     In their great heaven of blue :
> And some with thankful love are filled,
>     If but one streak of light,
> One ray of God's good mercy, gild
>     The darkness of their night.
>
> " In palaces are hearts that ask,
>     In discontent and pride,
> Why life is such a dreary task,
>     And all good things denied :
> And hearts in poorest huts admire
>     How Love has in their aid,
> Love that not ever seems to tire,
>     Such rich provision made."

# CHAPTER XVII

## *LA VIE DÉVOTE*

In 1607 Francis de Sales preached the Lenten sermons at Annecy. He writes to Mme. de Chantal :

" ANNECY,<br>" April 8, 1607.

" *Voyez-vous, mon enfant !* * Lent is, as you know, the harvest of souls. I had not preached during Lent in this dear town since I was consecrated Bishop, except the first year, when everyone stared at me, wondering what I would do, and I had indeed quite enough to do, to take up my position and look after the affairs of the diocese. Now I make my harvest with tears of joy and of love. It is seven or eight days since I have thought of myself or seen myself except on the surface, for so many souls have come to me for help that I have not had a moment to think of my own. But, in truth, this occupation is very profitable to me, and I sincerely hope it may be very useful for those for whom I labour."

" Holy Saturday, April 14, 1607.

" Yes, my dearest child, we are now at the end of Lent, and preparing for the feast of the glorious

157

---

*"See, my child!"

Resurrection. Ah, how I wish that we may all be raised up again with Our Lord! Yes, my dear child, we must have courage. Do not grieve because your patience in bearing domestic trials is called dissimulation. I am not exempt from such attacks, but I only laugh at them when I think of them, and that is very seldom indeed. Yet am I very sensitive to the injurious and bad opinion of others; they are not very stinging or very numerous; still, I hope that even if there were more, the Holy Spirit would give me courage to bear them patiently.

"Yesterday I preached a sermon on the Passion to the nuns of Ste. Claire. When I came to the part in which I contemplated the Cross laid on Our Lord's shoulders, and with what joy He embraced it, I said that with His own heavy Cross He also bore our little crosses, and kissed them all to sanctify them; and when I said that He kissed our drynesses, our contradictions, our bitternesses, I assure you I was much consoled, and with difficulty restrained my tears.

"I love our Celse-Benigne and the little Françon. May God be for ever their God, and may the angel who has guarded their mother bless them for ever! Yes, my child, for yours is a great angel, to have given you such holy inspirations. May he give you perseverance and the grace to execute them. *Vive Jésus!* Who made me, and Who keeps me always yours,

"FRANCIS."

In May, 1507, Mme. de Chantal paid her third
visit to the Château de Sales. A very real friendship had sprung up between her and Mme. de
Boisy. Indeed, both ladies were most anxious for
an alliance between their families. Mme. de Boisy
wished that her son, Bernard de Sales, would
marry Marie Aimée, the eldest daughter of the
Baronne de Chantal. In the meantime it was
arranged that Jeanne de Sales, the youngest child
of the house, then about fourteen, should be
removed from her convent at Puy d'Orbe and
return to Dijon with Mme. de Chantal, in order
to be educated with her three daughters. This
was the little sister Francis loved so devotedly—
"having baptized her myself, and she was the first
upon whom I exercised my priestly functions."

"I do not pause to deliberate whether or not I
ought to give you my little sister," he writes to Mme.
de Chantal, "for, independently of my own inclination, even mother wishes it very much, ever since
she learned that Jeanne does not wish to become a
nun, so that even if I did not myself wish it, I
should be obliged to yield to her desire. For this
purpose I send you thirty crowns to defray the
expense of removing her from the convent, where
she is at present. I am a little afraid that your
friend the Abbess will be annoyed at the with-
drawal of my sister, but it cannot be helped. It
would be unreasonable to keep a girl so long in a
convent when she does not intend to pass her life
in one. And as to you yourself? Ought I not to

use some ceremony in placing this burden on your shoulders? You must let me know what she requires—I mean for her outfit, for I know you will be vexed if I mention her board. I am writing to your respected father-in-law to beg his approval of the favour you are conferring on us, but I know nothing of fine words, and cannot make fine speeches. You will do all that for me."

This letter was received with great pleasure at Monthelon, for Jeanne de Sales was a general favourite. She had spent a short time there on her way to Puy d'Orbe, and had won all hearts by her grace and vivacity. Françoise, Marie Aimée, and Charlotte de Chantal welcomed her as a sister, and Mme. de Chantal devoted much of her time to the training of the four girls. Jeanne was a most lovable girl, light-hearted, good-humoured, gentle, and docile. Francis expected great things from her in the future, but she was only a very short time in Burgundy when she fell dangerously ill. In a few days all was over: she died in the arms of Mme. de Chantal.

Jeanne was broken-hearted. She grieved for her little namesake as though she were a child of her own. In her desolation she made a vow to give one of her daughters to the House of Sales to compensate for the loss of this dear little girl.

Thus it seemed likely that Mme. de Boisy would have her wish, and have a de Chantal for her daughter-in-law, and that one of the obstacles to Mme. de Chantal's entering the religious life would be removed. The Château de Sales was only a few miles from Annecy, and if one of her girls was settled there, she could easily arrange for Charlotte and Françoise to remain with her in the convent, and President Frémiot would take care of her son, Celse-Benigne.

Both Mme. de Boisy and Francis were plunged into profound grief when they learned of the sad death of their beloved Jeanne. Naturally, all the other members of the family mourned for their little sister; but she was particularly dear to these two—the mother, who loved her youngest born with a special affection, and the brother, who had been as a father to her.

Francis wrote to Mme. de Chantal, November 2, 1607:

"Yes, my dear child, it is right that the holy will of God should be done as much in the things we cherish as in others. But I wish to tell you that my good mother has drunk this chalice with an entirely Christian constancy, and her virtue, of which I had always a high opinion, has even excelled my estimation of it.

"On Sunday morning she sent for my brother, the Canon. She had noticed that he and all my other brothers had been very sad the night before, so she said to him : ' I dreamed all last night that my daughter Jeanne is dead. Tell me, I implore you, is she dead ?' My brother, who was waiting for me to break the news to her (I was on visitation), thought it better to tell her at once. ' It is true, mother,' was all he could say. ' God's will be done,' said my good mother, and wept abundantly for a long time. Then, calling her maid Nicoli, she said : ' I want to get up and go to the chapel to pray for my dear daughter.' She dressed immediately, and spent hours praying in the chapel, but without disquiet. Never did I see a calmer grief, such tears ; it was a marvel, but all from tenderness of heart, without any sort of passion. Ah! should I not love devotedly this dear mother?

" Yesterday, All Saints' Day, I was the confessor of the whole family, and with the Most Holy Sacrament I sealed my mother's heart against sadness. For the rest, she and my brothers all thank you for the care and maternal love you have shown to our dear Jeanne, and particularly our de Boisy, whom I love the more for the good disposition he has shown in his affliction. You will ask me, ' And you ?' Yes, my dear child, my heart was grieved more than I could have imagined possible ; but the truth is that my mother's sorrow and yours greatly increased mine. For the rest, Providence knows what is best. What a happiness for this child to be taken away ' lest wickedness should alter her understanding,' and to have died unspotted by the world! You may imagine, my dear daughter, how tenderly I loved this little child. I had brought her forth to her Saviour, for I baptized

her with my own hand some fourteen years ago.
She was the first creature on whom I exercised
my priestly functions. I was her spiritual father,
and fully promised myself one day to make something good out of her.

"You have, my dear child, four children, a
father and a father-in-law, a dear brother, and a
spiritual father. They are all very dear to you,
and rightly, for God wills it. But if God took
them all from you, would you not still have enough
in God? If He takes everything else from us, He
will never take Himself, so long as we do not will
it. Lord Jesus, without reservation, without an
'if,' or any limitation, may *Your will be done.*

"I send you an escutcheon to please you, and
since you wish the funeral services to be where the
dear child's body rests, I am content, but let there
be no great pomp, and only what Christian custom
requires. Of what use is anything further? You
will afterwards draw up a list of these expenses,
and of those of her illness, and send it to me, for
I wish it so, and meantime we will pray for the
repose of her soul, and do her some little honour.
But we will not have the *Quarantal;* so much
ceremony is not becoming for a child who has had
no rank in the world. You know me: I love
simplicity both in life and in death.

"Yours,

"FRANCIS."

As usual, the Bishop of Geneva had his hands
full, but in the midst of his episcopal labours he

found time to bring out " La Vie Dévote." The publication of this book came about in rather a curious way. As I mentioned in a former chapter, some of the instructions it contains were composed for the benefit of his mother, but the greater part is arranged from letters written by him to one of his penitents, Mme. de Charmoisy.

When in Paris in 1603, Francis de Sales met this lady for the first time. On January 24 in that year she heard him preach, and was so struck by the beauty and fervour of his discourse that she sought him out, and begged him to hear her confession, to advise her, and to become her director. She was a very beautiful woman, clever, accomplished, and attractive, and had led a very worldly life, moving in the highest circles, and being greatly admired for her beauty and wit. She was exposed to many temptations, and often placed in very trying and difficult positions. Now that she wished to lead a holy life in the world, she felt the need of a strong hand and clear head to guide her.

Francis de Sales gave her many counsels of perfection and plenty of sound, practical advice; but she often forgot what he said to her, and used to come to him frequently, asking him to repeat his instructions. These interviews took up so much of his time that he thought it expedient to jot down for her use a rule of life, and the principal devotions and practices of a devout Christian. When he left Paris, he continued to correspond with her.

Mme. de Charmoisy carefully preserved all his letters and memoranda, even to the tiniest note, arranging them, and reading them over and over again. When going on a long journey, she gave these precious documents to Père Forrier, S.J., to keep for her, and she also gave him permission to glance through them.

This saintly Jesuit had once been the director of Francis de Sales, and was himself distinguished for his virtues, his piety, and his learning, particularly in spiritual matters. He read the notes carefully and with profound admiration, and he earnestly requested Mme. de Charmoisy to permit him to have them copied. She willingly consented. Soon the copies increased and multiplied. Every Jesuit college possessed at least one copy; in fact, they created quite a furore among the *Saints Pères:* each and all longed to procure a special one for his own particular use.

Consequently, Père Forrier, S.J., wrote to the Bishop of Geneva, strongly recommending him to publish these letters and notes. Francis was quite puzzled; he could not imagine what his old director meant, but when he heard that he alluded to the instructions he himself had given to Mme. de Charmoisy, he was quite astonished. He went to her and asked her to explain.

"Do you not remember, Monseigneur," she said, "the good advice you so often gave me, and the letters you wrote me on various devotions and practices of piety?"

"What?" cried Francis in surprise, "those wretched scrawls! And the good Father has had the patience to wade through them?"

"Yes, Monseigneur, and he thinks them so beautiful that he tells me that never in his life did he read anything so useful and so devotional. All the Jesuit Fathers are of the same opinion. They have made several copies of your letters, and mean to publish them if you won't do so yourself."

"Well, it certainly is strange," replied Francis, smiling, "that, according to these good Fathers, I have written a book without knowing it."

Père Forrier, S.J., gave him no peace; he continued to urge him to arrange these notes and publish them. Henry IV. added his entreaties to those of the holy Jesuit.

"For there is no one," he told his secretary, M. Deshayes, "so capable of composing a devotional work suited to all sorts and conditions of men. No one understands true practical piety so well as the Bishop of Geneva."

Thus urged on all sides, Francis de Sales agreed to revise his letters to Mme. de Charmoisy, adding to them those he had written to Mme. de Boisy.

At last the longed-for book appeared, and was printed in Lyons in 1608, under the title of "L'Introduction à la Vie Dévote."[*] This wonderful book is just as well suited to the wants of the present day as though it had been written in the twentieth century. It takes the place of a director to many people, who, living in remote country

*The Introduction to the Devout Life

places, find it difficult to place themselves under
the guidance of a wise and prudent priest; indeed,
the Church in the Office of our Saint exhorts us
to be guided by his counsels—"admonished by his
directions." She assures us that his works have
diffused a bright light amongst the Faithful, to
whom they point out a way, as sure as it is easy, to
arrive at perfection. It gives minute instructions
on every point in the spiritual life—confession,
Holy Communion, Holy Mass, mental prayer,
examen of conscience, spiritual reading; on the
practice of every virtue—how to resist temptations; on amusements, friendship—in fact,
nothing is forgotten, and the instructions are
given in so clear and fascinating a manner as to
appeal to the people in general, as well as to the
more fortunate, cultured reading public.

Henry IV. was delighted with its sublime beauty
and exquisite grace, and was more than ever
desirous of persuading his "phœnix of Prelates"
to accept a See in France. He got M. Deshayes
to write to the Bishop of Geneva, entreating him
to come to Paris. "The See of Geneva," he tells
him, "is unworthy of your talents. Come to us,
and we will give you a position more suited to
your merits and ability."

Francis showed this letter to his brother Louis,
remarking with a quietly humorous smile: "Thank
God, I do not feel in the least tempted to accept
this brilliant offer. I prefer to stay where God
has placed me. Annecy is not a great city, but it

is big enough for me, who, as you know, dear Louis, am a good-for-nothing fellow."

However, he at once answered M. Deshayes' letter, begging him to thank the King for his great kindness, but most decidedly refusing to accept his offer.

" La Vie Dévote " was soon translated into several languages; it created an extraordinary sensation, and was undoubtedly "the book of the year." Everyone read it, and everyone declared it far surpassed their expectations. Marie de Medici, wife of Henry IV., sent a copy of it to James I. of England, who was so charmed with it that he always carried it about with him, and often remarked in an annoyed tone that he could not understand why some of his Bishops could not write as erudite, exquisite, and practical a book as the Bishop of Geneva.

# CHAPTER XVIII

## *THE PASSING OF MADAME DE BOISY*

M. DE BOISY made a strange will. He wished his property to remain intact, in order that his family might continue to live together at the Château de Sales with Mme. de Boisy. But if at any time they desired to separate and each take his portion, the eldest son was to make the division, but the youngest was to have the first choice. M. de Boisy was the father of thirteen children, but only seven survived him, and Bernard was now the youngest surviving son.

During the lifetime of M. de Boisy, Galloys had received the lands and title of Seigneur de Villaroget, always held by the eldest son. Francis had had it before he entered the ecclesiastical state, and on his doing so, Galloys had succeeded him. On the death of M. de Boisy, Galloys had also inherited the property and name of Seigneur de Boisy, and was henceforth known as M. de Boisy, and his father had conferred on Louis the lands of de la Thuile with the title of Seigneur. Francis and Jean-François were both priests, so after all it was only just that Bernard, who had neither lands nor title, should select as he pleased from what remained. The family had dwelt together in peace, love, and harmony up to 1609, when the wife of Louis de Sales took it into her head that it would be a good thing for them all if each received his portion.

Nevertheless, when matters were arranged and Bernard was declared Baron de Thorens and Seigneur de Sales, she was decidedly annoyed. She wished to dispute the will, and it was only with great difficulty that her husband succeeded in calming her, and getting her to consent to the arrangement. She died soon afterwards, yet though she was a somewhat wayward and intractable woman, Louis loved her passionately, and her death plunged him into the most profound grief. To add to his trouble, she left one young child, who was just at an age most to require a mother's care. This little boy was Charles Auguste de Sales, the future biographer and second successor of Francis in the See of Geneva.

The tender heart of the Bishop grieved for his brother's grief, and also for that of the father of Mme. Louis, the Baron de Cusy, his personal friend, and a most holy and excellent man. Only seven years previously Francis had performed the marriage ceremony, uniting his favourite brother to the daughter of his friend, and now this dear Louis was a broken-hearted widower.

But Francis sought consolation both for himself and those so dear to him in the Sacred Heart of Our Lord, and from it he gained courage and strength to continue his arduous ministry. The reformation of the Benedictine Abbey of Tailloires was his next important work. Like Sixt and many others, it had fallen into a state of great laxity. Arrived at the monastery, Francis pointed out their evil manner of life, broken rules, want of discipline, and the rest. The Prior and many of the monks refused to listen to him, but a few were not only willing but anxious to amend their ways.

Chief of these was Père de Coix. Francis appointed him Prior, and left the monastery hoping he would succeed in reforming the whole community. But the Bishop was no sooner gone than a regular rebellion broke out, and lasted some time. In the end, however, virtue triumphed, and the discontented monks were won over by the gentleness and kindness of the new Prior.

As soon as Francis reached Annecy he found awaiting him a summons from the King of France, asking him to go to Gex to confer with the Baron de Luz, Lieutenant-General of Burgundy, about the affairs of that most troublesome part of the diocese.

Francis set out immediately, accompanied by eight attendants, for he thought it advisable to take a larger suite with him than usual as he was going into the enemy's camp. Arrived at the Rhone, they found the recent floods had made it impassable, and the only other way of getting to Gex was to pass through the city of Geneva. To do so was to endanger the Bishop's life, for if the citizens recognized him they would certainly tear him to pieces.

His companions implored him to wait until the floods subsided, but Francis was resolved to run every risk to arrive quickly at Gex. Notwithstanding their entreaties and arguments, he decided to pass through the hostile city.

" At least you will go incognito ?"

" Certainly not," he replied, and arrayed in the violet robes of a Bishop, and with all the insignia of his office, he presented himself at the city gates.

The soldier on guard asked him his name.

" The Bishop of the Diocese and his suite," replied Francis quietly.

" The Diocese !" growled the rough Calvinist. " Never heard of that place. Pass." And he wrote in the register : " To-day the Bishop of the Diocese and his suite passed into the city."

Francis and his companions rode through it on their way to the gate that leads out towards Gex, but it was shut, so they rested awhile at an hotel, and when they heard the gate was open, they passed through it and arrived in safety at Gex.

The heretics were furious when they heard that the indomitable champion of the Catholic Faith had passed in safety through their city. They threatened to do all sorts of terrible things to this audacious Prelate if "they ever caught him in their Rome."

Francis smiled when he heard of these dreadful threats, quietly remarking that he was quite willing to go to Geneva and meet the Calvinist ministers, in order publicly to discuss religious questions ; but, as usual, the ministers fought shy of a conference with the learned and eloquent Bishop.

During his visit to Gex, Francis converted many of the inhabitants, and succeeded in restoring eight parish churches to Catholic worship. He went on from there to the Château de Monthelon, where he blessed the marriage of his brother Bernard, Baron de Thorens, with Marie Aimée, the eldest daughter of Mme. de Chantal. The wedding took place on October 13, 1609. Bride and groom were very young, and very much attached to each other ; they had been betrothed for more than a year. Francis dearly loved his brother, and had a great affection for "that little Aimée," as he calls her, "who will be one of the best-loved sisters in the world."

On the following day, President Frémiot, the Archbishop of Bourges, and the Bishop of Geneva conferred together on the subject of Mme. de Chantal's vocation. Both her father and her brother were opposed to her quitting the world and becoming a nun, and it took all her arguments, backed by those of the Bishop of Geneva, to induce them to give their consent. It was

decided that President Frémiot should take charge
of her only son Celse-Benigne, and that the Archbishop of Bourges should help him to look after
the boy's spiritual and temporal welfare. Mme.
de Chantal was, however, to return to Dijon; she
was not this time to bid a last farewell to her
family and friends; many matters connected with
her property had yet to be settled.

In the year 1609, Francis de Sales consecrated
John Peter Camus, Bishop of Belley; and this
was the beginning of a very true and warm friendship between the two Prelates. Their dioceses
adjoined, so they arranged every year to spend a
week in each other's house, not counting the days
of arrival and departure. The Bishop of Belley
was only twenty-five, and looked up to Francis as
a father, at the same time that he loved him as a
friend and reverenced him as a Saint, listening attentively to his every word, watching his every
gesture. The result of this unceasing observation
he has given us in his "L'Esprit de St. François
de Sales."

It is a really extraordinary book, for it makes
Francis live and breathe before us; he is no longer
a vague, distant, canonized Saint, he becomes
present to us; "his charming personality is real
to us, no longer a sanctified abstraction, but a
living, breathing man, suffering like us, thinking
like us; his daily life stands out distinctly; we
hear his conversations, we look upon his move-
ments; his character is painted for us, not only

with the loving hand of a friend, but with the unrelenting accuracy of a severe critic."

Among the many charming anecdotes there is one so characteristic of both men that I cannot refrain from quoting it. " They told the good Bishop, M. de Genève, that I took a dreadfully long time in saying Mass, and consequently was a nuisance to everyone. He wished to correct me. He was staying with me, and one day he had so many letters to answer that he was unable to say Mass before 11 a.m. He invariably offered up the Holy Sacrifice every day, unless prevented by serious illness. He came down in his rochet and mozetta, said a short prayer in the sacristy, vested, and proceeded to the Altar, where he said Mass; then he said another short prayer and returned to us; soon afterwards we went to dinner. I was surprised at the short time he took to prepare, celebrate, and make his thanksgiving, so I said to him, when we were alone : ' My Father, you go rather fast, don't you ? I noticed with surprise what a short time you spent this morning in preparation and thanksgiving.'

" ' Mon Dieu l' he exclaimed, ' you please me greatly by so candidly giving me your opinion. For three or four days I have had some remarks to make to you on the same subject, and was at a loss how to do so. Do you know that you weary people dreadfully, you are so slow ? Probably no one has had the courage to remonstrate with you, for few care to find fault with their

Bishop, but your people have asked me to speak to you. In the future you will endeavour to get on more quickly, and I will go slower. It is rather comical that the Bishop of Geneva should find fault with the Bishop of Belley for his slowness, and that the Bishop of Belley should remonstrate with the Bishop of Geneva for being too quick. But so it is, *mon ami;* this world is a strange place, and everything is more or less upside down. Just think, my dear fellow, of all the poor people who are in a hurry to hear Mass. They have their business to attend to; they are pressed for time; some of them want to ask your advice after Mass; and yet you keep them all waiting an interminable time, while you indulge your own love of prayer. It is unreasonable, *mon ami.*'

" ' But, my Father,' I protested, ' I must spend some time in preparing to offer the Holy Sacrifice.'

" ' Quite so,' he rejoined, ' but why not prepare early in the morning ?'

" ' But I rise at four,' I answered, 'and I do not say Mass until eight or nine.'

" ' Do you think,' he replied, ' that an interval of four or five hours is a very long space in His eyes, with Whom a thousand years are but as the day that has passed ?'

" ' And my thanksgiving ?' I inquired.

" ' Why not make it in the evening ?' he replied. ' You will have more time and leisure both morning and evening to perform these acts, and you will do them more thoroughly, and will inconvenience no one by taking as long as you please over them.'

" ' But,' I objected, ' will not people be shocked at my doing these things with such rapidity, since God does not wish to be worshipped on the run ?'

" ' Vainly do we run,' he replied. ' Run we ever so quickly, God runs faster than we do. He is a Spirit; all is present to Him; with Him there is neither past nor future. Whither can we go from His Spirit ?'

" I was convinced, and have since followed his advice, greatly to my own advantage."

Early in 1610, Mme. de Boisy*paid a long visit to her son at Annecy. She wished to prepare for death, and to do so thoroughly she made a long retreat under his guidance.

She was now sixty-eight. Though married at fourteen, she had not had a child until she was twenty-one, when Francis had been given to her in answer to her prayers and vows. Afterwards she had twelve children, and had always been a most devoted wife and mother, never sparing herself in the service of her husband and children. Now, when she felt worn out, and had no strength to continue the battle of life, she wished to enter into eternal rest ; and having a presentiment that soon her wish would be granted, she prepared in the most holy and fervent manner to

*St. Francis de Sales' mother. (See p. 1.)

meet her Saviour with a pure heart and a stain-
less soul. Her retreat over, she returned to the
Château de Sales. On leaving him, she said to
Francis : " Never in my life have I received so
much comfort and consolation as you have just
given me, my son and my Father."

On Ash Wednesday she heard three Masses in
the church, confessed, and received Holy Communion, and afterwards attended Vespers. Before
retiring to rest she read three chapters of " La
Vie Dévote," in order that her mind should be
full of pious thoughts. But in the morning, while
dressing, she fell, seized with apoplexy, and half
her body was paralyzed.

The Baron de Thorens rushed in and did all in
his power to revive her, sent for a doctor, and
despatched a special courier to Annecy to bring
back Francis. But I had better let Francis himself describe his mother's last moments.

*"March* 11, 1610.

" To Madame de Chantal :

" Yes, my dearest child, we must always
adore Providence, Whose ways are always good,
holy, and lovable. It has pleased Him to take
away from us the best and dearest of mothers, to
have her, as I believe, in His own presence, and
to hold her in His right hand. Let us confess, my
dearly-loved daughter, that ' God is good, and
His mercy endureth for ever.' His will is just
and His judgment is right. His will is always

good and His ordinances most amiable. As for me, I must acknowledge that this separation pains me greatly, for I ought to make this confession of my own weakness after making that of the Divine goodness. But yet, my child, it has been a quiet pain, though sharp, for I cried out with David : ' I was dumb, and I opened not my mouth, because Thou hast done it.' Without doubt, if it had not been so, I would have cried, ' Stop !' under this blow, but I feel I would not dare to do so, or to express unwillingness under the strokes of His fatherly Hand, which, thanks to His goodness, I have learnt to love tenderly from my youth.

"But you wish to know how this good woman ended her days. Here is the account of it ; I give it to you, to you to whom I have given my mother's place in my *Memento* at Mass, without taking from you the place you had. I could not do it, so firmly do you hold what you hold in my heart, and so you are there first and last.

" My mother came to me this winter, and during the month she stayed with me, she made a general review of her soul, and renewed her desire of perfection with great fervour. She went away well pleased with me, having, as she told me, got more consolation from me than ever before. She continued in this state of holy joy until Ash Wednesday, when she went to the parish church of Thorens, where she confessed and communicated, heard three Masses, and assisted at Vespers. At night, being in bed and unable to sleep, she got her maid to read her three chapters of the *Introduction* to entertain herself with good thoughts, and had the *Protestation* marked to make it next morning; but God was satisfied with her good-will, and arranged it differently, for when morning came, and my dear mother had got up and was having her hair dressed, she was taken suddenly ill, and fell as if dead.

" My poor brother, your son, was asleep, but as soon as he was told, he ran in without waiting to dress, lifted her up, walked her about, and made her take essences and other things usually administered in these cases. She recovered consciousness and tried to speak, but it was difficult to understand her, for both her tongue and her throat were affected.

" They sent for me, and I went at once with the doctor and the chemist. They found her in a lethargy and half paralyzed, but they were able to rouse her for brief intervals ; then she took the cross and kissed it, but then she became blind. She took nothing without making the sign of the Cross over it, and so she received Extreme Unction. On my arrival, though she was both blind and drowsy, she embraced me affectionately, and said: ' It is my son and my Father '; and she kissed my hand, saying, ' I owe you this in token of respect, my Father '; and then, extending her arms and embracing me tenderly, ' And I owe you this loving kiss, because you are also my son.'

"She remained in this state for two days and a half; after that we could not rouse her, and on March 1 she gave up her soul to God gently and happily, showing in death a dignity and beauty greater than she ever showed in life. She looked perfectly beautiful as she lay dead.

"I must also tell you that I had the courage to give her the last blessing, to close her eyes and her lips, and to give her the kiss of peace at the last moment. Then I gave way to my grief, and I wept over my good mother more than ever I have done since I have been in the Church, but, thank God, it was without spiritual bitterness.

"But I must tell you of your son's splendid behaviour. I was delighted with the care he took of our mother, and all the trouble and pains he took—and this he did so devotedly and lovingly that if he had been a stranger I would have adopted him as my brother. I know not whether I am mistaken, but I find him much changed for the better, both in worldly and spiritual matters.

"Well, my dear child, we must be resolved always to praise God, even if He sends us still heavier afflictions. And now, if you can manage it, I hope you will come here for Palm Sunday. Your little room is ready for you, and our simple fare will be prepared and offered with a good heart —I mean, with my heart—which, as you know, is yours. . . .

"Your dear little Charlotte is happy in leaving this world, while still unspotted by it. Yet we must weep a little for her, for have we not human hearts and sensitive natures ? Yes, we may indeed weep over our dead, since God not only allows us, but invites us to do so. I regret her, the poor little girl, but with a less intense grief, because the overwhelming sorrow I feel for the loss of my mother takes away the sting from this second trouble. I heard of your daughter's death while my mother lay dead. God giveth and God taketh away, blessed be His Holy Name."

Francis also wrote to his sister Gasparde, the wife of M. de Cornillon :

"*March* 4, 1610.

"MY DEAREST SISTER, MY CHILD,

"Let us console ourselves as best we can in this passing away of our good mother ; for the graces God conferred on her, to prepare her for so happy a death, are certain marks that He has received her soul into His heavenly kingdom, and she is blessed in being freed from the burdens and troubles of life. And we also, my dear Gasparde, shall be blessed in our turn if, like her, we live in the love and fear of Our Lord, as we promised each other that day at Annecy. . . . Be, then, quite consoled, my dear child, and if you cannot help feeling sorrow at this separation, try to moderate your grief—remember, we must reconcile ourselves to God's holy will. . . . And I must add that our dear mother was in a very holy and joyous state when she died, for Our Lord did not wish her to be in a melancholy mood when He took her to Himself.

"So, then, my dearest sister, always love me well, for I am more yours than ever, and I hope it will please God that you will be able to come to us for Holy Week. It would be a great consolation to me. *Bon jour, mon enfant.*

"I am your devoted brother,

"FRANCIS."

# CHAPTER XIX

## *HONOURABLE WOMEN—NOT A FEW*

" And what is so rare as a day in June ?
Then, if ever, come perfect days ;
Then Heaven tries the earth if it be in tune,
And over it softly her warm ear lays."

LOWELL.

ON June 10, 1610, Francis conducted his spiritual children to their long-desired home. Surely Heaven smiled that day on those devoted souls entering so courageously on their life of prayer and sacrifice.

" Voici, mes sœurs, le lieu de nos délices et de notre repos,"*Jeanne de Chantal cries, and then they and their friends kneel before the altar, while their saintly Bishop repeats three times the *Gloria Patri*, and after a short exhortation begs God's blessing upon their enterprise. Then, when the crowd of loving relations, of devoted friends, of curious or careless spectators, had gone away, Francis lingered for a few parting words with Jeanne. Mdlles. de Bréchard and Favre were doubtless talking it over as they stood at an upper window watching the people pass down the hill. Many among them were near and dear to the two novices, but they had parted with them for ever,

184

---

*"Here, my sisters, is the place of our delights and of our repose."

and as they caught the last glimmer of shimmering silk, and heard the last faint ripple of laughter, they must have felt that their strange new life had indeed commenced. Perhaps they stole quietly down to the little chapel to renew their consecration to God's service, and to kneel in silent prayer before His tabernacle, knowing where they could best quiet the first stirrings of their poor hearts, that felt a little restive on realizing the life of solitude and sacrifice to which they were being devoted.

Meanwhile the two holy founders were talking of what they hoped their Institute would be. Before he gave them a definite rule, Francis let them know his wishes. "I wish you to lead the life of Martha and of Mary," he often tells them, "to join works of charity to contemplation, not to remain cloistered, but to go forth into the lanes and alleys to tend the sick, to help the poor, to pray beside the dying. United thus, the active and contemplative life will help instead of interfering with each other. While the Sisters work out their own sanctification, they will also help their neighbours to lead better lives, by their example and by giving them assistance."

Francis then gave Mme. de Chantal a rough sketch of the constitutions, and, bidding her farewell, promised to come on the following morning to offer up the Holy Sacrifice and to give them Holy Communion.

Jeanne rejoined her companions, and, remembering her vision, reminded them that it was the

Feast of St. Claude, saying joyfully : " Here at last we find the rest of the children of God, not only through the Gate of St. Claude, but on the Feast of St. Claude."

They knelt down and thanked God ; then Mme. de Chantal read them the regulations just given her by the Bishop of Geneva. Finally, wishing each other an affectionate " good-night," they retired to their little rooms.

Marie Jacqueline Favre and Charlotte de Bréchard spent a peaceful night. They never slept so well, they said, as on that first night in the " Berceau." But Mme. de Chantal was troubled by doubts and scruples. The memory of her last interview with her father and son wrung her heart. Her father's grief, his tears, her son's passionate anger and despair. He had thrown himself prostrate across the threshold of the apartment, telling her that she must pass over his body. Then, had she been wise in bestowing all her property on her children and leaving herself almost penniless, having nothing in the world but a small pension her brother insisted on paying her annually.

However, her fervent faith helped her. Offering herself to God and trusting in His goodness, she prayed: "O God, Thou Who carest for the lilies of the field and the birds of the air, surely Thou wilt also care for the humblest of Thy servants ? It is enough for us to seek Thy kingdom ; the rest will be added unto us."

After Mass, Francis had to leave at once, but promised to return in the afternoon. In the meantime, they had nothing to eat. They had no provisions and no money. The good lay Sister, Jacqueline Coste, was in despair. She went to Mme. de Chantal, asking her how she was to prepare dinner when she had nothing. Jeanne smiled. " My child, God will provide," she told her.

But Jacqueline's faith was not so strong. Seeing no prospect of obtaining provisions, she went into the garden and gathered a few vegetables, borrowed a bowl of milk from a neighbour, and boiled them down together. They made a fairly good soup, and they all were enjoying it tremendously when a knock was heard. Jacqueline Coste hastened to open the door. President Favre had sent wine, meat, and bread. Poor Jacqueline felt quite remorseful that she had doubted Divine Providence.

President Favre had opposed his daughter's quitting the world almost as strenuously as President Frémiot had objected to Jeanne's entering religion. Indeed, a year before no one would have guessed that brilliant, beautiful Jacqueline Favre would bury herself in a convent.

She, however, always displayed a great repugnance to the married state. " If you will guarantee that my husband will die two hours after we are married and leave me free, then I will accept one of my suitors." For she had many, among them

Louis de Sales. Naturally her father favoured him, for was he not the well-beloved brother of his own dearest friend and more than brother, Francis de Sales?

Louis was greatly attached to this young and charming girl. He appreciated her keen intelligence, her good sense, and her light-heartedness. Not only would she make an ideal wife, but she would also, he was sure, prove a loving and devoted mother to little Charles Auguste.

Marie Jacqueline had confided her wish to enter religion to the Bishop of Geneva, and the trouble his brother's suit caused her, her father insisting that she should accept so desirable a husband. Francis promised to arrange matters. One day after dinner he said to Louis:

"My poor brother, you will have to give up your sweetheart; you have a powerful rival."

"Except His Highness," cried Louis, with hot anger, "I know of no one bold enough to dispute my claim."

"Oh," replied Francis, with a somewhat mocking smile, "this rival I refer to is so great you would not dare to look Him in the face."

Louis was indignant, and turned on his brother in angry surprise.

"Do you doubt my courage?" he asked hotly.

"Certainly not," Francis answered, with his humorous smile; "but Mdlle. Favre has chosen Jesus Christ for her spouse, so you must give her up to Him."

"Ah! if it is so, certes I will no longer seek her hand. May His holy will be done."

He went to Marie Jacqueline, and said to her: "If you refused me in order to marry another I should be inconsolable, but since you wish to give yourself to God, I leave you to Him gladly."

Charlotte de Bréchard had long wished to become a nun, but she could not make up her mind to enter any particular Order. She thought of the Poor Clares, the Carmelites. While in this state of indecision she had a strange dream. She saw in a splendid chapel a beautifully decorated altar, and a nun in an unknown habit performing some devotions. The nun rose from her knees, blew a horn, and, turning to Charlotte, said: "Will you join us?" "With pleasure," the girl replied. Then the nun gave her a bouquet of flowers, and, continuing to blow her horn, several other girls joined her.

After this dream Charlotte ardently longed to find the Order, but, of course, failed. Unable to discover it, she joined the Carmelites, but she had to leave at the end of the month, her delicate health preventing her from following their severe rules. Then she entered the Ursuline Order, but again her health prevented her remaining in it. She was so ill and fragile that President Frémiot, a great friend of her father's, brought her into the country to spend some time with Mme. de Chantal at Monthelon. There she met Francis de Sales, and felt irresistibly impelled to confide in him.

He was equally impressed by her, at once appreciating her greatness of soul and her strong character. He told her of the Institute he hoped soon to organize, and asked her:

"My child, would you be willing to run with Mme. de Chantal for the same prize?"

She remembered the bouquet of flowers given to her in her dream, and answered eagerly:

"With the greatest pleasure, Monseigneur."

"Then wait patiently, my daughter, and only think of loving God more and more, for He wishes you to devote your life to His service."

Anne Jacqueline Coste was the humble servant Francis first met at the Hôtel de l'Écu de France in Geneva, when he had stopped there at the time he endeavoured to convert Théodore de Bèze. Afterwards she got a situation in an hotel at Annecy, and at once placed herself under the direction of the saintly Bishop. One day she said to him:

"My Father, will you allow me to be a lay Sister in the Order you are going to found?"

"Who told you I intended founding an Order?" he asked in surprise.

"No one," she answered; "but my heart tells me you will do so."

These four chosen souls were thus specially called by God to be the first Sisters of the Visitation.

When Francis arrived in the afternoon, he found his "little doves," as he playfully called them, attired in the garb of novices—a black dress with a white linen collar, a black cap half covering the forehead and completely hiding the hair, and a hood of black taffeta that, when lowered, quite hid the face. Francis was very much amused at their costume, and, when he returned home, laughingly told his brothers : " Our ladies are indeed dead to the pomps and vanities of this world, for they have selected a most unbecoming head-dress."

On June 8 he composed the chant used by the Sisters of the Visitation, and got them to begin the study of Latin in order to recite every day the Little Office of Our Lady. Every day the Bishop managed to pay them a short visit, and gradually to instruct them in the rules he intended them to observe. "You are no longer to call each other Madame and Mademoiselle," he informed them ; "but by the sweet and homely names of Mother and Sister."

Mother de Chantal relates :

"It is impossible to relate all the graces and favours God lavished upon us during this happy time. In our community there was fervent piety, strict obedience, the spirit of prayer and of self-sacrifice, and childlike candour. We spoke continually of God and the means of loving Him more and more. We made the least observances a matter of conscience. Our beloved Father inspired us with so great a love of simplicity and exactitude that we felt the deepest remorse for the least fault. So great was our sisterly union, that to be among us was a Paradise on earth.

Indeed, we spent six such happy weeks, that Sister Jacqueline Favre used to remark that, were it not for the glory of God, she would wish thus to pass our whole life together without increasing our numbers."

Many young and innocent girls were longing to join the new Institute. Everyone spoke of the holy and happy life led by the Sisters, who, notwithstanding all their privations, often suffering hunger and thirst, never complained, but were always gay, light-hearted, full of holy joy, and of love of God and of their neighbours.

On July, 1610, Claude Frances Roget left her father's house at Annecy and joined the little community. She came like a flash of summer: and like it she passed away.

"The first of my daughters," says Francis, "who has gone to Heaven to see what God is preparing there for her sisters."

On July 26, 1610, Marie Peronne de Châtel was received into the Order. She was a bright, clever girl of twenty, loving dancing, singing, and poetry. Indeed, she composed several ballads and rondeaus. Having thoroughly enjoyed life for a couple of years, she accidentally came across Granada's "Memorial of a Christian Life." She read it attentively, and the perusal of it completely changed her point of view. She resolved to give up the world and to consecrate herself to God. But, like Charlotte de Bréchard, she could not decide to enter any existing Order. She, too, thought of becoming a Poor Clare or a Carmelite, but she also was too delicate. In her distress she prayed to Our Lord with the simplicity of a loving child : " Oh, my dear Lord, You see my weakness and You know my distress. You must show me by next Whitsun-tide how I am to consecrate myself to Your service. If You will not do so, I shall be obliged to enter a mitigated Order."

God heard her prayer, for during Whitsun Week she met Mme. de Chantal, and she at once knew that under her direction she would serve her Lord.

On July 28 Marie Marguerite Millot received the habit. She was the daughter of a Councillor of the Parliament of Burgundy. Shortly after Marie Adrienne Fichet joined the Institute. She was a great favourite of the holy founder. He had himself baptized her, and had watched over her childhood and youth, helping her to advance rapidly on the thorny road that leads to Heaven. She was gladly welcomed by Mother de Chantal, who, though ill and unable to leave her room, insisted on giving her the habit herself. So Adrienne was robed in sombre black and donned the ugly cap, kneeling on the hearthrug in Jeanne's cell.

Claude Marin Thioller was the eighth received into the little community. The house was rather small for the rapidly increasing numbers, but as yet they had not sufficient funds to purchase a larger one.

While occupied with the care and guidance of his "little doves," Francis continued to govern his diocese with his usual watchful solicitude and paternal anxiety. His desire to reform the clergy only increased, and to do so effectually, he begged the Pope to allow him to found a diocesan college. But although Paul V. said to M. de Coex, who had gone to Rome to solicit the Sovereign Pontiff's approval on the reform of Tailliores, "Your Bishop is a perfect Saint. I have always esteemed and respected him. Tell him I have the greatest confidence in his prayers, and beg of him to remember me in them," yet Rome saw so many difficulties in the way of granting the request of the saintly Bishop that in the end nothing was done.

The year 1610 had indeed been a memorable one in the life of Francis de Sales—full of sorrow and of joy, of meetings and of partings, of bitterness and of gladness. His dear mother had passed away in March, full of years and of honours. Scarcely recovered from the shock of her somewhat sudden death, he as well as the rest of the civilized world was thunderstruck at the news of the assassination of Henry of Navarre by the mad fanatic, François Ravaillac. This terrible event, as all students of history know, happened on May 14. Henry was on his way to visit his friend, the Duc de Sully, at the Arsenal, when his carriage was blocked in a narrow thoroughfare, traffic was impeded, and in the confusion the wretched lunatic sprang forward and stabbed the King with a knife. Henry raised his arm, crying out, "I am wounded." Another blow pierced his heart. He survived only a few moments, though some historians say he lived long enough to receive absolution.

The Bishop of Geneva and the King of France had mutually esteemed and loved each other, therefore Francis was much grieved at the tragic end of his royal and generous friend. "The death of this great King," he writes, "grieves me infinitely; he is indeed deserving of sorrow and of tears." And to M. Deshayes he speaks more freely:

"A greater calamity could not have happened than the death of this great monarch. So noble, so generous, so kingly, who would have thought that he would fall under the dagger of an unknown wretch? He deserved to die gloriously and heroically. His greatest happiness was that he had become a son of the Church and the Father of France. I hope that in his last moments God gave him the grace of perfect contrition, and that the Almighty will show mercy to him who was so merciful to others, will forgive him who so nobly forgave his enemies."

In June Francis had had the great joy of founding the Order of the Visitation, thus realizing the dream of his life, and during the succeeding months he had the happiness of receiving into the new Institute honourable women—not a few, many of them personal friends.

But towards the end of the year yet more trials tested his courage and resignation to God's holy will. His good old tutor, M. Déage, passed away, and though he had become rather tiresome and petulant in his old age, yet Francis loved him dearly. So much, indeed, did he feel the death of this venerable man that, when offering up the Holy Sacrifice for the repose of his soul he reached the Pater, he burst into tears, and could not articulate a word. It was only after a long interval, during which, notwithstanding his wonderful self-control, he could not restrain his emotion, that he was able to finish the Mass. When he retired to his room, his chaplain, in trying to comfort him, asked him why he wept so bitterly at the Pater.

"Ah, if you wish to know why," he answered, "it is because this good, holy man first taught me to say the Our Father, and though I know that he is now a Saint in Heaven, enjoying in fullest measure the Beatific Vision, yet my heart grieves for him, who was my lifelong friend and counsellor."

While still sorrowing for this second Father, Francis lost—but fortunately not by death—the friend he called his *cher frère*, Antoine Favre. The Duke of Savoy conferred on M. Favre the dignity of First President of the Senate of Chambéry, and he was obliged to quit Annecy to take up his abode in the capital.

Before leaving he insisted that the Bishop of

Geneva should take up his residence in his magnificent dwelling-house, the grandest and most splendid mansion in Annecy, consequently, as Antoine Favre remarked, best suited to become the episcopal palace. As we know, Francis finally consented, to the great joy of his friend, who set out for Chambéry, feeling he had at last been able to do something for this dear Francis who, so generous himself, never asked anything from others, but adhered to his rule: "Ask nothing, refuse nothing."

# CHAPTER XX

## *THE LIFE OF MARTHA AND OF MARY*

"You ask me, dear brother," Francis de Sales writes to one of his friends, a priest, "what we are doing here in this little town in the midst of our mountains. You say reports have reached you that I am much occupied. Yes, it is so, my dear brother, for since I have placed holocausts on God's altar, does it not follow that they should send forth an odour of sweetness? But it is God's work, not mine.

"My brother, de Thorens, went to Burgundy for his little wife, and brought back with her a mother-in-law whom he never deserved to have, nor I to serve. You already know how God made her my daughter; and now this brave woman has left all for God, but not without providing for her children, and leaving her affairs in perfect order.

"On Trinity Sunday she and two companions, with the maid, Jacqueline Coste, took up their abode in a small house, and entered on their novitiate. They have since been joined by young ladies from Chambéry, Grenoble, and Burgundy. I hope this Congregation will suit the infirm and delicate, for without corporal austerities they lead a most devout life.

"They say the Office of Our Lady and meditate. They observe strict poverty, humility, obedience, and silence; they are most industrious, and their life is as edifying, peaceful, and holy as in any monastery in the world. After their profession they will, if it please Our Lord, go out humbly to nurse and care for the sick."

Again he writes:

"In the beginning, enclosure will be thus observed: no man will be allowed to enter, except on such occasions as they are allowed to enter the reformed monasteries. Neither will women be permitted to enter without the Superior's leave. After their year of novitiate they will go out, but only to nurse the sick. They will sing the Office of Our Lady, and the rest of their time will be spent in all kinds of good works, particularly in prayer and meditation."

The year of novitiate passed rapidly. The Sisters lived in a perfect Eden of peace and affection. Every day they advanced in grace, and every day all drew closer together, and were more and more united in spirit and in ideas, for their saintly founder constantly visited them, gradually unfolding the plan of the Order, teaching them little by little the rules and constitutions. Under such a guide, listening to the words of wisdom which fell from his lips, no wonder their hearts burned within them, and they longed for the glorious day when their sacrifice would be accepted by their loving Redeemer, and He would place on their fingers the ring of espousals, and cover their hair with the veil which would hide them from the eyes of men.

At last the day came, the first anniversary of their entrance into that humble, quiet house in the midst of the busy town—June 6, St. Claude's Feast. Francis de Sales officiated. Robed in full pontificals, he ascended the pulpit and addressed to them words flowing with Divine love, words eloquent yet simple, full of encouragement and of consolation.

We can easily imagine the seraphic love and overwhelming joy that filled his tender, gentle soul, when, later on, he placed the veils on their bowed heads, fastened the little silver cross round their necks, and placed the crucifix in their hands. The ceremony over, turning to them, "Go, my children," he said. "Return to your abode. You are indeed the chosen ones of your loving Saviour."

And as they withdrew from the sanctuary into the choir, Mme. de Chantal sang in a glad and joyous voice: "This is my rest for ever and for ever: here will I dwell, for I have chosen it" —words now always used in the ceremony of profession.

Their friends wished to remain and converse with them, but Francis said:

"Leave them this day alone in peace to enjoy the gift of God."

A few days later Francis wrote to Mother de Chantal :

"ANNECY,
"*June* 10, 1611.

"GOOD MORNING, MY DEAREST MOTHER.

"Last night God made known to me that our House of the Visitation was noble and great enough through His grace to have an escutcheon, a coat of arms, and a motto. So, subject to your approval, we will take for our arms a heart pierced with two arrows, encircled by a crown of thorns, the heart surmounted by a cross, engraved on which will be the sacred names of Jesus and Mary. The next time we meet I will tell you of a thousand ideas of mine on this subject, for, indeed our Congregation is the work of the Hearts of Jesus and of Mary. Our dying Saviour has brought us forth through the wound in His Sacred Heart."

There were as yet so few professed Sisters that Francis thought it wiser for them to postpone visiting the sick until January 1, 1612. On August 11, 1611, he wrote to Charlotte Bréchard, who had been left in charge of the Community during Mme. de Chantal's absence :

"MY DEAREST DAUGHTER,

"You must rest yourself, and sufficiently. You really must generously let the others do their part, and not seek to gain all the crowns. Your dear Sisters will be only too delighted to share them with you. The ardour of holy love which inspires you to do everything yourself ought also to inspire you to restrain yourself and allow the others to do their share of work.

"God will be good to us, my dearest daughter. I hope He is only threatening you, and does not intend to strike, and that our dear Mother will soon return to her dearest lieutenant and well-beloved daughter. Yes, my child, I wish you to work in a spirit ardent yet gentle, fervent yet moderate, not trusting to yourself, but leaving the happy ending of all things—sickness, labour, everything—to the loving care of your Spouse. May He deign to bless you now and always, and all the dear flock of our beloved Mother, absent, yet so present to our hearts, in the presence of Him Who is the Supreme All of the hearts of Mother and of daughters.

"Pray to Him to be this also to the Father, that all may be holily equal in our dear, humble little Visitation.

"FRANCIS."

True to her promise, Mother de Chantal arrived in Annecy late in December. She was determined that nothing should prevent her beginning the great and new work of visiting the sick and infirm, and bringing consolation and assistance to the poor in their own homes.

It is almost impossible for us, in the go-ahead

twentieth century, to realize what a strange innovation this visiting the sick and afflicted by nuns
was in those days. That a nun should leave the
strict enclosure of her convent and walk about
the streets, no matter what the object, was quite
unprecedented.

Women who entered religion were, in deed and
in fact, shut in by "narrowing nunnery walls,"
and to break through the traditions of centuries
required the originality and the courage of a gallant
and unconventional Saint like Francis de Sales,
and the resolution and freedom from all worldly
respect, of a Jeanne de Chantal; for the Mrs.
Grundy of those days and her friends turned up
their eyes to Heaven in horror. Men and women,
saints and sinners alike, cried out against such an
innovation.

"Nuns walk about the streets! go into houses!
Dreadful idea! Unheard of, and not to be
tolerated!"

Nevertheless, on January 1, 1611, Mother de
Chantal and her companions started on this
difficult and somewhat dangerous task, for they
had to brave the god of many—public opinion;
but confident in the loving mercy and goodness of
their God, their crucified Saviour, He Who cured
the sick, and healed the infirm, and went about
doing good, they set forth through the streets of
Annecy, up and down the dark old passages into
the dilapidated old gloomy houses, bringing sunshine into those noisome dwellings, helping not in

words only, but in deeds. But Madame de Chantal's own account of these visits is so vivid and so realistic that I must give a few extracts from it :

" In these visits we not only consoled the sick and assisted them with the service of our hands, but we gave them all they required in the way of linen, food, etc. Some of them were in the most abject poverty, misery, and filth, full of vermin and smelling vilely, so that such a love as that of our dear Sisters was necessary in order even to touch them. But they went about their task with marvellous courage, cleaning and making the poor souls comfortable. Some of these poor people were wet to the shoulders, not being able to get up, and having no one to help them ; some of them were covered with ulcers, some full of vermin. The Sisters dressed the sores of the former, and cut the hair of the latter ; in fact, they did everything necessary for the relief of the poor sufferers, making their beds, changing their linen, arranging fresh straw for those who were lying on the ground, and cleaning up their wretched dwellings. They sent doctors to visit them, and when it was time to administer the Last Sacraments, they told the priest, spread white sheets on the bed, and covered as well as they could the hideous and unsightly parts of the room. They also buried the dead. The poor people were full of gratitude and love, and, indeed, they taught us many a great lesson. Their patience in their sufferings astonished us, and we were much edified by their resignation to the will of God, to suffer and to die."

Needless to say that among the heroic little band of devoted souls, none were more heroic, none more generous and self-sacrificing, than the former Châtelaine of Bourbilly and Monthelon. Mother Marie de Chaugy says in her deposition in the process for the Canonization of Mother de Chantal, after having related several incidents of her zeal and charity:

"She displayed such courage and heroism, she showed so little disgust at the filth of the poor, that one of the Sisters asked her one day how she could endure such revolting things. The Saint replied that she did not consider that it was to a mere creature she gave her services, but that it always seemed to her that she was dressing the wounds of Our Lord in the person of His poor."

Thus the nuns of the Visitation led the life both of Martha and of Mary, as their saintly founder intended, giving much time to prayer and contemplation, mortifying their wills more than their bodies; for Francis de Sales held the same views as Ignatius of Loyola, and considered dying to self and to self-love a nobler, a more heroic, and an infinitely more difficult task than practising exterior austerities and severe corporal mortifications.

Two Sisters in turn were selected to visit the sick, one acting as Superior. One day when Mother Favre and Sister Fichet were on their visitation, they passed the Episcopal Palace. The Bishop was confined to bed with an ulcer on his leg, so when he heard they were passing, he sent out for them and asked them to dress his leg. They were only too pleased to be able to do anything for their beloved Father, and with hands trembling with joy, and, alas! also with nervousness and inexperience, they proceeded to dress the wound. Francis endured agonies under their kindly ministrations, but he said nothing until they had finished; then he remarked quietly and with a gently humorous smile:

"My children, when you dress the sores of the poor, do it quietly, with a steady hand, and not too quickly, for when the raw flesh is roughly handled it causes great pain."

On their return to the convent, they related their adventure. Charlotte de Bréchard, who was a splendid nurse, begged leave to attend the dear patient, but he refused.

"I will not see any of you," he told them, "until I can walk with my bad leg into the parlour."

No sooner did Francis de Sales recover his health and strength, than Jeanne de Chantal fell ill of a mysterious malady, that sorely puzzled the most eminent physicians. Several times she was on the point of death. The Sisters were inconsolable; it seemed that the beautiful Institute they loved so much would collapse utterly if their saintly Mother was taken away from them. In this sad state of affairs Francis had recourse to prayer.

He invoked the intercession of his model, the holy Archbishop of Milan, promising to go on a pilgrimage to his shrine if Mother de Chantal were cured, then mixing the powder of a relic of the Saint with the drink she was about to take, he gave it her. No sooner had she swallowed it than, with a deep sigh, she opened her eyes and said: "My Father, I shall not die this time: I feel I am quite cured, thanks to God and to St. Charles Borromeo."

Enraptured at these words, the Bishop and all the community recited the *Te Deum*, and in a day or two Mother de Chantal was able to resume her duties.

The little Maison de la Perrière was much too small for the daily increasing number of postulants, and Mother de Chantal succeeded in buying a much larger house near the lake, and on Tuesday, October 30, 1612, they moved into it. She intended to buy up more houses and to found on that spot the first monastery of the Visitation. But many obstacles had first to be overcome, and it was not until September 18, 1614, that the Countess de Tournon, acting for the Duchess of Mantua, daughter of the Duke of Savoy, laid the foundation-stone of the new edifice. Francis de Sales naturally officiated, and blessed the foundation-stone, on which the following inscription was engraved in Latin: " To the great and good God, to Jesus Christ, and to His Most Holy Mother under the title of the Visitation.

During the reign of Charles Emmanuel, Duke of Savoy, Henry of Savoy being Duke of Nemours and of Geneva, in the year 1614, on September 18, under the protection of Margaret of Savoy, widow of the Duke of Mantua, and during the episcopacy of Francis, who was present and performed the ceremony, this foundation - stone was laid and blessed as a monument consecrated to the devotion of the Oblate Sisters of the Visitation."

# CHAPTER XXI

## *TEMPORAL POWER*

AT this period all Europe was discussing the vexed question of the temporal power of the Pope. James I. of England set the ball rolling by the many books he wrote to justify the oath of allegiance he demanded from his Catholic subjects. Cardinal Bellarmine retorted by a very clever work, " De Romano Pontifice."

But, clever and erudite as it was, it pleased no one, for Sixtus V. put it on the Index, considering it did not sufficiently vindicate the authority of the Holy See, and from the opposition there was a cry of universal indignation, not only heretics but good Catholics considering he went too far. He then published a second book, " Tractatus de Potestate Summi Pontificis in Temporalibus." It was really only a repetition of the principles advocated in his former work—namely, that the Pope had an *indirect* right over matters temporal.

This, then, was the bone of contention. The war of words waged fast and furious. The faithful were divided into two camps; the Sorbonne took one side, the Jesuits another. Matters had reached such a crisis that it almost seemed a schism would result. And for what? For absolutely nothing. Francis de Sales frequently remarked, and endeavoured to impress on these turbulent people, the Pope did not claim temporal power. He had no desire to exercise it. He had not the faintest intention of deposing Kings, upsetting existing constitutions, or of interfering in any way with the government of kingdoms. Then why in Heaven's name discuss the subject, particularly in so bitter and hostile a spirit? He endeavoured to throw oil upon the troubled waters, for he feared that dissension among Catholics would lead to grave evils, as, indeed, was the case later on, during the reign of Louis XIV.

On June 2, 1612, Francis de Sales addressed a memoir to Cardinal Scipione Cafferelli Borghese. In it he proves himself a true and loyal son of the Church, grieving with her grief, troubled over her troubles, studying how best to remedy them, and suggesting what he considered the surest way of obtaining peace and concord among Christian Kings and nations. Though so loyal a son of Holy Church and devoted adherent of the Holy See, he does not seem to have thought that the Pope did possess temporal power, for he writes to a lady who consulted him on the subject:

"The Pope is the Sovereign Pontiff and spiritual Father; the King is the Sovereign Prince and temporal lord. Their different powers do not clash; on the contrary, they help each other.

If our sovereign lord His Holiness is in any difficulty or danger, or threatened by his enemies,
then will his loyal children, the Kings and Princes
of this world, hasten to aid him, uphold his
dominion, and fight for and protect him. Then
he in like manner will treat them as his dearly
beloved children, bless and love them, and confer
on them spiritual graces and benefits. But, as I
have often before remarked, this discussion is
utterly vain and useless, for our Holy Father does
not claim temporal power."

He often repeated to people who over and over
again asked his opinion on this burning question
of the day, " Pacem habete, et Deus pacis et
dilectionis erit vobiscum."*

While endeavouring to bring about a more
cordial feeling between the controversialists,
Francis was doing his utmost to obtain from
Rome the canonization of Amadeus III., Duke of
Savoy, a truly holy man, a just and generous
Prince, one whose memory was revered by all
good Savoyards.

In the spring of 1613 the Bishop of Geneva set
out to visit the shrine of the Archbishop of Milan
in accordance with the vow he had made when,
through the intercession of St. Charles Borromeo,
Mother de Chantal was miraculously cured. On
his way he stopped at Turin to pay his respects
to his Sovereign, Charles Emmanuel, and to
entreat him to confer on the new Order of the
Visitation the patronage of the House of Savoy.

*"Be at peace, and the God of peace and love will be with you."

He also asked the Duke to give the charge of the college at Annecy to a religious Order, as the lay-teachers were not working it in a satisfactory manner. These requests the Prince graciously granted. He mentioned to Francis that he thought the Barnabite Fathers eminently suited to carry on the work, but left the Bishop of Geneva free to select them or not as he pleased. Having thoroughly pondered the matter, and prayed and fasted to obtain the Divine guidance, Francis interviewed the Barnabites at Milan, and, having found them in every way capable of directing the college, he offered the care of it to them, and they gladly accepted.

Francis also pleaded the cause of several gentlemen who were accused of complicity in the murder of the Secretary of the Duc de Nemours. Charles Emmanuel promised thoroughly to investigate the matter, and Francis proceeded on his pilgrimage to Milan. He arrived there on April 25, and was royally welcomed by Cardinal Frederic Borromeo, cousin and successor of St. Charles, and by Don Juan de Mendoza, the governor of the city.

Mendoza pressed him to stay with him at the palace, but the chief wish of the Bishop of Geneva was to find some humble lodging, to pass to and fro from it to the cathedral unnoticed and unknown, indulging freely his devotion, and spending long hours in prayer before the shrine of his sainted model.

It is a curious fact that Francis de Sales, who was himself so genial, gentle, and indulgent towards others, should have chosen as his guide, and have wished to imitate, one of the most austere of the servants of God.

One little instance will illustrate the difference in their dispositions. The Bishop of Belley relates it:

"St. Charles Borromeo could not endure that after meals the company he received should amuse themselves by spending their time in useless conversation, saying that it was unworthy of a pastor charged with the care of so large a diocese to encourage such frivolity, and that there were many better occupations. This was natural in a Saint so austere, and no one was surprised when on such occasions he broke off the conversation. Francis de Sales was of a more indulgent spirit, and did not withdraw from conversation after meals. When I was staying with him, he always tried to amuse me. He would take me out boating on the beautiful lake of Annecy, or we would go for a walk in some pleasant gardens on the lovely shores. When he visited me at Belley, he did not decline similar recreations which I provided for him, but he never proposed them or sought them of his own accord. In everything he saw, flowers, birds, paintings, splendid buildings, glorious scenery, snow-capped mountains, and lakes, he found means of raising his soul to God, and of helping others to do likewise."

Yet, as Charles Borromeo devoted his whole

life to labouring for and tending his flock, and was consumed by the most ardent charity, and governed his enormous diocese with marvellous wisdom and consummate prudence; so Francis de Sales followed in his footsteps, thinking he was but a humble and inefficient imitator of a great Saint, while he himself carried out the Gospel counsel of perfection: "Let your light so shine before men that they may see your good works, and glorify your Father Who is in Heaven."

But the revered and popular Bishop of Geneva could not remain, like the humble violet, hidden and unknown. He was requested to celebrate Holy Mass the following morning at the tomb of St. Charles Borromeo. The Archbishop insisted, moreover, that he should be robed in magnificent vestments glittering with jewels and precious stones. The ceremony over, Francis went to pay his respects to the Archbishop, accompanied by several priests and cavaliers. On their way they went into raptures over the beauties of the great cathedral and the splendour of the ornaments and decorations. Then, surprised that Francis made no remark, they asked his opinion.

"I must honestly confess," he answered, smiling, "I saw absolutely nothing."

"But at least, Monseigneur, you must have noticed the beautiful vestments you wore and the exquisite vessels you used at Mass. It is impossible that your eyes were not dazzled by the brilliancy of the jewels and the glitter of gold."

"I noticed nothing," replied Francis quietly, "for I was so engrossed in meditating on the interior ornaments of virtue and holiness of the great Cardinal that I did not perceive the magnificent exterior of the cathedral nor the sacred vestments."

Having spent some days of peaceful devotion at Milan, he returned to Turin to take part in the celebration of the Feast of the Holy Winding-Sheet, as he was one of the Prelates selected to expose the precious relic to the veneration of the faithful.

Francis fulfilled with celestial joy this holy office; but even as he held it the intense heat of the church caused some drops of sweat to mingle with his tears of devotion and to fall on the sacred sheet. The Cardinal of Savoy, perceiving it, was very much annoyed, and severely reproved Francis for his carelessness, but he, raising his eyes to Heaven, prayed thus to his Lord in secret: "O my Saviour, deign to allow me to mix my sweat with Thine, to saturate my blood, my life, my thoughts in Thy most precious Blood. This good Cardinal is vexed, but Thou, my Saviour, art not so fastidious. Thou didst shed Thy Blood and Thy Sweat in order that ours should mingle with Thine, and we should obtain life everlasting. May my sighs and prayers unite with Thine, so that the Eternal Father may graciously receive them."

Having returned to Annecy, he hardly gave himself time to rest a little after his long and tiresome journey across the Alps, but set out for Gex. As usual, that unhappy country was in a disturbed state. Religious differences continued, and party spirit ran high. It taxed the almost superhuman patience of the gentle Bishop of Geneva to establish some degree of order and of peace. He, however, succeeded in reconstructing eight more parishes, and in having priests and people more closely united. He had the consolation of settling the Barnabites at the college of Annecy and the Carthusians at Repailles.

In 1614 he received an invitation from the Emperor, Matthias I., to attend the Diet at Ratisbon on February 1, 1615. For nearly a century the Bishops of Geneva had been unable to dwell in their episcopal city, but the sovereignty of it was still theirs, and they were recognized by the holy Roman Empire as the only true and legitimate Princes, for the Empire quite refused to have any dealings with or to countenance the Calvinist Republic.

The herald, according to an ancient custom, marched into Geneva, went to the Episcopal Palace, knocked at the door, and announced that he had a message to give to the Bishop from His Imperial Majesty. Of course he was informed that the Bishop was not there, and that he must go to Annecy if he wished to see him. This he accordingly did, and delivered the summons to Francis. To it the Bishop of Geneva replied that he would only be too delighted to accept, but that he was too poor to undertake so long a journey, and that the only way in which he could show his devotion to the Emperor was by constantly remembering him in his prayers. " More things are wrought by prayer than this world dreams of."

# CHAPTER XXII

## *"NOT WHAT I WILL, FATHER, BUT WHAT THOU WILT"*

" I am called the Founder of the Visitation. Is there anything more unreasonable ? I have done what I did not wish to do, and what I wished to do I have left undone."

Surely no words are sadder or more pathetic. What did Jeanne de Chantal do when she heard of the change ? Was she capable of the same sublime renunciation ? or did she struggle and weep vain tears over the destruction of her life's purpose ? " Closed about by narrowing nunnery walls," did her soul long for the fuller, more active existence she had hoped to lead ? Probably she forgot her own disappointment, having resolved to devote her life to God's service in whatever manner God chose to have that service ; and now she accepted the decision of her saintly guide as the expression of God's will in her regard, and endeavoured to console and sympathize with him. Not that he would have required much consolation ; the sacrifice once made, he was not likely to look back and waste time in futile regrets, but

rather at once to set about modelling the Order
on its new lines.

But at first, while Francis was yet undecided,
Jeanne protested against the change, entreating
him to stand firm, and in no way to alter the rules
and constitutions of the Institute.

Cardinal Bellarmine also urged him to adhere
to his original design, writing to him the following
letter in reply to a note Francis had sent him to
ask the Holy See for several favours for the Visitation, at the same time telling him of Cardinal de
Marquemont's desire to change the whole life of
the nuns and alter the rules of the Institute :

" I will give you the counsel to act as I would
myself act if I were in your place. I would leave
these widows and spinsters precisely as they are,
and I would not change what has been well done.
Before Boniface VIII. there were nuns both in
the East and West. We have the authority of the
Holy Fathers for this. Now, these religious could
go abroad when necessary, consequently they
had not strict enclosure. And you, Monseigneur,
are not ignorant of the fact that simple vows are
not less binding or less meritorious before God
than solemn ones, since the solemnity as well as
the enclosure dates only from the Bull of Boniface VIII. Even in our own day the convent of
noble ladies founded by St. Frances of Rome is
in a flourishing condition, and gives us an up-
to-date example of an ancient custom, for they
have neither enclosure nor solemn profession. If

then, in your country, widows and spinsters live as holily, and can be as useful to seculars by their charity and good example, without being cloistered, I do not see why their way of life should be altered."

However, Cardinal de Marquemont won, or rather, the Divine will, for Francis came to the conclusion that it was not God's will that he should lead maidens and widows forth from cloistered cells into the fuller and more active life he had dreamed of for them. It was Vincent de Paul, not Francis de Sales, who was destined to succeed in so glorious an undertaking ; to him the honour and glory of success, to Francis the triumph of failure. For surely to resign one's most cherished ambition, to give up the dream of one's life, requires more heroic courage, greater strength of will, and a more virile and noble character than to carry it out in spite of all obstacles. Renunciation is the highest, as it is the most difficult, virtue to practise, yet, though the Visitation was not formed on its original lines, it and its generous founder received a reward exceedingly great to compensate, if compensation were needed, for the spoiling of the original purpose ; for unto them it was given to propagate the devotion to the Sacred Heart of Jesus.

It was to a humble daughter of Our Lady and of St. Francis de Sales that Our Lord chose to manifest the greatness of this love of His Sacred Heart for us, and this lowly maiden, guided and

directed by her Jesuit confessor, made it known
to the whole world. From the simple convent
in quiet little Paray-le-Monial this devotion has
spread throughout the universe. If it is true that
the sun never sets upon our empire, it is equally
true that there is not a spot upon God's earth
where the Sacred Heart of His Divine Son is not
adored. And everywhere, in the gorgeous East
as well as in the enlightened West, under the
Southern Cross, and in the uttermost regions of
the snow-bound lands, wherever the Heart of Jesus
is held in veneration—and that is everywhere—the
daughters of Holy Mary and of Francis de Sales,
and the Sons of Jesus and of Ignatius of Loyola,
are the chosen propagators and apostles of this, the
most beautiful and inspiring devotion of the Holy
Catholic Church.

But what were the reasons that caused the
Bishop of Geneva to alter his plans ? Principally
the determination of Cardinal de Marquemont
not to allow the nuns under his jurisdiction to
visit the sick.

In 1615 Mme. de Chantal founded a convent at
Lyons at the express wish of the Archbishop of
that city, Cardinal de Marquemont. But, greatly
to her surprise and annoyance, no sooner were
they all settled in their new abode, and ready to
begin their daily duties of tending the sick and
helping the poor, than the Archbishop sternly for-
bade them to leave the convent and go into the
streets.

Cardinal de Marquemont was old-fashioned, and, like all old-fashioned people, he hated innovations. What was good enough for his forefathers was good enough for him ; and he probably forgot, or, more probably, never knew, that in the early days of Christianity holy women had lived in community as religious, but without strict enclosure, and had consequently gone forth to succour their weak and helpless brethren. Anyway, that was a very long time ago.

The Archbishop had no recollection of such an order of things, so he would have no reforms. Not for him " The old order changeth, giving place to new"; no changes for him, thanks. Keep within your cloistered walls, O my Sisters ! If you wish to wander over the world, then, in God's name, remain in the world. Do not take the veil ; but if you insist on taking it, then remain within the monastery walls, remain there like all other women consecrated to God—Carmelites, Dominicans, Poor Clares. They do not seek to leave their cloistered cells. Do as they do ; pray and pray, and work, and occupy your hands and heads within your narrow walls. It is not given to you to perform the corporal works of mercy—to visit the sick, to bury the dead, to comfort the afflicted, to give meat to the hungry and drink to the thirsty, to clothe the naked, and to alleviate physical pain. No, no, a thousand times, no. Pray, my Sisters, and let your prayers rise like incense day and night before the Tabernacle, and help the poor, the sick, the afflicted, by means of supplications before the Lord; and, as for the dead, pray for their souls.

So it was settled. That was to be their life's work.

In October, 1617, Francis wrote to Mother Favre, then at Lyons:

"MY DEAREST DAUGHTER,

"If my Lord Archbishop says to you what he has written to me, you must tell him that you have been left to establish our Congregation as well as you can, and to guide your Sisters according to our rules; and that if it is God's will that our Congregation should change its name, state, and condition, you will refer yourself to his good pleasure; and add that in whatever way God may best be served, you will be content with that way.

"That must be the spirit of our Congregation, for it is the perfect and apostolic spirit.

"On the points the Cardinal proposes to me, without which he will not allow our poor Congretion to remain in his diocese, I leave him the choice without any reserve. I am quite indifferent, so long as good is done, whether it is done in this way or in that, although I should have dearly loved the title of simple Congregation, where in love only and fear of the Beloved would be the only enclosure.

"I agree, then, that we make it a formal religious Order, and, my dear daughter, I speak to

223

you in confidence and in simplicity. I agree to this
quietly and tranquilly—nay, even with a certain
pleasure, and not only my will, but my judgment,
is glad to give this homage to a great and estimable Prelate.

" For what do I aim at in all this but the greater
honour and glory of God, and that He may be
better known and more dearly loved by those who
dedicate themselves wholly to His service ?

" Rest assured, my child, that I truly love our
little Congregation, but without anxiety. It is
true that love seldom exists without anxiety, but
mine is not ordinary love, and so lives without
solicitude through a particular confidence which I
have in the grace of Our Lord. His Sovereign
Hand will do more for our little Institute than
men can think.

" I am, more than you can believe, yours,

" FRANCIS."


About the same time Francis de Sales wrote to
a priest who told him that a religious did not
approve of the nuns of the Visitation reciting only
the Little Office of Our Lady.


" REVEREND FATHER,

" As to the question that good gentleman
asks about the occupations of the Sisters of the
Visitation, by which they make up for not saying
the Divine Office, I have two things to say.

" Since they recite the Little Office with great

solemnity and with long pauses, they employ as much time over it as other nuns do in saying the Divine Office, with this difference, that they say it with more edification and better pronunciation than the latter. Certainly, a week ago, in a monastery near this city, I saw things that would make the Huguenots laugh, and some of the nuns told me they never had less devotion than at Office, where they always committed a number of faults, partly from not knowing the accents and quantities, and also from not knowing the rubrics, or again because they were obliged to recite it so rapidly that, they said, it was utterly impossible for them among so many distractions to remain recollected. I do not, however, wish to say that they ought to be dispensed from saying it unless when the Holy See, taking compassion on them, will think it advisable to do so.

" But at the same time, I consider that there is no impropriety, but rather great advantage, in the nuns of the Visitation reciting only the Little Office. In fact, Rev. Father, this Little Office is the spring of devotion among them. Secondly, in the Visitation every moment is employed most usefully in prayer, examination of conscience, spiritual reading and other exercises. I am sure that the Holy Father will favour this work, which is against neither the law nor the religious state, and which gains it so many houses of obedience at a time when, and in a kingdom where, it has lost so many ; and because also convents of women can be of no consequence to other Orders, nor yet occasions of complaint to nuns living under other rules.

"It is solely for the greater glory of God that I desire that this little Congregation shall recite only the Little Office of Our Lady, for I consider that by saying it they can more perfectly serve God, and that also they are incapable of saying the Divine Office.

"Is it not much to be desired that there should be a retreat to which those poor daughters can retire, who have strong and vigorous hearts, but weak eyes and delicate constitutions?

"Your friend and servant, etc.,

"FRANCIS."

So the little Congregation of the Daughters of Holy Mary was converted into a religious Order with strict enclosure, under the title of the Visitation.

Cardinal de Marquemont had wished to change the name also, and call it the Presentation, remarking that as they no longer visited the sick and poor the name Visitation was a misnomer; but it pleased Our Lord to show in a remarkable manner that He willed the old name to be retained; for in the letters patent for the new Institute, instead of the words "Congregation of the *Presentation*," and in all the letters and documents, Congregation of the *Visitation* was written clearly and distinctly, even in the letters the Cardinal had

himself written to the King.   " Truly," exclaimed
the spectators, " it is the hand of God."

On April 23, 1618, Paul V. sent Francis de Sales
a Bull authorizing him to form into a religious
Order, under the Rule of St. Augustine, the Institute of the Visitation, and on October 9 of the
same year the saintly founder gave to his daughters
the constitutions and rules of the new Order.

# CHAPTER XXIII

## *THE SPIRIT OF THE VISITATION*

"JE suis grand partisan des infirmes," Francis de
Sales writes to one of the Sisters of the Visitation.
Again, he says: "I am the champion of the weak;"
and it was in this spirit that he laid down the
rules that were to guide his spiritual children
homewards. Following the Rule of St. Augustine,
he yet changed and modified it to a certain extent
in order to suit the needs and the strength of his
children.

"There is no one more lenient than St. Augustine," he says. "His writings are sweetness itself; his Rule is animated by the spirit of charity;
it breathes mildness, benignity, and indulgence,
and suits people of all nations and all constitutions. But at the same time it is somewhat
vague. It comprises only the great counsels, the
fundamental duties of the religious life; it indi-
cates no form of government. St. Augustine has
traced the great circumference of a vast religious
city, not a cloister. Many of the devout female
sex, secretly drawn by the Holy Spirit to aspire to
a religious life, are prevented from joining the
religious Orders where extreme austerities, cor-

poral penances and mortifications are the rule. These girls and widows are not strong enough to undertake so religious a life. They are consequently obliged to remain amidst the distractions of the world, exposed to occasions of sin, or, at least, of losing the fervour of their devotion, and of tarnishing the purity of their souls. In order, therefore, that these generous souls who wish to live only for God, but are prevented from doing so by infirmities, delicacy of constitution or age, may be able to follow their vocation and retire from the world, this Congregation has been formed. In it there are no hardships to deter the feeble and infirm from entering it, and seeking in it to serve God. Widows also may be received into it. Persons who, on account of their age or corporal infirmities, would be refused admittance into more severe Orders, are gladly welcomed."

As all sorts and conditions of women were received, much of the severity of the existing Orders was relaxed. The Sisters did not sleep on a plank like the Daughters of Carmel; they did not rise at midnight to recite the Divine Office. Instead, they said the Little Office of Our Lady at half-past eight, and retired to rest at ten. They were not obliged to abstain from eating meat, nor yet to fast from September to Easter—only the fast on Fridays, during Lent, and on certain vigils, was retained. Severe disciplines and other macerations of the flesh were also forbidden. The spirit of the Order was essentially a spirit of love and of self-denial. The mortification of the soul was substituted for that of the flesh, the crucifixion of the will for that of the body. The aim of the Sisters was to rise higher, ever higher, in the spiritual life, striving to attain the highest degree of perfection, and to die to self-love, though Francis tells us that self-love never dies.

"Self-love may be mortified in us, but it never dies; from time to time it sends forth shoots which prove that, though cut down to the root, it is never completely destroyed. Self-love never leaves us. It sleeps sometimes like a fox; then suddenly springs upon the chickens. We must therefore be constantly watchful of it, and patiently defend ourselves against it. Ah! how suddenly self-love insinuates itself into our affections, however devout they may appear."

Yet his spiritual children ran it almost to death in their daily sacrifice of their inclinations. In their thorough unselfishness they attained a degree of perfection that brightened the declining years of their beloved Father, and consoled him for the great sacrifice he had made. Perhaps one of the strictest rules of the Order is the one of absolute poverty, for the Sisters possess nothing of their own, not even their crosses and Prayer-Books. Every year the cells, the beds, the medals, the pictures, and the books are changed, so that they "may live in a perfect abnegation of the things they use, and not become attached to them. On no pretext may a Sister have anything of her own."

Their time is certainly not their own, for every day the Superior tells them what they are to do until night, and every half-hour their occupation is changed, so that they never have a moment to themselves. But to grasp the real spirit of the Visitation, we must listen to the counsels Francis one day gave to a little lay Sister, who, on account of her childlike innocence, was called Sister Simplicienne by the community. She said to the Bishop one day:

"Monseigneur, I would like to perform all my actions as you would if you were here."

"Is that so, dear Sister Simplicienne? Well, I fear I should not act as well as you do, for I am good for nothing. Yet, with God's grace, I would endeavour to be so attentive to all the little petty observances that, by being so, I might please Our Lord. I would keep silence, but in time of silence, I would speak if charity required me to do so, not otherwise, and I would always speak in a low voice, for such is the rule. I would open and close doors gently, because our Mother wishes it, and you must always try to please her. I would always keep the custody of the eyes, as well as of all my senses, for God and His angels are always watching us, and they love best those who act well. If I had much to do I should endeavour to do it well, but if I was given no employment I should avoid interfering with others, be obedient, and love Our Lord. And in order to love Him and serve Him with all my heart, I should apply myself to attend to the exact observance of the rules and constitutions. Ah, my dear daughter Simplicienne, we must do this as well as possible. Shall I tell you still more, my child? I should be very joyous, and I should never be in a hurry. This, thank God, I do already, for I am never eager, but I should then practise it even more. I should humble myself and make acts of humility whenever I had a chance; and if I had not done so I should at least humble myself for not having done so. I should try to live always in the Presence of God, and to perform all my actions for Him. I should often read the chapters of our constitutions on humility and modesty. Yes, my dear daughter, they ought to be often read and faithfully practised."

Francis impressed on Mother de Chantal the following counsels of perfection:

"I wish you to be little and lowly in your own eyes, yielding and gentle as a dove, to love lowliness and faithfully practise it. Employ willingly all the opportunities of doing so which occur. Do not speak quickly, answer slowly, humbly and gently, and let your silence often speak for you. Gently support and make allowances for others, with great kindness of heart. Do not dwell on contradictions and troubles; look only on God and submit yourself completely to His Divine will. Do everything for God, turning your eyes and your heart always towards Him.

"Do not agitate yourself over anything—do all

things with tranquillity and in a spirit of repose; do not lose the peace of your soul even if everything should be turned upside down, for what are all the things of this life compared to interior peace? Our Lord loves you; He would have you all His, that nothing may come between. Forget all the rest, troubling yourself about nothing. Have good courage, and keep yourself very humble; abase yourself before your Saviour, and desire nothing but to love Him more and more.

"Refuse nothing, painful though it may be; clothe yourself with Our Lord crucified, love Him in His sufferings, and frequently make ejaculatory prayers over them. Do this, my dearest daughter; and may Jesus Christ do all in us, with us, and through us, for His own sake and His most holy will. Amen. I have, thank God, my eyes always fixed on Providence, whose decrees will always be the laws of my heart."

Such is the spirit of the Order of the Visitation: a spirit of profound humility, gentleness, kindness. The Sisters are to have sweet and winning words upon their lips and love in their hearts; they are to bear one another's burdens, to help one another, to abound and superabound in gentleness and charity. They are to practise simplicity in thought, word, and action. They are indeed to become as little children, docile, affectionate, innocent, and they are to have special love for and take particular care of the aged and infirm.

Francis de Sales writes most strongly on this

point: "I have a great love for the sick, and I fear that perhaps the inconvenience they occasion might, through a spirit of prudence, cause some of the convents to send them away; but remember the spirit of our Order is a spirit of love and of charity. I take the part of the poor sick Sister, and, provided she is humble and acknowledges herself indebted to you, you must receive and keep the poor invalid. It is also a continual exercise in patience and holiness for the other Sisters."

The Visitation was now in working order. Foundations were made—not only at Lyons, but at Moulins, Grenoble, Bourges, and later on, but still during the lifetime of Francis, at Paris, Orleans, and Dijon. But Francis de Sales, like Ignatius of Loyola—like, in fact, all the great Saints and servants of God—was not to escape detraction and calumny. "Be thou as chaste as ice, as pure as snow, thou shalt not scape calumny."

The beautiful, and humble little Order of the Visitation, lowly though it was, did not escape the sneers and jeers of men. That powerful *vox populi* which has crushed so many reformers, and taken the hope and the heart's blood out of martyrs and patriots, cried out in horror against it. Men called it the Confraternity of the *Descent* from the Cross, and people shrieked out that it was to amuse a few idle women and coddle a few sick ones that the Bishop of Geneva was founding what he called monasteries, but they were really hospitals, or else houses of rest and dwelling-places of pleasure. He had found out the secret of going to Heaven in a coach-and-four over a road strewn with roses without thorns, of entering Paradise with a different key, and by another way than the royal way of the Holy Cross.

Francis, however, having finally decided on the constitutions, and having got them approved by Paul V., was resolved that they should not be tampered with or altered, but that each and all of the communities should abide by them. The following extract from a letter to Mother Favre gives his views on this subject:

" I cannot think, my dearest daughter, that my Lord Archbishop will introduce any further laws into your convent, since he sees that those laid down are well observed. But if he wishes to make any changes, you must ask him to make his rules compatible with the holy uniformity that should exist in all our convents, for I consider it would be most disedifying to have a separate and different spirit in the different houses. I hope Our Lord will give you the mouth and the wisdom, indeed, to answer with humility and gentleness."

# CHAPTER XXIV

## "THE LOVE OF GOD"

" I AM going to put my hand to the book on the
Love of God, and will try to write as much on my
heart as on the paper." Francis de Sales writes
thus to Mother de Chantal, who was constantly
urging him to write this *Treatise*. He promised
her to do so, but with the affairs of his large
diocese weighing on his mind and taking up his
time, and interruptions from outside, he found it
almost impossible to begin. Every spare moment,
however, he devoted to this great work, and in
composing it felt his heart so inflamed with Divine
love that his tears flowed in such abundance over
the paper that he had to cease writing. On
March 25, when he returned from Vespers, he was
so overwhelmed by the burning love that consumed
his soul that he fainted away. His brother Louis
soon after entered the room, and saw that a globe
of fire from which several flames descended was
over the head of Francis, shedding on his face a
radiant light, and causing it to seem like the face
of an angel, and the flames played round him, and
mingled with and touched his garments without
consuming them. Louis remained spellbound for

a time, but when the phenomenon vanished he summoned up courage to ask his brother what it all meant, at the same time inquiring if he were ill, for the face of the Saint was still a brilliant scarlet.

" No, my brother, I am not ill; and do not call anyone," Francis replied, still trembling from the effects of the prodigy. " I will tell you what has happened, but you must solemnly promise me never to relate what I will reveal to you to anyone else."

The love Louis had always felt for his eldest brother from this day deepened into a feeling of profound veneration, and he looked upon him as a Saint. In memory of this miraculous favour by which the Divine Spirit had infused itself into his heart and soul, and filled him as it did the Apostles of old with the fire of celestial love, and given to him knowledge and wisdom passing that of men, he wrote the following lines in a book he always carried about with him: " Die vigesima quinta Martii, hodie, servum suum Franciscum misericorditer visitare dignatus est Dominus " (To-day, March 25, the Lord has mercifully deigned to visit His servant Francis).

In July, 1616, this wonderful book appeared, and at once attracted the attention of all, creating a profound sensation, not only in France and Italy, but more particularly in England.

James I., as we know, was so delighted with " La Vie Dévote," that he always carried it about with him, but when he read " L'Amour de Dieu," his admiration was such that he was quite carried away, and cried out : " O if I could only once see the author of this evangelical book! His language is that of Heaven not of Earth. He must be a great saint."

These words were repeated to Francis, who exclaimed : " O that I had the wings of a dove, that I might fly to the King of that fair land, once the Island of Saints, now the abode of heresy. Ah! dear Lord, if my Prince allows it I will go to this King, and preach the truth to him, and to his subjects even at the peril of my life." But Charles Emmanuel would not allow him to go.

The " Love of God "[*] is a beautiful book, almost too beautiful for most of us, for it is scientific, theological, and philosophical, as well as devout and seraphic. In it we see the exercises of contemplation, that loving repose of the soul in God. We follow the soul through transports, in courage, and in sadness, and in complete abandonment to Providence. It contains instructions on the science of the love of God, and it irresistibly impels us to that love. St. Vincent de Paul calls it " the goad of the slothful, and the stimulus of love," and the General of the Feuillants says : " It is the most perfect book that mortal hand ever composed, a book that one would always wish to read again and again. He who reads it must become better, and having become better, must again read it and become perfect."

238

*Usually called *Treatise on the Love of God.*

# "The Love of God"

When "La Vie Dévote" appeared, the General of the Carthusians advised Francis never to write another book, lest he might lose the reputation it had gained for him, but after the publication of "L'Amour de Dieu," the General hoped and begged of him that he would never lay down his pen.

The book had a wide circulation, and its extraordinary success made everyone long to know, or at least to see, the author. He was requested to preach during Advent and Lent in several cities, but it was finally decided that he should preach the Advent of 1616, and the Lent of 1617, in Grenoble. The Parliament of Dauphiny were so eager to secure him that they besought the Duke of Savoy to use his influence with the Bishop on their behalf.

It was while engaged in arduous missionary work in this beautiful city, preaching, hearing confessions, helping and comforting all who came to him, that he met the Maréchal Duc de Lesdiguères, who was Governor of the Province. This nobleman was a stern and obstinate Calvinist, and looked upon by the heretics as a shining light, one on whose constancy they could always rely, and who would remain impervious to the subtlest argument, and the most persuasive sermons; but having seen Francis, the Saint's gentle dignity and courteous manners made such an impression on the haughty but chivalrous old man that he was determined to hear him preach.

Francis approved of shortness in sermons; in this

he agreed with his seraphic namesake, St. Francis of Assisi, who recommended the preaching of his Order to be brief, quoting to them the verse of St. Paul's Epistle to the Romans ix. 28 : " Because a short word shall the Lord make upon the earth."

" Believe me," the Bishop of Geneva says to his friend the Bishop of Belley, " I speak from experience, the more you say the less will be remembered, and the less will your hearers profit. By overloading their memory you cause it to break down, as lamps are put out by too much oil and plants killed by too much watering. A preacher cannot have a greater fault than lengthiness. Say little, but say it well and to the purpose."

And so, at Grenoble, numbers of Protestants preferred to attend his sermons to going to listen to the tedious and long-winded discourses of their own ministers. They said he was free from the spirit of contention, and yet he always employed the first part of his sermon in setting forth the truths of the Catholic Religion ; the second part he devoted to moral and devotional subjects. But yet these discourses which were not specially directed against heresy, possessed such power against it that many Huguenots were converted.

" I have always maintained," Francis says, " that whoever preaches with love, preaches sufficiently against heresy, although he may not utter a single word of controversy. During all these years that God has called me to preach His Word to the people, I have remarked that practical sermons, where the subject is treated with zeal and devotion, are so many burning coals cast upon the heads of the Protestants who hear them; and they are always pleased and edified by them, and are thereby rendered more docile and reasonable when we confer with them on disputed points. This is not my opinion only, but is also that of the most celebrated preachers I know. They all agree that the pulpit ought not to be made the battle-ground of controversy, and that we must demolish more than we build up if we attempt more than a passing allusion to it."

Such, then, was the style of preaching which touched the soul of the old Maréchal and of his soldiers. The attractive personality of Francis de Sales won his heart; his short and practical discourses appealed to his reason; the result was a warm and sincere friendship between the two. So great, indeed, was this friendship, and so often did the Duc de Lesdiguères invite the Bishop of Geneva to dine and sup with him, and so many hours did they spend together in social intercourse, that the Calvinist ministers became alarmed, and actually had the audacity to remonstrate with the Maréchal and warn him against so dangerous a friendship. The Duc was half angry, half amused.

"Tell them," he said "that I am old enough to take care of myself. They are much too young and insignificant to attempt to teach a man of my age and position how to behave. I know how Bishops should be treated; they are quite different from our ministers, who certainly are never more than Curés, since they have rejected the episcopal dignity, although we have the authority of the Scriptures for it. When I see Sovereign Princes, sons and brothers of Kings, become ministers, as they now consider it an honour and a distinction to become Bishops and Cardinals, I will consider what respect I shall pay to these ministers and their opinions."

Unfortunately, the Maréchal had to set out from Grenoble on December 19, 1616, to the assistance of the Duke of Savoy, who was fighting against the Spaniards, and he was unable to return until September, 1617. Thus his intercourse with Francis was interrupted for a time. But finally, in 1622, the Duc de Lesdiguères was reconciled to the Catholic Church. During the Advent and Lent Francis converted many distinguished Calvinists, among others the Minister Barbier, one of the most learned and virtuous of the heretics, Claude Boucard, a gentleman of distinction and renown, and several of the nobles of the province.

No sooner was Lent over than Francis hastened back to Annecy without delay. Asked why he left so soon a city where he was so much honoured and esteemed, he replied simply : "In these big cities, and receiving honour and applause, I am not in my element. I am like a fish out of water. I love my little town of Annecy, and I prefer my own little room to the palace of a King."

It was in it he constantly prayed for peace and concord among Christian Kings and peoples, and, above all, for the welfare of the Church and the propagation of the Faith. There he united himself in prayer with his Divine Master, and there, his soul on fire with love of God, he tasted even in this life the joy of the blessed.

In and near Annecy were his three favourite churches—St. Dominic's, the Church of the Visitation, and the Parish Church of Thorens. One day he preached so splendid and convincing a sermon on faith in the Church of St. Dominic that, on leaving the pulpit, he was met by Père Blanc, a Dominican Father, who remarked to him :

" Monseigneur, never have I heard you preach with such unction and fervour as to-day."

" My friend," replied Francis, " I was confirmed in your church, and the remembrance of that happy day inspired me."

" Ah, Monseigneur, you are always kind and gracious to us and to our poor church !"

" Père Blanc," replied Francis, with his winning smile, " you need not thank me. I am only doing my duty, and at the same time pleasing myself, when I officiate in your church. I love all the churches in my diocese, but I have a particular affection for three—Thorens, where I was baptized and consecrated Bishop ; yours, where I was confirmed ; and the little Church of the Visitation, where I shall be buried."

"Oh, Monseigneur," cried Père Blanc, falling on his knees in supplication, "surely you will not deprive our church of your body? For many centuries your ancestors have all been interred in our poor church, and we possess their tombs. Surely you, too, will be buried here."

Francis smiled.

"I have said too much," he said; "nevertheless, I wish you to know that neither in life nor in death do I belong to this world, and I desire that after my death my wretched body may be hidden away in some corner of the little Church of the Visitation. I consecrated it, and our Sisters will remember to pray for my soul."

# CHAPTER XXV

## *HUMAN LOVE*

BERNARD, Baron de Thorens, and the little wife
he had brought from Burgundy, led an ideal
life in the old Château de Sales, *filant le parfait
amour,** and supremely happy in each other's
society and in that of their dear ones.

Francoise de Chantal, Jeanne's youngest
daughter, spent part of her time with her mother
in the convent, but she often went off to the
Château for long visits. Marie Aimée was always
delighted to have her sister with her; then they
often drove in to Annecy to see their mother, and
to pay their respects to Mgr. de Genève.

The little Baroness would have been spoiled but
that she had such a sweet and gentle disposition,
for her big husband adored her, and her saintly
brother-in-law loved this little sister dearly; even
stern Jean-Francois unbent towards her, and
Louis petted and indulged her as much as he did
his own young son, Charles-Auguste, to whom
she made the most charming aunt in the world.
But, alas! this joyous and happy existence could
not last. Marie Aimée and Bernard had been
married for eight years, and she was for the first

245

---

*"spinning out perfect love"

time about to become a mother, when her husband's regiment was ordered into Piedmont.

Both were broken-hearted at having to part. "They wept so bitterly that all present shared their grief, and such was the violence of their sorrow that they were themselves surprised that they could endure it and live." So they said farewell. They never met again. De Thorens was only gone three weeks when they heard that he was dangerously ill in camp.

"O dear Lord," writes Francis de Sales, "dimitte me, ut plangam paululum dolorem meum.* Every moment I expect to hear of my brother de Thorens' death. I shall need time to console his poor widow, and to calm my own heart."

Next day the news arrived that the gallant and chivalrous Bernard had passed away. Francis wrote to his sister, Mme. de Cornillon, to announce the sad news :

"ANNECY,
"*May* 27, 1617.

"O MON DIEU, MY DEAREST SISTER,

"How troubled I am for the pain you will feel at the death of our poor brother, who was so dear to all of us ! But it cannot be helped ; we must resign ourselves to the will of God, Who, when we calmly consider it, has shown much favour to our dear Bernard in taking him away at an age and from a vocation in which there is so much danger of damnation.

---

*"Dismiss me, that I may mourn a little."

" As for me, I have wept more than once, for I tenderly loved our brother, and could not but give way to the feelings of nature. But now I am quite comforted and resigned, having heard how devoutly he passed away in the arms of our Barnabite Father and of our Chevalier, having made a general confession, received absolution three times, and received Holy Communion and Extreme Unction with great fervour and piety.

" It cannot be expressed what virtue his poor little widow has shown. We will keep her here at the Visitation some days longer, until she is quite restored. Never was man so generally regretted as this one. This letter is intended also for your husband. In the hope of seeing you soon,

" I am,

" Most devotedly yours,

" FRANCIS."

But the little Baroness never left the Visitation. She pined day by day, her soul resigned to God's will, but her frail body wasting away. Her child was born in the monastery, but only lived a few moments, just long enough to be baptized by Mother de Chantal. Then Marie Aimée asked to be received into the Order of the Visitation, and in her agony was clothed in the garb of a religious. Suffering intense pain—her mind was clear—and pronouncing the Sacred Name three times, she calmly expired.

The following account of her last moments, written by Francis de Sales, is in the register of the convent :

" Marie Aimée de Rabutin, daughter of our Mother, and widow of Bernard de Sales, Baron of the said place and of Thorens, having frequently expressed a wish to be received into our Congregation here, was taken suddenly ill in this house. After having confessed and received absolution with unparalleled resignation, rare meekness, and deep humility, her mind being extremely tranquil, in a sweet, clear, and distinct voice she asked for the habit of the Visitation. Her request was granted on account of the great devotion she had shown, and, having received the Sacrament of Extreme Unction, she begged to be allowed to take her vows. This request also was granted, and she pronounced them with great courage, expiring three hours later, repeating until her last breath, constantly, gently, and devoutly, ' Vive Jésus !'

" She was admitted to the habit and profession by her Bishop, the brother of her late husband, and by her Mother, the Superior of the Congregation, and by all the Sisters who were present at her holy and beautiful death, September 6, 1617. On that day, at eight in the evening, she fell into her death-agony. At nine she received the habit ; at ten she was professed ; and between one and two in the morning on the seventh day of the said month, the Eve of the Nativity of Our Lady, she passed into a better life, leaving behind her a rare example of devotion and wonderful spiritual consolation to those who, otherwise afflicted at her death, saw and admired the pious circumstances attending it.

"FRANCIS, *Bishop of Geneva.*"

Mother de Chantal added the next lines: "Who administered to her the Sacraments of Penance, Holy Eucharist, and Extreme Unction, and received the vows of the beloved deceased, who was nineteen years, two months, and six days old.

"SISTER JEANNE FRANÇOISE FRÉMIOT."

To Mother Favre, who was then Superioress at Lyons, Francis wrote:

"You ask about our domestic afflictions. No, it is not the dear little sister-in-law, Marie Aimée de Thorens, that you knew, but quite another Marie Aimée, who has lately died. For the last year the dear little Baroness became so perfect that she could no longer be recognized, but particularly since her widowhood, when she vowed herself to the Visitation. And oh, how she died! Certainly one of the holiest and happiest deaths that could be imagined. I loved her with a far greater than fraternal love, but as it has pleased God, so be it done: may His Holy Name be blessed!"

The Bishop of Geneva, having performed all

the Offices for the Dead, drove off to visit his friend, the Bishop of Belley, and from him received consolation and comfort. On his return to Annecy, he found Mother de Chantal not only consumed with grief for the loss of her daughter, but a prey to the greatest remorse. She feared that she had not properly baptized her grandson, that in her hurry and confusion she had forgotten an important part of the Sacrament, and that he would never see the face of God.

"O my Father," she cried, throwing herself at his feet in a passion of tears and sorrow, "that I should be the cause of his never seeing God, that I should be the cause!"

And she wept bitterly.

With his usual penetration and keen discernment Francis immediately touched the weak spot.

"My daughter," he said incisively, "are you thinking only of yourself?"

At these words Jeanne de Chantal at once recognized her fault, and as the mists cleared from her soul she remembered distinctly every circumstance connected with the Baptism, and that she had in deed and in truth performed the ceremony most accurately.

At this time Francis wrote two letters to the Sovereign Pontiff—one to ask him to allow the Poor Clares to possess some property in common. Up to this time they had lived completely on the alms of the charitable, but of late, owing to much private distress and poverty, these offerings had fallen off and they were in a most deplorable state, almost starving, and without warm covering or fuel.

Needless to say the Bishop gave them all the help he could, but he had not sufficient money to enable him to support unaided a whole community. He at the same time wrote to Cardinal Bellarmine, entreating him to use his influence with the Pope; but it was of no use, the Cardinal failed to obtain this favour, and the poor nuns remained in a most pitiable state of want and destitution.

The second letter, addressed by the saintly Bishop to the Head of the Church, was in reply to one in which Paul V. had asked his advice on the subject of the beatification of his great friend Giovanni Giovenali Ancina, Bishop of Saluzzo.

In this letter Francis draws a most vivid and exquisite picture of the holy Oratorian, but the most curious and interesting thing about this life-like portrait is that Francis, while describing Ancina, is really, though quite unconsciously, describing himself. It runs as follows:

"I was delighted to hear that the life of the most illustrious Bishop, Giovenali Ancina, would soon be published; for since, as St. Gregory tells us, Bishops are the painters of virtue, and as they have to paint so excellent a thing by their words and their works as accurately as possible, I do not doubt that in the life of our admirable Ancina we shall see a complete and perfect image of Christian Justice—that is, of all virtue.

"And, indeed, during the four or five months that I spent in Rome, negotiating the affairs of this See, in compliance with the command of my most devout and illustrious predecessor, Mgr. Claude de Granier, I saw many men excelling in sanctity and erudition, but, amongst all these great personages, I was most particularly struck by the virtues of the venerable Ancina.

"For I admired the profound knowledge of this man which embraced so many different subjects, and he possessed with this wonderful erudition a corresponding self-contempt; I also admired the perfect gravity of his appearance, of his discourse and of his manners, his modesty and grace, his great solicitude for devotion, an equal remembrance of politeness and courtesy, 'so that he did not tread down pride by another pride,' as happens with many, but by a true humility, and he did not display his charity by 'knowledge which puffeth up' but made his knowledge fruitful by the 'charity which edifieth.' He was a man beloved of God and men because he loved them with the purest charity. Now, I call purest charity that in which can scarce be found the smallest trace of self-love or *philantia*, a rare and exquisite charity, which is very seldom met with even among those who make profession of piety, wherefore 'from far and from the uttermost coasts is the price thereof' (Prov. xxxi. 10). I have noticed that when an occasion presented itself this holy man used openly, frankly and lovingly, to praise the different Institutes, virtues, teaching, and ways of serving God of various religious, ecclesiastics, and laymen, as if he were a member of their Congregations and meetings. And while he embraced with a loving and filial heart his own dearly loved Congregation of the Oratory, he did not on that account, as often happens, more coldly or the less love, esteem, and extol other houses or assemblies of persons serving God. This was why, seeking only the greater glory of God, he most lovingly guided into the society he thought most suited to them those who, touched by Divine grace, desired to lead a holier life, and who asked his advice; he was a man who was neither of Paul, nor of Cephas, nor of Apollo, but of Jesus Christ, and who listened not to those cold words *mine* and *thine* either in temporal or spiritual matters, but did all things solely for Christ and in Christ.

" I will give you an example of the perfect charity of this Apostolic man. William Cramoisy, of Paris, died lately in the College of the Clerks Regular of St. Paul, here in Annecy. Speaking to him one day shortly before his death, I casually mentioned Giovenali Ancina. His face was illumined with joy, and he cried out : ' O how grateful, how precious to me is the memory of this holy man ! For he it was who brought me forth again in Christ.'

" Then he told me the story.

" ' When I was twenty-four,' he said, ' God called

me to the religious life, but, from weakness and want of courage, I was a prey to many temptations, and was even thinking seriously of getting married. But one day I went to the Oratory at Vallicelle, and I heard Father Giovenali Ancina preaching, first on the inconstancy and weakness of the human heart, then on the generosity with which we should follow the impulses of grace.

"'When the discourse was over I went to him in a corner of the Oratory, where he was praying, and I told him how I felt, and opened my heart to him.

"'"Come to me to-morrow," he said; "in the meantime I will attentively consider your case and pray for light."

"'So I went to him next day, and attentively heard and weighed all he said:

"'"It is for this reason that there are so many different Religious Orders in the Church—namely, that those who are unable to lead lives of great austerity and penance may yet be able to devote themselves to God's service in less severe Congregations. I advise you to enter the Congregation of the Clerks Regular of St. Paul, for in it the discipline of religious perfection flourishes, but yet it is not weighed down by bodily labours or strict observances."

"'Accordingly I entered the Congregation, and have been most happy in it.'

"From this, one sees how great was the power of Giovenali Ancina in preaching, how wise he was in counselling, and how zealous in helping others. And for myself I honestly confess that through the many letters he has written to me, my desire to practise the Christian virtues was greatly increased and strengthened. After he was transferred from the admirable life of the Congregation of the Oratory to the most holy episcopal office, his virtue shone even more splendidly and more clearly, as was indeed fitting, sending forth its rays as 'a burning and shining light placed on a candlestick, that it may give light to all that are in the house.'

"When, in 1603, I went a little out of my way to visit him at Carmagnola, a town in his diocese of Saluzzo, where he was then engaged in his pastoral Visitation, I saw with what love and veneration his people regarded him. For, when they heard of my arrival I cannot sufficiently express the ardour with which by a certain friendly violence they brought me from the public hospice to the house of a noble citizen, saying they would like, if it were possible to lodge in their hearts, the man who had gone out of his way to honour their beloved pastor.

"Nor could they sufficiently satisfy themselves in joyously showing in their words and looks, their delight in the presence of their beloved pastor, whilst he, with a certain dignified familiarity and kindly goodwill towards all, drew to himself at once their eyes and their souls, and as a glorious and loving-hearted shepherd, *called his own* sheep by name to green pastures, and with his hands full of the salt of wisdom enticed them—nay compelled them—to follow him. I will say one word more—may I say it without offence? Never have I seen a man so abundantly, so splendidly, adorned with the gifts the Apostle desired so earnestly for all Apostolic men."

# CHAPTER XXVI

## *THE HOLY MOUNTAIN*

FRANCIS DE SALES preached during the Advent of 1617, and the Lent of 1618, at Grenoble. The Maréchal de Lesdiguères had earnestly entreated the Duke of Savoy to persuade the Bishop of Geneva to accept the invitation of the Parliament of Dauphiny. Some good people thought it rather foolish of Francis to preach two years in succession in the same city, saying he would repeat himself and lose the reputation he had made, but the saintly Bishop was foolish with the foolishness of the Word of the Cross.

"For the Word of the Cross, to them indeed that perish, is foolishness ; but to them that are saved, that is, to us, it is the power of God.

"For it is written : I will destroy the wisdom of the wise, and the prudence of the prudent I will reject !

"Where is the wise ? Where is the scribe ? Where is the disputer of this world ? Hath not God made foolish the wisdom of this world ?

"For seeing that in the wisdom of God, the world by wisdom knew not God : it pleased God by the foolishness of *our* preaching to save them that believe.

"For the foolishness of God is wiser than men: and the weakness of God is stronger than men."

And so, as it always happens when one trusts solely in God, not relying on one's own strength or wisdom, but leaving all to Him, the missions of the Bishop of Geneva were a complete success. His sermons were even better attended and more appreciated than during the previous stations. Crowds flocked to hear him, there was not standing room in the church, and conversions were so numerous that, as frequently happened, Francis had not a spare moment, his time was so fully occupied, preaching, admonishing, instructing, receiving converts, administering the Sacraments.

It was in the small hours of the morning that he wrote in great haste to Mother de Chantal, who had been seriously ill, but was convalescent.

"GRENOBLE,
"*March*, 1618.

"MY DEAR DAUGHTER,

"This night during my wakeful hours, I have had a thousand good ideas for my sermons, but strength has failed me to bring them forth. God knows all, and directing all to His greater glory, and adoring His Providence, I remain in peace.

There is no help for it: I must do what I will not, and the good which I will I do not. I am here in the midst of preachings, and of a large audience, much larger than I expected, but if I do nothing here it will be no consolation to me. Meantime, I think constantly of you and of your soul, for which I incessantly pray to God and His angels that it may be filled with the abundance of His grace.

"I feel, my dearest daughter, the most intense desire for your advancement in heavenly love. While offering up Holy Mass this morning I again dedicated you to God. . . .

"Nor did I forget to make a special memento for your dear husband. In truth I have had deep feelings lately of the obligations I am under to Providence, and over and over again, with fervour and zeal, I have resolved to serve Him with the greatest fidelity, and to keep my soul more continually in His Divine Presence, and with all this I feel a certain gladness, not impetuous, but I think efficacious, at undertaking this mine amendment. Will you not rejoice, my dear daughter, if one day you see me well fitted for the service of Our Lord? Yes, you will, because we are inseparably and interiorly united. You perpetually wish many graces for me, and with all the fervour of my soul I pray God to make you entirely His. God knows, O dearest daughter of my soul, how I long to die for love of my Saviour! But at least if I cannot die for it, may I live for it.

"I am in a desperate hurry, so, what more can

I say to you save, may God for ever bless and protect you?

"Adieu, my dear daughter; keep close to your crucified Redeemer. Adieu, again. I am far advanced into the night, but still more in picturing you united to Jesus. I pray Him to unite Himself to you ever more and more, and to abide in your heart for ever. Adieu, yet once more, my dear daughter, whom I cherish beyond compare, in Our Lord Who liveth and reigneth world without end. Amen. Vive Jésus!"

The citizens of Grenoble entreated Francis to found a Monastery of the Visitation in their city, promising it generous support, and adding that if Mother de Chantal would come herself to start it, everything would be in readiness for her reception and for the community. Accordingly, when Jeanne arrived, on the Eve of Palm Sunday, she found the house they were to occupy *pro tem.* in perfect order, amply provisioned, and supplied with all the necessaries of life. On the following day the Bishop of Geneva officiated at a magnificent ceremony, that of founding the new community. It was carried out with great pomp and splendour. Then he and Mother de Chantal selected a site for the new building at a considerable height above the city, in the midst of rocks, where the air was pure and salubrious, and the Sisters could live retired, unspotted from the world.

Having successfully arranged matters, Mother de Chantal returned to Annecy, but Francis had long wished to ascend the Holy Mountain, so he stayed a little longer in order to do so.

Arrived at La Grande Chartreuse, a curious incident happened. Dom Bruno d'Affringues was at that time Prior, and also General of the whole Order, for the Grande Chartreuse was the parent-house, having been founded by St. Bruno in 1084, whence it gained the distinguishing title of *Grande*. Dom Bruno was a most holy and learned man, but almost childlike in his simplicity and innocence.

He received the popular Bishop of Geneva with great cordiality, conducted him to the room allotted to him, conversed with him for a short time on spiritual matters, and then went off to prepare for Matins, mentioning that it was the Feast of one of the greatest Saints of their Order. On his way to his cell the good Prior was met by one of the community, who asked him where he was going, and where he had left Mgr. de Genève.

"I left him in his room," replied Dom Bruno, "and have taken leave of him that I may prepare myself in my cell for the Matins of to-morrow's Feast."

"My Father," the monk said, surprised and distressed, "you are sadly ignorant of etiquette. What! do we every day receive Prelates as distinguished as the Bishop of Geneva that we leave them thus alone, especially when it is only a question of a Feast of our own Order? Do you not know that God takes pleasure in the sacrifices made in the cause of hospitality? You will always have plenty of time to sing the praises of the Lord; but who can entertain so great a Prelate save you? It were a disgrace to our monastery that you should leave him alone."

"My child," replied the humble General, "you are right, and I am wrong."

Going back to Francis, he said to him with childlike simplicity: "Monseigneur, I have just met one of our Fathers, and he tells me that I have committed a grave fault in leaving you by yourself. He is right, and I have come back to beg your pardon, and I hope you will forgive me, for I am telling you the truth when I say that I committed this fault through pure inadvertence."

So much candour, ingenuousness, and simplicity quite won the heart of the man who loved simplicity and frankness so dearly, and he and the worthy Dom Bruno became the best of friends.

It was doubtless with regret that Francis descended from the holy abode of peace and beauty. Here indeed for a little while he enjoyed that tranquil happiness and freedom from worldly cares which is surely a foretaste of Heaven. Wandering in the thickly wooded forest that the Brothers call the Desert, he could raise his heart to the God Who created this beautiful world; and when he returned at night to the monastery, the silent, white-robed monks were like ministering angels waiting on him, and later on, like Cherubim and Seraphim, when they sang the praises of the Lord in their dimly-lit devotional church.

But the Bishop of Geneva had too much to occupy him to allow him to linger long in this peaceful retreat, and he had to return to his diocese to take up the burden of life; but he was greatly refreshed and invigorated in soul and body by his short sojourn on the Holy Mountain.

One of the first things he did on his return to Annecy was to get his picture painted. This he did to satisfy his friends, who often begged him to do so. In the end a clever artist succeeded in overcoming his repugnance, telling him he was the cause of many sins, so many people grumbled and were annoyed that he would not allow his portrait to be taken. However, the first picture was a failure, because he did not give sufficient time to the sittings. Again the artist attacked him.

"Monseigneur," he said, "in the name of charity and of virtue I entreat you to give me a long sitting; in the name of charity, because you will thus enable me to earn money to support myself; in the name of truth and virtue, because the shop-people say that the picture is like you, in order to sell copies, and that is not true, so you are the cause of their telling lies. I love you so much, Monseigneur, that when I have not you before my eyes, I make you much handsomer than you really are."

Certainly an adroit and subtle pleader! Francis yielded, and the painter was delighted. Soon after one of his friends, having heard that at last he had allowed his portrait to be taken, wrote to ask him for it. In reply Francis remarked:

"Here is the portrait of this carnal man; as you wish to have it I send it you, for you know I can refuse you nothing. They tell me I have never been really well taken, but I think that matters little. I have to borrow this to send you, as I have not one of my own. 'Man passeth as an image, yea and is disquieted in vain.' Would that the likeness of my Redeemer were imprinted on my heart! O Jesus, by Thy light, heal, renew, make perfect those who have been redeemed by Thy Blood, and make them conformable to Thee!"

This picture is probably the one that hangs in the salon of the modern Château de Sales. In it we see Francis in the full maturity of his manhood. The lines round his mouth and eyes and on his broad, open brow have deepened, but those blue eyes smile on us with kindly humour and with much good-humour; they are the clear, frank eyes of a man who could never threaten nor deceive, but who would always be loyal and true and tender and gentle. The mouth is beautifully shaped, the lips resolute and determined, yet a smile lurks round them. Grave and dignified as is the air and countenance of Francis de Sales, yet there is nothing severe or solemn or austere in that noble dignity, for Francis always had, and never lost, a saving sense of humour. That is what makes him so attractive, because so very human. Great Saint as he is, Doctor of Devotion as the Church styles him, what appeals most to many of us is that touch of humour and of spontaneous good-fellowship. " One touch of nature makes the whole world kin."

Francis was, indeed, so kind-hearted that he could never say " No," unless, of course, when to say " Yes" would have been wrong. He was always ready to preach, hear confessions, give alms. As an instance of his unselfish kindliness I mention the following incident : He officiated and preached one day at the Cordeliers on the Feast of St. Bona-venture ; the Capuchins who were also celebrating the Feast of this great Saint, came to him at five in the afternoon, complaining that he had spent the whole day with the Cordeliers, and had not honoured their church with his presence.

" You are right," he said, " but it is not yet too late." Accordingly he gave Benediction and preached an exquisite sermon to these good Fathers. The ceremony over, they asked him to forgive them for the fatigue and trouble they had caused him.

" I belong," he said, " to the Order of St. Francis, and I am bound to all the different branches of that Order by a double tie, that of Baptism—for I was christened Francis Bonaventure—and that of my affiliation to your holy Order."

The text of St. Paul's Epistle to the Corinthians

that he applied to his friend Giovenali Ancina, Bishop of Saluzzo, applied quite as aptly to Francis de Sales, Bishop of Geneva—"A man, in sooth, who was neither of Paul, nor of Cephas, nor of Apollo, but of Jesus Christ": "For all things are yours, whether it be Paul, or Apollo, or Cephas, or the world, or life, or death, or things present, or things to come; for all are yours: And you are Christ's, and Christ is God's" (1 Cor. iii. 22, 23).

While thus loving and venerating all religious Orders, Francis had always a particular affection for the Sons of St. Ignatius. Therefore it was with great devotion and pleasure he received a letter breathing admiration from the celebrated Jesuit, Père Leonard Lessius, S.J., Professor of Theology at Louvain. His reply to it is well known.

"For a long time," the Bishop wrote, "I have felt the greatest esteem and friendship for you, and not only because I know and appreciate your merits. I have read your 'Traité de la Prédesti-nation,' in which you teach the doctrine that God predestines men to glory only on account of their foreseen merits—*ob prævisa merita*—a doctrine with which I thoroughly agree, and which has always seemed to me the most conformable with the mercy and the grace of God, the most likely to enkindle in our hearts the fire of Divine love, as I have endeavoured to explain in my little book of 'L'Amour de Dieu.'

"Feeling so warm a friendship for you, it gives me intense pleasure to find you reciprocating my sentiments, and in order that we may continue friends, you may rely on me to do all in my power to serve you."

# CHAPTER XXVII

## *THE THEATRE OF THE WORLD*

In the year 1619 Francis de Sales accompanied His Eminence the Cardinal of Savoy to Paris, to be present at the marriage of the Prince of Piedmont, son of the Duke of Savoy, with the King's sister, Mme. Christine of France. Arrived at the " Theatre of the World," as St. Vincent de Paul called Paris, Francis had to take his part upon its stage. He was invited to preach in the Church of the Oratory on November 11, the Feast of St. Martin.

As usual, he consented. When it was known who was to preach, great excitement prevailed. The King, the two Queens, several Bishops and learned men, the nobility, the *bourgeoisie*, rich and poor, the ignorant and the erudite, all rushed to hear the saintly Bishop of Geneva, a man so famous for learning, knowledge, and piety. Indeed, so crowded was the church that Francis de Sales, when he arrived, found it impossible to get in, and had to climb a ladder, as he could only get in through one of the windows. Great things were expected of him, and the Bishop of Geneva had only to preach with his usual zeal and fervour to win all hearts and make for himself an undying reputation. But Francis did not rise to the occasion, or, rather, he rose above it, and putting from him all vainglory and desire of praise and honour, delivered a pithy and somewhat dry discourse on the life of St. Martin.

As he spoke he heard some of the audience murmuring: "Just listen to this man from the mountains! How roughly he speaks! It was not worth his while to come from such a distance to talk as he does, and to bore us all to death." These unkind remarks caused Francis supreme joy, for nothing delighted him more than to be despised by men. However, all were not of the opinion of these captious critics, and invitations to preach poured in upon him, and, according to his rule, he never refused. He could never understand why people flocked to hear him, having a very low opinion of his own style and manner of delivery.

The following anecdote, taken from " L'Esprit de St. François de Sales," will convey an idea of his own opinion of his discourses:

" ' Apropos of sermons,' said Francis de Sales to me one day, ' I am told you have lately taken to mimicking the Bishop of Geneva's sermons.' I replied: ' Have I, then, chosen a bad model? Don't you think he preaches better than I do ?' ' Oh, come now, this is a personal attack. Well, certainly, he sometimes preaches moderately well; but the worst of it is, I hear you imitate him so badly that people can make nothing of it. They say it is an imperfect attempt that spoils the Bishop of Belley, without giving them the manner of the Bishop of Geneva; so that, as for a bad painter, it is necessary to write the names of the persons whose portraits he has taken under the face he has daubed.'

" 'Let him alone,' I retorted, 'and you will see that he will rise from the rank of an apprentice to that of a master, and that his copies will pass for originals.'

" 'Putting all jokes aside,' he replied, laughing, 'you only spoil yourself. Oh, if it were possible to exchange qualities, what would I not give for yours! I do my best to stir myself up to get on rapidly, but the more I try the slower I seem to become. I have a difficulty in finding words, more still in pronouncing them. I am heavier than an old tree-stump. I can move neither myself nor others. I perspire a great deal, but I make little way. You get on like a ship in full sail, I toil heavily at the oars ; you fly, I crawl or creep along heavily like a tortoise ; you have more fire in your fingers' ends than I have in my whole body ; you have a wonderful rapidity and the liveliness of a bird, and now I hear that you weigh your words, measure your periods, drag your wings ; that you droop and flag, and make your hearers do the same.' "

The rest of the world did not hold the same opinion regarding the sermons of the Bishop of

Geneva, for, notwithstanding his seeming failure
and the adverse criticisms directed against him on
the Feast of St. Martin, he again became the rage.

The Church of St. André des Arts, where he
preached the Advent and Lenten sermons, was
always full, and he was constantly implored to
preach in other churches. He could not understand why he was so popular.

"Are you not surprised," he remarked to a
friend, "to see all these good Parisians come to
hear me — I, who have so unready a tongue,
such stupid ideas, and who preach such tame and
uninteresting sermons?"

"Do you think," retorted his friend, "that it is
a beautiful and flowing style they expect from
you? Not at all. It is quite enough for them to
see you in the pulpit. Your heart speaks in your
eyes, in your voice. If they only heard you say a
short prayer they would be satisfied. The simple
words you use are so full of fire and of Divine love
that they penetrate their hearts and move them
strangely. There is a something—I cannot tell
what—in your discourses that goes home. Another
would say three times as much, and no one would
pay any attention to him. You have a certain
rhetoric of Annecy, or, rather, of Paradise, that
succeeds beyond ordinary words, and is simply
marvellous."

One day, preaching at the Church of St. Martin,
Francis took for his text "Jesus was obedient,
even unto the death of the Cross." A Calvinist

who was present came to him afterwards and remarked in a pompous manner that the text of his discourse was most inopportune. " Monsieur," retorted Francis readily, and with a slightly sarcastic smile, " it is most opportune for you, since you disobey the Church." The Calvinist was so struck by this reply that he asked to be instructed in the Faith, and shortly afterwards abjured his errors.

Francis during his stay in Paris put up in the Rue de Thournon at the house of the Maréchal d'Ancre. His old friend, President Favre, was also there; consequently, there was a certain amount of splendour about the appointments, and the humble Bishop of Geneva frequently drove in a magnificent carriage, with high-stepping horses and gorgeous flunkeys in attendance.

One day a Huguenot sought him out in his own sanctum, and, without even saying *Bon Jour*, asked rudely : " Are you the person they call Bishop of Geneva ?"

" Monsieur," replied Francis courteously, " I am so styled."

" Then I want you to tell me, since everyone says you are a holy and Apostolic man, did the Apostles drive about in carriages ?"

" Occasionally," replied Francis, with a gleam of humour, " when it suited their convenience."

" I should like you to give me a proof of that. Is it mentioned in the Scriptures ?" the Huguenot said sceptically.

"In the Acts of the Apostles it is mentioned," continued Francis, with a quiet smile, "that St. Philip drove about in the chariot or carriage of the eunuch of Candace, Queen of Ethiopia."

"But that carriage was not St. Philip's; it belonged to the eunuch," retorted his interlocutor.

"Just so," replied Francis, still smiling. "Did I not say so? And I said that when the opportunity presented itself they drove in carriages."

"But not in gilded embroidered carriages, drawn by splendid horses, and driven by coachmen in such gorgeous liveries that not even the King has a grander equipage. I am shocked at you—you, who are reputed so holy. You are a nice sort of Saint, travelling to Paradise in a coach-and-four!"

"My good friend," replied the Bishop, "I never had a carriage of my own in all my life. The citizens of Geneva, who keep possession of the property of the See of Geneva, leave me hardly enough to live upon in the plainest manner."

"Then that splendid carriage is not yours?"

"Certainly not," replied Francis; "and you may well call it splendid, for it is His Majesty's, and is one of those the King has allotted to us who belong to the suite of the Prince of Piedmont and the Cardinal of Savoy. Why, the livery the coachman wears is the King's. Did you not notice that?"

"Well, I am delighted to hear it, and I like you all the better. You are not rich, then?"

"I do not complain of my poverty, since I have enough for the necessaries of life; and even if I suffered from straitened means I should not mind, for did not Our Lord Jesus Christ choose poverty for His lifelong portion? However, my family owes allegiance to the House of Savoy, and so I esteem it an honour to belong to the suite of the Princes of that House, and to be present at the marriage of my Prince with a daughter of France."

The Huguenot was delighted with the gentle dignity of the Bishop of Geneva; but we do not hear that he became a Catholic.

As usual, Francis de Sales made many friends. There was something so kindly and sympathetic about him that people felt irresistibly drawn towards him. He united in his striking and attractive personality gravity and gentleness. Those who loved him also revered him, and many reverenced him so much that they actually trembled when conversing with him, not from the fear of displeasing him—for he was never angry, and he received the roughest and rudest people graciously—but for fear of not pleasing him enough. Like St. Paul, he made himself all things to all men, studying their characters, their tempers, and succeeding, by his penetration and affability, in winning their hearts.

Among his greatest friends in Paris at this time

were Père de Condren, who was so saintly, and whose teaching was so sublime that Cardinal de Bérulle used to kneel while listening to him and M. André Duval, whose peculiar gift was to restore peace to troubled souls, and who was the spiritual director of St. Vincent de Paul and of Mme. Acarie. Francis de Sales selected him also as his director, and he in his turn confessed to the Bishop of Geneva, each remarking of the other, in the words of John the Baptist: "One mightier than I, the latchet of whose shoes I am not worthy to stoop down and loose."

Another great friend of the Bishop of Geneva was Père Sufferin, S.J., Confessor of the King and Queen, and a man of rare learning and piety; then there were Père Bourdoise, founder of the Community of St. Nicholas, and Cardinal de Bérulle, with whom he renewed the friendship of bygone years; but among all these distinguished men, famous alike for holiness and for learning, the one that Francis loved and honoured above all others was Vincent de Paul. These two heroic souls understood each other at once, Vincent de Paul proclaiming that the Bishop of Geneva was so dignified, so gentle, so gracious, and so modest, that it seemed as though Christ Himself once more walked the earth, so like unto Him was Francis de Sales; and Francis always spoke of the apostle of charity as the "holy priest, the best and noblest man" he had ever known. So high an opinion, indeed, had Francis of Vincent de Paul that it was to him on his own departure from Paris he confided the direction of his beloved Daughters of the Visitation.

Mother de Chantal had also come to the "Theatre of the World" with a few Sisters, and they had established themselves in what they hoped would prove an abode of peace. Peace there certainly was, as always within the convent walls and in the hearts of the nuns; but the house was situated between two tennis-courts, and they were disturbed day and night by the noise of the players.

At last, Mother de Chantal had the chance of purchasing a most suitable dwelling—the Hôtel Gamet in the Rue St. Antoine—but the sum asked was enormous. "My God, where, then, shall I lodge Thy spouses?" she cried to Our Lord, half in despair. And Jesus, Who never abandons those who trust in Him, came to her aid, for a very wealthy heiress, Mdlle. Lhuillier, begged to be received into the Order. She was a clever and virtuous girl, belonging to a noble family; and as her vocation was a true and real one, Mother de Chantal gladly received her; and her dowry paid for the Hôtel Gamet.

It was not quite suited for a monastery, so many repairs and alterations were made, and it was not until 1621 that the nuns of the Visitation took formal possession of it, having to spend over two years listening to the turmoil and noise of the tennis-players.

# CHAPTER XXVIII

## *THE ABBESS OF PORT-ROYAL*

Marie Angélique Arnauld, Abbess of the Benedictine Abbey of Port-Royal, was one of the most
remarkable women then playing their part on the
stage of the theatre of the world. Abbess at fourteen; at seventeen she had reformed her own
abbey, in spite of opposition; and she was now, at
twenty-eight, engaged in the still more difficult
task of introducing reform into the Abbey of
Maubuisson. She met Francis de Sales, and at
once fell under his influence. Extracts from his
letters will clearly and vividly show her character,
and the adroitness with which he guided her
somewhat intractable but ardent spirit.

> "*August,* 1619.

"You shall no more address me as *My Lord*,
nor will I call you *Madame;* the dear names of
Father and Daughter are sweeter, and express
better the sacred love Our Lord has willed we
should have for each other.

"So, my dear daughter, I do not know when I
may have to leave Paris, therefore I cannot promise
myself the consolation of seeing you again; but if

I have leisure I will do so, and if I consider my
doing so will benefit your soul, I will do all I can
to insure my meeting you. In any case, remember
what I have told you ; God wishes to make use of
you in matters of consequence, and He desires
you to lead an excellent and holy life. Continually animate your courage with humility and your
humility with confidence in God, so that your
courage may be humble and your humility courageous ; season your conduct, both interior and
exterior, with sincerity, gentleness, and cheerful-
ness, according to the direction of the Apostle :
' Rejoice in the Lord alway : again I say, Rejoice.
Let your modesty be known to all men ;' and, if
possible, be equal in temper, and let your actions
always show the resolution you have made ever to
love God with all your heart. Do not burden
yourself with too many vigils and austerities, my
dear daughter. I know well what I am saying.
Enter the *royal port* of the religious life by the
royal road of the love of God and your neighbour,
by humility and gentleness."

" PARIS,
" *September* 12, 1619.

" I start to-morrow, my dear daughter, since
such is God's will. I hope that God will
strengthen you more and more. If He thought
you had need of a more present assistance than I
can give you from so great a distance, He would
have given it to you, and He will always give it to
you when required.

"Beware, my dear daughter, of that word 'fool,' and remember the saying of Our Lord: 'He who shall say to his brother, *Raca*, shall be guilty of the Council.' Gradually tame down the vivacity of your spirit to patience, sweetness, and affability amid the littleness, childishness, and feminine imperfections of the Sisters, who are tender with themselves, and inclined to weary their Mother with complaints. Sleep well. Little by little you shall return to the six hours, since you wish it; but to eat little, work hard, have much anxiety of mind, and refuse sleep to the body, is to try to get much work out of a horse in poor condition without feeding him up."

*About the end of* 1619.

"You see, my daughter, these inclinations to pride, vanity, and self-love, mingle in all we do; but, at the same time, they are not the motives of our actions. St. Bernard, while preaching, was annoyed by them, and he cried: 'Depart, Satan; I did not begin for thee, and I will not cease for thee.'

"Do not burden your weak body with any austerity but those inspired by the rule. Preserve your physical strength to serve God with in spiritual exercises, which we are often obliged to give up when we have indiscreetly overworked ourselves."

" ANNECY,
" *February* 4, 1620.

" It is a great thing that exteriorly you are more observant of the rule. God first formed the exterior of the man, then ' He breathed into him the breath of life,' and he became a living soul. Humiliations, says Our Lord, very often precede and produce humility. Continue in the exterior, which is easier, and little by little the interior will become like it. Accustom yourself to speak softly and slowly, and to walk composedly. Do everything quietly and gently, and you will in a few years have regulated your impetuosity."

During the time that Angélique was under the direction of Francis de Sales—indeed, as long as he lived, she succeeded in moderating her impetuosity and desire of supremacy. She even wished to leave her own abbey and enter the Visitation Order, imploring Francis to receive her. But he felt, as he told her, that she was better suited to command than to obey, and did not encourage her. A letter he wrote to Father Binet, S.J., expresses his views on the subject.

" ANNECY,
" *November* 11, 1621.

" REVEREND FATHER,
" A thousand thanks for your letter. I say in reply that when in Paris I would never acquiesce in Madame de Port-Royal's desire to leave

her own Order; but when I returned here she frequently wrote imploring me to enter into her ideas and approve her wishes. I temporized as much as I could, and showed myself not only cold, but altogether opposed to her wishes, until later on a distinguished person wrote to me in such a way that I considered I ought not to make myself the sovereign judge. I refrained from giving her any advice, but wrote to her that, since her heart did not find rest in what I said to her, she might present her petition. If His Holiness granted it, then doubtless it would be God's will, inasmuch as it was a difficult matter, and could not succeed without a special concurrence of the Divine favour. On the contrary, if His Holiness refused, she should then humble herself and abase her heart.

"This, Reverend Father, is what I did. I clearly saw that the design was extraordinary, but I also saw an extraordinary heart. I saw, indeed, the inclination of this heart to command, but I saw also it was in the hope of conquering this inclination that she wished to bind herself to obedience. I saw she was a woman, but I also saw she was more than a woman in commanding and governing, and that she might well be so also in obeying. As for the interests of the Visitation, I protest before God and your Reverence that I never thought of it, or, if I did, it was so little that I do not even recollect it. I acknowledge that I have a particular affection for the Order of the Visitation, but I told Madame de Chantal, your dear daughter and mine, that I would not withdraw from her vocation the most excellent and most esteemed creature in the world, even though she might become a canonized Saint in the Visitation. I rejoice when God draws good and holy women to enter it, but I will never employ either word or act, no matter how holy, to attract anyone. The most I would do is to pray humbly to God. The inconstancy of woman is to be feared, but one can never tell, and constancy in this case may be hoped for."

On the same subject Francis de Sales wrote to Mme. de Chantal. Jeanne ardently loved the haughty, impetuous, but generous and noble, young Abbess. She saw her strength and her weakness, her unceasing craving to know whether she would be among the high or the low, her hot indignation against anything low or mean, her hatred of evil, her love of sacrifice and desire of perfection; but, at the same time, Angélique was imperious, sarcastic, inclined to laugh at others, to mock at and deride their childishness. Loving her so dearly, Jeanne would have been delighted to receive her as a daughter. She writes to her beloved Father:

"I send you some letters from our dear child at Port-Royal. Her desires increase amid contradictions. She tells me that, in spite of all her efforts to drive away the thought, she feels that

God is calling her to the Visitation. I am of the same opinion. I cannot refrain from adding that, since God has given her so strong an inclination to enter our Order, I believe it is for the increase of His glory by the services she will render Him in it."

Francis again strongly expresses his views in the following letter :

" I have seen the account of the consultation held about our very dear daughter, Mme. de Port-Royal, and I can only say that, on account of length of time and office, notwithstanding her dislike and increasing distaste, she is, strictly, obliged to stay, for though this may be a matter of conscience, it is not acknowledged by all, and besides, the Pope can dispense from it. I also consider the comparison between the Rule of St. Benedict and the Visitation narrow and unfair. The comparison should be made between the Rule of St. Augustine and of St. Benedict, and though perhaps the Rule of St. Benedict might still appear more perfect, yet the comparison would remove all contempt from the Visitation— I mean, all temptation to contempt. But what I tell you is not to be brought forward, but only humbly considered, and the decision to be left unreservedly to Rome.

" Therefore, tell our good daughter to moderate her impulsiveness, not to defend herself or to retort. In this, at least, she must follow the spirit of the Visitation ; and, in any case, she will be able to console herself from time to time by visiting you, and I hope that she will resign herself wholly to God's good pleasure, and He will comfort her at last."

But Rome seldom permits a subject to leave a severe Order for one less so, and many obstacles were in the way in this case.

In the meantime, Angélique entreated Francis de Sales to preach at Port-Royal, where her sister Agnes was Superior, during her absence. He gladly consented, but in the midst of his discourse he was quite overcome, and could not restrain his tears. Asked the reason of his distress, he replied: " God revealed to me that your monastery will lose the Faith. Your only chance of preserving it lies in obedience to the Holy See."

Alas! he was right : the poor young Abbess, left lonely and desolate after the death of the Bishop of Geneva, without anyone to guide and control her undisciplined heart, fell under the fatal influence of the Abbé of St. Cyran, that unhappy apostle of Jansenism.

Quite wanting in the qualifications of a director for so proud and ardent a soul, he urged her on, instead of, like Francis de Sales, moderating her zeal. He perplexed her mind with discussions about grace, and finally led her into heresy.

But even in spite of the morbid and severe tenets of Jansenism she retained the nobility and grandeur of her soul, and of her and her Sisters

it could truly be said, in the words of the Archbishop of Paris, "They were pure as angels, but
proud as demons."

Honours were showered on the popular Bishop
of Geneva, but he refused all except the position
of Grand Almoner to the Princess Christine. This
post he only accepted on condition that it should
in no way interfere with his work in his diocese,
and that no salary should be attached to it.

He was offered the Abbey of St. Géneviève, an
enormously rich benefice, but he refused it most
decidedly. "I want nothing," he said; "I will
not take this abbey."

Cardinal de Retz, Archbishop of Paris, begged
him to become his Coadjutor, with right of succession, offering him considerable emoluments, even
promising much freedom of action, and that his
brother, Jean-Francois de Sales, should be appointed Bishop of Geneva in his stead; but
Francis was adamant.

"I did not enter the Church to make my
fortune," he said quietly. "My diocese is poor,
but it is the portion of His vineyard that God has
given me to cultivate, and I cannot abandon it
without risking my eternal salvation."

Later on he remarked to a friend, probably the
Bishop of Belley: "My See is worth as much to
me as the See of Toledo to its Archbishop, for it
is worth to me Heaven or Hell, even as his is to
him. 'Godliness with contentment is great gain.'

My revenue suffices for my necessities. Anything more would be too much. Those who have more have to keep a larger establishment, so they themselves do not profit by it. He who has less has less account to give, and less solicitude in reflecting to whom he must give it. The King of glory will be served and honoured with judgment. Those who have great revenues often spend so much that they are as poor as I am by the end of the year. If we desire only what nature requires, we shall never be poor ; if more, we shall never be rich. He will never have enough to whom enough suffices not."

# CHAPTER XXIX

### "HE MUST INCREASE, BUT I MUST DECREASE"

HIGH up in the mountains, where Mont Voiron looks down on the Lake of Geneva, and faces Mont Blanc, is an ideal place in which to live unspotted from the world, and in close communion with nature and with God.

> " Mont Blanc is the monarch of mountains,
>     They crowned him long ago
> On a throne of rocks, in a robe of clouds,
>     With a diadem of snow."

Surely the eyes could never weary of gazing across the blue waters of the lake at that splendid monarch, snow-capped on the warmest midsummer day, " canopied by the blue sky,"

> " So cloudless, clear, and purely beautiful
>     That God alone was to be seen in Heaven."

So the souls of these solitary men would wing their way heavenward while still they lived and toiled here below.

For centuries hermits and holy men had taken refuge in this wild and beautiful eyrie, and spent their lives in solitude and peace, growing daily nearer to God. There they realized that—

> " There is a pleasure in the pathless woods,
> There is a rapture on the lonely shore,
> There is society where none intrudes
> By the deep Sea ; and music in its roar :
> I love not man the less but nature more."

Many had heard of this quiet retreat, and many from time to time came to it. Some remained there until Death called them; others, after a long or short sojourn, returned to the world ; but they had no fixed rule, and each and all lived more or less according to his individual taste.

But in 1620 Antoine Rigaud, Secretary to the Governor of Milan, wished to leave all, and retire to this haven of rest. He asked the Bishop of Geneva to allow him to join these pious men, at the same time requesting him to draw up a rule for their guidance.

Francis de Sales gladly complied. He established the Hermitage under the title of the Visitation of Mary, giving it for patrons Our Lady, St. Joseph, St. Zachary, St. Elizabeth, and St. John the Baptist, adding also those famous hermits of old—St. Paul, St. Anthony, and St. Hilary. The rules he drew up for their use were simple and easily observed, tending to lead them gently upward, and to enable them to attain to a high degree of perfection without hurry. *Doucement* was always his advice to those too eager souls who, in their anxiety to climb to sanctity, often neglected the ordinary little duties and courtesies of daily life.

Having wished these good hermits farewell, and left the glorious mountain heights to return to the valley of Annecy, Francis did not forget his latest foundation, frequently writing to Rigaud and his companions, exhorting them to love God daily more and more.

"The love of Christ is gentle, patient, long-suffering," he writes. "God is Love; may He, then, watch over and keep you in His holy service. I, for my part, devote myself to your service as a faithful friend and loving brother. I will watch over you and care for you. Rest, then, in peace, and confide in my promise. Arm yourselves with humility, patience, and gentleness, and sing joyously:

"'I will bless the Lord at all times: His praise shall be always in my mouth.

"'O magnify the Lord with me: and let us extol His Name together.

"'The Lord is my helper and my protector: my heart hath trusted in Him, and I have been helped.

"'The Lord is my light and my salvation: whom shall I fear?

"'The Lord is the protector of my life: of whom shall I be afraid?

"'Wait on the Lord, do manfully, and let thy heart take courage: and wait thou on the Lord.'

"Rest, then, my dear Brothers, under the protection of Our Lady; fear nothing; and 'may the peace of Our Lord Jesus Christ, which surpasseth all understanding, be with you for ever and ever.''

Francis de Sales would have dearly loved to spend the rest of his life among these good, holy men, in the midst of the everlasting hills, for his failing health made the unceasing labours of the episcopate almost more than he could perform. Having worked all his life for the salvation of souls, he ardently longed to devote the little time left him to care for his own soul, and to have leisure to enjoy closer communion with his Divine Master.

When he visited Talloires the same desire seized upon him. He even got four or five cells prepared for himself in the vain hope that some day God would permit him to retire from the hurry and bustle, the fret and toil, of his too-well-filled days.

"Oh, who will give me the wings of a dove," he exclaims, "to fly into this sacred desert, and breathe awhile under the shadow of the Cross? Then, while enjoying a holy leisure, I could trace out for the greater glory of God and the instruction of souls what I have treasured in my mind for more than thirty years, the various ideas I have used in my sermons, discourses, and meditations. I have abundance of material, and God would not fail to inspire me. There in that heavenly solitude great and beautiful thoughts would fill my mind, as thick, as soft, and as abundant as the snowflakes that fall in winter."

But he never realized his dream. Daily there were fresh calls on his time and patience.

The Abbey of Sixt was again in a disturbed

state. Twice already he had visited it, and succeeded, as he fondly hoped, in restoring order and regularity; but no sooner was he gone than the old spirit of disobedience revived, the monks became unmanageable, and relaxation and discord reigned.

Indeed, the worldly-wise were inclined to laugh and jeer at his attempted reforms, remarking that the Bishop of Geneva "gained nothing from his two journeys but to return half-frozen from the cold, the snow, and the ice of the mountains."

To this the genial prelate replied with his usual kindly good-humour: "It is true I have sown only beneath the snow, but the harvest-time will come. When the snow melts, then we will gather in the crops. We must do God's work according to God's will, and God is patient and merciful. He wants our repentance. He is not as we are— prompt to anger and unforgiving, and merciful only to ourselves."

So Francis continued to write to the Abbot and monks, exhorting them to observe faithfully the rule. His gentleness and patience were at last rewarded. In January, 1618, they wrote, telling him they intended to take his advice, and were sending him, signed and sealed, the renewal of their vows of fidelity to their rule. Rejoiced at the good news and resolved to do all he could to help and encourage them, the Bishop of Geneva paid them a third visit.

During his stay at Sixt he performed a well-authenticated miracle, attested by several witnesses in the process of his canonization. While he was guiding and directing the community, the people living far and near flocked to see him and to receive advice and assistance from so clear-sighted and saintly a director. These good folk were hospitably entertained at the monastery, but, as their numbers increased, the Father-minister feared that his provisions would run out, and that a famine would ensue. Francis divined his thoughts, and, telling him not to fear, blessed the wine-cask, the oven, and the river. As a result, never was the river so full of fish, the bread baked for the monks was sufficient to feed the crowd, and the wine never decreased, though all partook of it.

Francis de Sales returned to Annecy, but shortly after his arrival the sad intelligence reached him that the Abbot and the monks were again at variance. Once more he traversed the mountains and valleys, and, notwithstanding the severe weather, quickly regained Sixt.

He endeavoured to restore discipline, and finally his prudence, gentleness, and wisdom so impressed the Abbot that he sincerely repented, and made a general confession to the Bishop. As a result, the Abbot resolved to devote himself completely to prayer, meditation, and good works. His conversion was a true and real one : thenceforth he led a most exemplary life, and soon died a holy and happy death, as Francis had foretold would happen.

In 1620 the Bishop of Geneva endeavoured to reform the Bernardine nuns at St. Catherine's. It was an undertaking of the greatest difficulty, for the nuns proved even more intractable than the monks. The Abbess headed the opposition, firmly refusing to accept a reformed rule, and determined to remain in the lax state into which they had fallen. They were supported by the civil authority.

It proved a most tedious and uncongenial task to the peace-loving Francis. His persuasive eloquence and the soul-stirring discourses and instructions he gave them seemed to fall on barren ground. Finally, he permitted the five Sisters who desired reformation to found a convent at Rumilly, and to retire there, leaving the haughty Abbess and her adherents in possession of St. Catherine's.

Rumilly soon became a flourishing house. Many novices joined the faithful five, and in a short time so numerous was the reformed community that they were obliged to establish several convents for those desirous of following the strict observance.

No wonder that, in the midst of all this worry and trouble, Francis should write:

"As for me, I am in a continual turmoil, which the variety of the business of the diocese increasingly produces. I have not a moment to look at my poor books—books I once so truly loved. I fear to love them any longer, lest I should feel more bitterly and more deeply my divorce from them."

However, in this same year of grace, 1620, it pleased Our Lord to lighten a little for His faithful servant the weighty burden of his high office, and to brighten his declining days with the constant presence and devoted affection of his brother and nephew.

Jean-François de Sales was appointed Coadjutor of Geneva, with right of succession, and the title of Bishop of Chalcedon was conferred upon him.

Francis de Sales, writing to Mother de Chantal, tells her:

"So you see, my dear Mother, my brother is now a Bishop and my Coadjutor. I am delighted, though I am no better off in the matter of money than I was before; but this appointment gives me reason to hope that I may soon be able to retire from the world, and that, as you know, is the dearest wish of my heart. I long for it more than for a Cardinal's hat."

Jean-François held the appointment of Chief Almoner to the Princess Christine, and was therefore obliged to spend much of his time at the Court of Turin. However, shortly after his consecration he visited Annecy.

Francis, who was desirous of paying him the greatest respect and reverence, notwithstanding the lateness of the hour, went forth to welcome him at the gates of the city, and during his visit treated him with much deference and veneration, insisting that the new prelate should celebrate pontifically, and, on every occasion, giving him the place of honour. Some of his friends and admirers remonstrated, but he quietly said : "He must increase, but I must decrease" (Oportet illum crescere me autem minui). "He must act, but I must rest." Speaking to his brother, he said : "I never asked the Duke of Savoy to give you to me as my right hand and appoint you as my successor. It is to God alone we owe this great favour, and I thank Divine Providence with all my heart, hoping that you will act the part of Martha, leaving to me the part of Mary."

The Bishop of Chalcedon could only remain a few days at Annecy, his duties as Chief Almoner necessitating his return to Turin; but he was soon permitted to resign this post and to return to help Francis in the government of the diocese.

Charles Auguste de Sales, the only son of Louis de Sales, came to live with the two Bishops at the Palace, and it was during his residence with them that he learned to know and love his saintly uncle. In the close intimacy of domestic life he was enabled to study the character, and treasure the sayings, and note the actions of the gentle and humble Francis, thus gleaning ample material for his beautiful and minute "Vie du Bienheureux François de Sales."

To mould and perfect this young soul was a congenial task to the Bishop of Geneva, and Charles Auguste fully responded to the thought and care lavished upon him. He was a gentle, studious lad, and in after-years, when he in his turn was Bishop of Geneva, he proved that he had graduated in a school of Saints, for Jean-François de Sales, though quite different in character and temperament from the genial, warm-hearted Francis, was a just and good man, a trifle too austere and rigid, perhaps, but most severe to himself, always endeavouring to attain to his own ideal of perfection, truly a holy and righteous man according to the light given him.

So the young son of Louis "advanced in wisdom and age, and grace with God and men"; and the Bishop of Chalcedon grew daily more ascetic, more mortified; and the Bishop of Geneva, our gentle, unselfish, generous Francis, grew more ethereal, more spiritual, nearer and ever nearer and closer to the Sacred Heart of our loving Lord.

"I must tell you, my dear Mother," he writes to Mother de Chantal, "that this morning, having a little solitude, I made an act of supreme resignation, but one I cannot write, but will tell you when we meet. How blessed are those souls that live in God and for God alone! Ah! what spiritual sweetness does not the acceptance of His holy will give us! What a blessing in all things to abandon ourselves to Him! We have said we will do so, we have so resolved, and our hearts have for their sovereign law the greater glory of the love of God. Now, the glory of this holy love consists in burning and consuming all that is not itself, in order to reduce and convert everything to and into itself. It exalts itself on our annihilation, and reigns on the throne of our servitude. Oh, my dearest Mother, how this affection has expanded my will! May it please His Divine Goodness to continue to give me this abundance of high courage for His honour and glory and for the perfection and excellence of this most incomparable unity of heart which it has pleased Him to give us. Vive Jésus!

" I beg of Our Lady to protect you, and of your Angel Guardian and mine, to conduct you, so that you may arrive here safely, where your dear daughters await you, and where I, your poor Father, long to see you, when I will tell you why, and how I have at present no chance of writing more, though I am quite well, thank God.

" The bearer of this note wishes me to hurry, as he hopes to catch you at Dijon; and, indeed, I am myself pressed for time, having numerous affairs of importance to attend to.

" All goes well here, and I am, in Our Lord, more yours than I can say in this world; for there are no words to express this love. I am more and more your most humble and devoted,

" FRANCIS."

# CHAPTER XXX

## *TOWARDS EVENING*

IN 1622 Gregory XV. empowered Francis de Sales to act as his representative at the Chapter held by the Feuillants to appoint a General. Accordingly, the faithful Prelate journeyed to Pignerol, though the state of his health caused considerable anxiety to his friends and relatives. They implored him to remain at Annecy, but Francis de Sales was not the man to spare himself; as long as life lasted he would be up and doing, absolutely regardless of the pain and suffering his exertions caused his frail body. At any cost he was resolved to obey the mandate of the Holy See. At Pignerol it was not only on the election of a General that the monks could not agree; they disputed over several other points. Francis spoke to each in turn, reasoning, calming, persuading, throwing light on the many subjects under discussion. With his usual clearness of vision and sound judgment he discovered remedies for all complaints, whether fancied or real, and succeeded in restoring peace and unity.

Dom Jean de St. François was unanimously elected General. Everyone agreed that he was the best and most suitable man for so important a position, combining, as he did in a marked degree, considerable tact with great strength of character and executive ability.

But the strain told on the enfeebled frame of the Bishop of Geneva. Frequently he was so indisposed that he was compelled to leave the church and cease from fulfilling the duties of the sacred ministry. As soon as he recovered a little, he returned to the church to preach and administer the Sacraments.

One day he became quite unconscious, and had to be carried out by the monks. Recovered from this prolonged fainting-fit, he remarked, with a sad smile: "It is a shame for me to be so weak and delicate a follower of a Chief crowned with thorns."

He insisted on returning to his duties, for he never spared himself.

> " O God all-conquering ! this lower earth
> Would be for men the blessed abode of mirth
>   If they were strong in Thee,
> As other things of this world well are seen ;
> Oh, then, far other than they yet have been,
>   How happy would men be !"

The election held at Pignerol brought to a satisfactory conclusion, Francis de Sales, in obedience to the wish of his Sovereign, proceeded to Turin to pay his respects at the Court. Princess Christine prepared a sumptuous dwelling-place for her Chief Almoner, but the humble

Prelate refused to occupy these gorgeous rooms, preferring to stay with the Feuillants at the Monastère de la Consolata.

"Will you not allow me," he said to the Fathers, "to live for a few days among you as one of yourselves, for in truth I am one of you; I also am a son of St. Bernard, for I am affiliated to your Order? Therefore let me stay here in your calm abode at the feet of Our Lady of Consolation."

The Archbishopric of Turin became vacant, and the Duke of Savoy wished to confer it on his well-beloved Apostle of the Chablais, promising at the same time to give the See of Geneva to Jean-François.

But Francis de Sales remained constant to the bride of his youth, refusing to leave his dear Annecy and his faithful and devoted flock. Not for all this world could offer would he abandon his beloved Savoyards, his own people, the sheep God had given unto him to guard and cherish, to watch and tend.

At Turin he meditated, as he had years previously meditated in Paris, on the vanity and folly of the life of a courtier. These ideas he expresses with his usual clearness and candour in one of his letters to Mother de Chantal.

"I assure you, my dearest Mother, that the sight of the grandeur of the world makes the grandeur of the virtues of a Christian appear grander to me, and makes me more highly esteem its contempt. What a difference, my dearest Mother, between the assemblage of various suitors—for the Court is this, and nothing else—and the assemblage of religious souls who long only for Heaven! If we but knew in what consists true good! Do not think that I can be attracted to the Court by any favour. O God! how much more desirable it is to be poor in the House of God than to dwell in the palaces of Kings! I am here making my novitiate in the Court, but, with God's help, I will never make my profession in it.

"On Christmas Eve I preached before the Queen at the Capuchins, and she received Holy Communion; but I assure you that I preached neither better nor with greater willingness than I do in our poor little Visitation at Annecy.

"We must rest our hearts in God alone, and never take them from Him; He alone is our peace, our consolation, and our glory. Let us, then, unite ourselves more and more to our Saviour, *that we may bring forth good fruit.*

"Are we not indeed blessed, my dear Mother, that we can graft ourselves on the stock of the Saviour? For this sovereign essence is the root of that tree, whose branches we are, and whose fruit our love is. This was my subject this morning.

"Courage, my own dear Mother. Let us cast our hearts unceasingly into God; they are the perfume-balls He loves to compound. Let us allow

Him to fashion them as He wills. Yes, dear Jesus, do as You will with our hearts, for we wish neither part nor portion therein, but give, consecrate, and sacrifice them to You for ever.

"But much time elapses before we become quite despoiled of ourselves, and give us the right of judging what is best for us and desiring it. I admire the little Infant of Bethlehem, Who knew so much, Who was so powerful, and Who, with-without saying a word, allowed Himself to be bound and handled and fastened and wrapped up as required. May God be ever in the midst of your heart and of mine, my dearest Mother."

While at Turin, Francis de Sales fell dangerously ill, and was laid up for several weeks— indeed, the doctors feared he would not pull through.

> "Think not I dread to see my spirit fly
> Through the dark gates of fell mortality.
> Death has no terrors when the life is true;
> 'Tis living ill that makes us fear to die."

The seraphic Bishop of Geneva only pined to fly heavenward, but not yet was he to enter into eternal rest. And while he lay worn and exhausted on his bed of pain, there came to him the sad tidings that there was a famine in Annecy, and that his dear flock were suffering the pangs of hunger and of thirst. Of course the worry and trouble this news caused him only retarded his recovery. The fact that he was unable to go to their assistance was torture to him.

"Ah!" he cried, "as soon as I am able I will return to Annecy, and will sell my mitre, my crozier, my silver, even my garments; all I possess I will give to my poor people."

From another quarter he heard good news: Maréchal de Lesdiguères abjured heresy on July 22, 1622, and was received into the Catholic Church by the Archbishop of Embrun.

Francis de Sales longed to meet his old friend to congratulate him, and also to give him needful help and counsel. He entreated Princess Christine to allow him to leave Turin. She consented, so, as soon as he had recovered sufficient strength for the long and tiring journey across the Alps, he set out homeward bound. When wishing farewell to the Princess she presented him with a magnificent ring worth thousands of francs.

Francis was overjoyed to receive this generous gift, intending to sell it and give the proceeds to the poor, but when they halted for the night the ring could not be found. Rolland was in a terrible state, but the gentle Bishop heard of his loss with his usual calm.

"Thank God!" he exclaimed. "Such beautiful gems might have proved a distraction, and I might have grown attached to them and wished to keep the ring for myself; but now God has taken the matter out of my hands, and probably enriched some poor starving fellow."

However, the ring turned up. It had only fallen into the folds of a coat.

Francis heard of its recovery in the same spirit of supreme detachment. When he arrived at Annecy, he immediately pledged it, and gave the money to the poor. His friends, when they heard what he had done, redeemed it and restored it to him ; but no sooner was it in his possession than Francis de Sales once more pledged it. It was redeemed again by his relatives, repledged, and so on, until it became a saying in the country that the ring of the Bishop of Geneva did not belong to him, but was the property of all the beggars in the town.

Francis was scarcely rested from his journey from Turin when the Duke of Savoy requested him to accompany him to the Court and attend the Princess Christine as her Chief Almoner on the occasion of their visit to Avignon, where they were to meet Louis XIII. to congratulate him on his recent successes against the Huguenots of Languedoc.

His family feared he would never be able to bear the fatigues of the journey, and implored him to refuse.

" I must go where God calls me," Francis said ; and he might have added the words of Epictetus : " I am always content with that which happens, for I think that what God chooses is better than what I choose."

Nevertheless, he clearly foresaw that never again would his eyes rest on the glories of lake and mountain, on the quaint beauty of the grey old town, on the honest, kindly faces of his people. At a parting interview with his brothers he told them that he was about to start on a journey from which he would never return, and he read his will to them.

" We, Francis de Sales, by the grace of God and the Holy See, Prince and Bishop of Geneva, make known to all whom it concerns our last will. First, begging Almighty God to receive our soul and to give us a share in His Eternal Kingdom, purchased for us by the Blood of our Redeemer. Secondly, imploring Our Lady and all the Saints to intercede with God for us both in life and in death. Thirdly, if it please Divine Providence that the One, True, and Holy Catholic Religion should be re-established in the City of Geneva; and then, that being so, we wish that our body should be interred in the Cathedral; but if the Catholic Religion is not re-established, we wish to be buried in the nave of the Church of the Visitation of Annecy, consecrated by us— that is, in case we die in our diocese; but if we die away from it, we leave the choice of our burial-place to those with us at the time. Fourthly, approving with all our heart of the rites and ceremonials of the Church, we wish that at our funeral thirteen candles should be lighted round our coffin; but we will have no escutcheons but the holy names of Jesus and Mary to testify that we embrace with all our heart the Faith preached by the Apostles.

"For the rest, detesting the pomps and vanities of this world, we absolutely forbid any other lights to be employed at our funeral, begging our relatives and friends, and directing our heirs, to add nothing, but to show their affection for us by causing to be offered up for us the adorable sacrifice of the Mass."

The following day, November 7, 1622, he made a general confession. He then confided his papers and documents to his brother, the Bishop of Chalcedon, gaily remarking to him: " It seems to me that I have only one foot on earth. By the grace of God the other is already lifted heavenwards."

To Père Anselm, one of his greatest friends, he remarked: " This journey will cost me my life, and you and I will next meet in Paradise. We must be obedient, like our Divine Master, even unto the death of the Cross."

# CHAPTER XXXI

## "ASK FOR NOTHING, REFUSE NOTHING"

ON the morning on which Francis de Sales left Annecy, he bade farewell to his beloved daughters of the Visitation. He offered up the Holy Sacrifice of the Mass in their little chapel, using a beautiful chasuble given to him by the Princess of Savoy, and he left it with them as a souvenir.

"When friends say good-bye, they give each other presents," he said to them. Then he spoke a few words burning with love of God and zeal for souls: "My dear daughters, ask for nothing, refuse nothing, desire nothing, resign your cares to Divine Providence, allow God to do with you whatever He pleases. A heart indifferent to all things is like a ball of wax in the hands of God, capable of receiving all the impressions of His eternal good pleasure. It does not place its love in the things which God wills, but in the will of God which decrees them. My dear children, always act as God and your Superiors wish. Let the aim of your life be to love God more and more, your ambition to possess Him. Adieu, my daughters, until eternity."

"O my Father, we will pray God to bring you back to us soon," the Sisters cried in tears. When leaving the convent, he met Sister Anne Jacqueline Coste, who threw herself on her knees before him, weeping bitterly.

"My daughter," he said to her, "I have often before left you, and you have never wept. Why do you do so to-day?"

"My lord," the good lay Sister replied, "my heart tells me that you will never return, and that we shall never see you again."

"And my heart tells me," Francis de Sales replied, "that we shall see each other sooner than you think." For he foresaw that Jacqueline Coste would not long survive him.

Francis de Sales broke his journey at Belley. He spent a few days there, saying Mass every morning at the little Convent of the Visitation. It was very tiny. He said: "I am delighted to see my doves in so small a cot." The first day he went to the convent, Sister Simplicienne, when she saw him, burst into tears.

"What is the matter with you?" he asked kindly.

"O my Father," replied the gentle nun, "you will die this year."

"Oh, that is it, my dear little daughter Simplicienne, I am, then, to die this year?"

"Alas! yes, Monseigneur, but I will beg of Our Lord and His Blessed Mother to leave you to us yet a little while. Oh, I will pray so fervently, I

will weary them with my prayers; they will have
to grant my request!"

"Ah! no, my dear daughter Simplicienne, you
shall not do that. Do you not know how much
I need rest? I feel so exhausted and worn out, I
have no strength left. You do not require me any
longer; you have your constitutions, and I leave
you our dear Mother de Chantal. She is sufficient
for you; and, besides, you must put your trust in
God, not in men."

After this touching interview with Sister Simplicienne, Francis de Sales went into the chapel
and offered up Mass in honour of St. Martha.
While officiating, he appeared surrounded by
light; those present thought he looked as if he
were already in Heaven.

Having spent a few days at Belley, the Bishop
of Geneva started for Avignon. At Lyons he
stopped to celebrate Mass at the Visitation of
Bellecour and to say a few words to the Superior,
but he had to hurry off to catch the boat. Arrived
at the quay, the boatman would not allow him to
go on board without a passport, so Rolland had
to fly off to get one. Francis had to wait over an
hour; it was bitterly cold, and his attendants all
grumbled and growled, but the gentle Bishop only
smiled, remarking: " The man is quite right; he
knows his business as boatman better than we
know ours as travellers." He succeeded in calming the irritation of his companions, and they were
all very pleased when Rolland returned with the

passport and they were able to embark. Francis
sat beside the boatman, saying: "I wish to make
friends with this good man, and to talk to him of
our dear Lord."

Arrived at Avignon, "because there was no
room for them in the town," they had to wander
about for hours seeking shelter, while the rain fell
in torrents, and they were frozen by the keen
wind. At last they found a lodging, and Francis
promised to pray for their guide. All the time
they had been tramping through the mud he had
talked to this poor man of God and of His love
for us.

Avignon was crowded. The Courts of France
and of Savoy were there in regal splendour. The
Queens Marie de Medici and Anne of Austria
were surrounded by a magnificent suite of courtiers and ladies. All was pomp and glitter, the
glory of this world and the beauty of it; but
Francis refused even to look at all the gorgeous
processions, and never attended the sumptuous
entertainments, though the Duke of Savoy entreated him to do so.

On November 25 the two Courts left Avignon
*en route* for Lyons. Francis de Sales accompanied
them, but he stopped at Valence to visit the
Convent of the Visitation. There was an old
lady there as a parlour-boarder: as a matter of
fact, she was the foundress of the monastery,
Mme. de la Granelle, aged, some say, eighty-four;
others, eighty-eight. In spite of her advanced

age, this estimable woman wished to enter the
Order of the Visitation. She had begged to be
allowed to begin her novitiate, but had been
refused. When Francis heard her request, he
immediately granted it, saying to the Sisters:
"Why refuse her? At no age is one unworthy
of being consecrated to God."

He wished to pay his respects to a most
holy and admirable woman, Sister Marie de
Valence, and as he did not know where she lived,
he asked one of the lay Sisters to show him the
way. This girl had left some work undone that
she was anxious to finish, and walked at so fast
a pace that Francis, what with his swollen feet
and his enfeebled body, was unable to keep up
with her. He begged her to go more slowly: "Un
peu plus doucement, s'il vous plait." For a few
minutes the Sister adopted a more leisurely pace,
but soon rushed on again at headlong speed. The
Bishop followed, panting and gasping, and did not
again ask her to go less quickly, remarking good-
humouredly: "They who are led must follow."

When they arrived, the girl knelt down, and
Francis, putting his hand on her head, blessed
her three times, telling her: "You will one day
wear the veil of a religious of the Visitation."

He had a long conference with Marie de
Valence; indeed, it was so late when he left her
that his attendants were indignant, murmuring
that it was a shame to keep them all waiting.

"Sir," the Bishop said to one of them, smiling

genially, "you must know what a benefit it is to a sinner like me to converse *cœur à cœur* with a holy spouse of Christ like Sister Marie. She will say a Hail Mary for you, and after a good night's rest you will forget your grievance."

When the Bishop of Geneva arrived at Lyons, several distinguished people disputed with each other who would have the honour of entertaining the illustrious and saintly Prelate. M. Jacques Olier, Lieutenant of the Province, offered him half of his splendid mansion. The Jesuits begged him to be their guest at St. Joseph's. He replied to each and all that, knowing how difficult it would be to procure rooms in a city where France and Savoy were holding their Courts, he had already made his arrangements. His would-be hosts were quite satisfied with this reply, believing that he really had a suitable lodging; but the abode Francis had selected for himself was a little room in the house of the gardener of the Monastery of the Visitation—a wretched room, exposed to all the winds of heaven, draughty, cold, and with a smoky chimney.

" I am never so well off as when I am badly off," he remarked, with his usual dry humour. "Que jamais il n'était mieux que quand il n'était guère bien. Besides," he continued, " I shall be at the beck and call of my dear daughters of the Visitation, and so shall be of more use to them; and I shall be able to receive quietly any poor sinners who may wish to see me."

His friends entreated him to allow them to put
a carriage at his disposal—his legs and feet were
in a dreadful state, so swollen and inflamed that
walking was a torture to him—but he refused.
"What a nice thing it would be for me to go
round preaching evangelical poverty, and the
necessity for penance and mortification, in a
carriage and pair! A nice example I should
give!"

Some people remarked that the Bishop of
Geneva encouraged women to seek his spiritual
advice and to come to him too often.

Francis replied to this that many women followed Christ, and that many murmured at it.

"At any rate," said one of his friends to him,
"I really can't see what amusement they find in
coming to you, for I notice that you say very
little to them."

"And do you think it nothing to let them talk?
They prefer a good listener to a good talker.
They talk enough for themselves and for me;
probably that is why they like coming to me, for
there is nothing a talkative person likes so much
as a patient and attentive listener."

His friend then said that he had often watched
his confessional, and had noticed that there were
far more women than men besieging it.

"Surely that does not surprise you," said the
Bishop, with his humorous smile and a merry
twinkle in the kindly blue eyes. "Does not the
Church particularly mention the devout female

sex, and are not women as a rule far more pious than men? Would to God that men, who are far greater sinners and commit more mortal offences, were as prone to penance!"

"Then," asked his friend, encouraged by the Saint's urbanity, "are more women saved than men?"

"Seriously speaking," said Francis, with grave serenity, "it is not for us to pry into the secrets of the Lord, or to be His counsellors."

M. Jacques Olier frequently visited the gardener's humble abode, bringing with him his little son, Jean Jacques, a most troublesome boy, self-willed and unmanageable. His father was much distressed about him, but Francis de Sales, placing his hand on the lad's head, blessed him, and said: "Fear nothing; your young son will one day be a great Saint. God has chosen him to be an honour and a glory to His Church, and to save and perfect many souls."

In after years this unruly boy, Jean Jacques Olier, founded the Order of St. Sulpice, and was indeed a burning and a shining light, and of the noblest and most saintly men of his century.

Francis de Sales had founded thirteen monasteries of the Visitation — namely, at Annecy, Lyons, Moulins, Grenoble, Bourges, Paris, Montferrand, Nevers, Orleans, Valence, Dijon, St. Étienne-en-Forez, and Belley. He had done all that man could do for them; it now only remained for him to wish them an eternal farewell, and to give them parting words of assistance and counsel. He devoted all his spare time to them.

"My Father," a Sister said to him one day, "here are ink and paper; please write down the virtues you most wish us to practise."

Francis took the pen, and wrote one word, "Humility."

Mother de Chantal had not seen Francis de Sales for three and a half years. She longed for an interview with him, and hastened to Lyons. As soon as he entered the parlour of the convent she was immediately struck by his altered appearance. His face was transfigured; the brightness of the love of God shone on his countenance, giving it an unearthly radiance; the burning fire that consumed his soul shone in his deep eyes, and he looked more like a seraph than a man; it was as though Our Lord had imprinted on his brow the rays of the beatitude that awaited him. It seemed that after years of labour he had attained the plenitude of perfect manhood and that maturity of the soul in Christ that God grants only to a favoured few.

"Mother, which of us two shall speak first?" Francis de Sales asked Jeanne de Chantal.

"I, my Father," she answered, with her usual impetuosity; "I have much to tell you of the state of my soul."

"Ah, my dear daughter, you are as eager as ever. When will you become absolutely indifferent ? I had hoped to find you quite seraphic. We will speak of your soul at Annecy, but now we must discuss the affairs of our Congregation. Oh, how I love our little Institute, for the dear God loves it."

For several hours they discussed various points concerning the solid establishment of the Order. Francis de Sales particularly desired each convent to be free and independent of the others, under the government of the Bishop of the Diocese and the Holy See. He said that the more he prayed and asked for guidance the more convinced he felt that such was the will of God, and that such an arrangement would be productive of greater fervour, and would in no way diminish unity and stability.

" Remember," he told Mother de Chantal, " that our daughters are the daughters of the clergy, and the clergy form the first Order in Religion."

When saying good-bye, Mme. de Chantal exclaimed fervently :

" My Father, I am certain that you will be canonized one day, and I hope to take part in your canonization."

" God could work that miracle, my Mother," Francis replied very gravely, " but they who are to negotiate my canonization are not yet born."

These were their last words. They never met again in this life; but when a short time later the remains of the saintly Bishop were laid in the convent chapel at Annecy, Jeanne de Chantal knelt before the coffin, and remembering that he had said at their last interview that he would listen at Annecy to her account of her own soul, she poured out her heart to her beloved Father. Surely he heard and counselled her, for when she returned to the community her face was as that of an Angel, and the Sisters knew that she had received sublime communications and heavenly consolations from a Saint in Heaven—their own dear dead Father.

# CHAPTER XXXII

## "*THE DAY IS NOW FAR SPENT*"

At Christmas, 1622, Francis de Sales offered up the Holy Sacrifice at midnight in the Church of the Visitation. He appeared to the Sisters like an angel from Paradise, his face radiant, transfigured by the glory of the Beatific Vision. Mother de Blonay states that it seemed to her she saw the Archangel Gabriel at his side when he intoned the *Gloria in Excelsis.*

"My lord," she asked him, when speaking to him at the grate of the sacristy, " is it true that the Angel Gabriel was beside you during the *Gloria,* or did I dream I saw him ?"

"My daughter," replied Francis humbly, " my heart is so very dull to God's inspirations that He has to send His angels to speak to my corporal ears and wake my soul with their melody."

But Mother de Blonay was not satisfied with this answer. She persisted in questioning him, and Francis acknowledged :

"It is true that I was never more consoled at the altar. The Divine Infant was there, visibly and invisibly. Why should they not be there ?

But I will tell you no more; there are too many listening to us."

In a letter to Mother de Chantal, Francis expresses clearly the beautiful thoughts that filled his soul on Christmas night.

" Ah! how sweet is this night, my dearest daughter! 'The heavens,' sings the Church, 'rain down honey over all the world.' And, for my part, I think those holy angels who thrill the air with their glorious music have come to gather this honey from the lily as it lies on the breast of our dear Lady, and of St. Joseph. But am I not ambitious to think that our dear angels, yours and mine, were amongst the glorious band of heavenly musicians who sang that night? Ah, if they would once more intone in the ears of my heart that heavenly song! What joy! what happiness! I beg them to do so, that there may be 'glory to God on high and on earth peace to men of goodwill.'

" Returning from the Sacred Mysteries, I say good-morning to my dear daughter, for I think that even the shepherds, having adored the Blessed Babe, whom Heaven itself had announced to them, rested a little. But what sweetness they must have felt in their sleep! They must have heard in their dreams the sacred melody of the angels who had saluted them so joyously in their canticle. They must have seen the dear Infant and the Mother whom they had visited.

"What shall we give to our little King that we have not received from Him and from His Divine liberality? Well, I will give Him at High Mass the beloved daughter He has given me. O Saviour of our souls, make her to be all gold in charity, all myrrh in mortification, all incense in prayer, and then receive her within the arms of Your holy protection, and let Your Heart say to hers, ' I am thy salvation for ever and ever.'

"Your very affectionate Father and servant,

"FRANCIS."

As Chief Almoner to the Princess Christine, the Bishop of Geneva had to go to the Church of the Dominicans to hear her confession and that of her husband, offer up the Holy Sacrifice for them at break of day—the " Aurora " Mass, and give them Holy Communion. He then returned to the Visitation, intending to say there his third Mass, but when he reached the sacristy he found their chaplain already vested. This good priest at once offered to allow the Bishop of Geneva to officiate first, but Francis refused, remarking graciously that he was only too pleased to have a little time to spend quietly in prayer and meditation. He assisted at the chaplain's three Masses, hidden in a dark corner of the chapel, and only said his own last Mass towards midday. He partook of a very light repast; and then gave the habit of the Visitation to two novices, and preached on the Epistle of the day.

" Instructing us that, denying ungodliness and worldly desires, we should live soberly and justly and godly in this world, looking for the blessed hope and coming of the glory of the great God and of our Saviour, Jesus Christ."

Having rested for a short time, he then conversed with his blessed daughters on the Love of God, gave audiences to several people, paid a farewell visit to Marie de Medici, and was not able to leave the Court until late at night.

On the Feast of St. Stephen he said Holy Mass, and gave Holy Communion to the Nuns of the Visitation. He dined with one of his greatest friends, the Vicar-General of the diocese, talked over several important matters with him, and at five o'clock went to the Visitation to say good-bye to his dear daughters. He said to them :

" My children, we shall never meet again here below. Remember, my last words to you are : Ask for nothing, refuse nothing, desire nothing but to do the Divine will. What happiness to resign ourselves absolutely to Our Lord, submitting our will to His, adoring Him in tribulation and in consolation, in sorrow and in joy, doing whatever He wills like little children ! Let Him carry you on His right arm or His left—an infant does not mind which. Let Him lay you down or lift you up, for, like a good nurse, He knows best what we need. Therefore, my children, desire nothing, refuse nothing ; enough is said in those words."

"But, my Father," asked one of the nuns, "ought one to warm one self if one feels cold?"

The Bishop smiled indulgently.

"When the fire is lit," he replied, "it is evident that it is intended that we should warm ourselves; but let us do so moderately, and without hurry or eagerness. Good-bye, my children; adieu until eternity." His attendants arrived with torches to light him back to his lodgings. "I must go, my children," he said. "I would willingly spend the night here conversing with you. I had no idea it was so late. Obedience calls me, and I must go."

"Before you leave us, my Father, tell us what you wish us to have most deeply engraven in our souls."

"Have I not already told you?" he said. "Ask for nothing, refuse nothing, imitate Jesus in His cradle. He accepts poverty, nakedness, the companionship of beasts, cold, the inclemency of the season, everything His Father ordains, without a murmur. He accepts the services of His Mother and of St. Joseph, the adoration of the kings and the shepherds, all in the same spirit of indifference. Imitate Him."

Francis de Sales returned to the Visitation the following morning, offered up the Divine Sacrifice, and gave Holy Communion to the Sisters. He then heard Mother de Blonay's confession.

"My Father," she asked, "are you ill? You do not look well."

"My daughter," replied the Bishop, "all turns

to good to those who love God. Adieu! I leave
you my spirit and my heart."

Outside the church he conversed for some time
with the Duc de Bellegarde and M. de Villeroy.
He stood bareheaded. A sharp wind was blowing, and it was cold and foggy. He felt chilled,
but went on to pay his respects to the Duc de
Nemours. On leaving him, he went on to visit
the Prince de Piedmont. When at last he got
home, he was quite exhausted, and fell almost
fainting into a chair. His attendants brought
him food and drink. He barely touched them,
but, as soon as he was a little rested, he wrote
two letters, and then interviewed several priests
and noblemen. He was so ill and weak that he
was unable to accompany them to the door, as
was his custom. Rolland remarked this, and
asked him if he were very ill. He smiled.

" You think I am," he answered.

Rolland told him of a sermon he had just
heard, in which the preacher exhorted the Queen
to love her servants.

" And you, Rolland," asked Francis in an
exhausted voice, " do you love me well?"

The devoted servant replied by bursting into
tears.

" Ah! it is well," said Francis. " I love you
also, my good Rolland; but let us love God best
of all, for He is our Divine Master."

As he pronounced the last words he fainted.
The servants immediately opened wide the

windows, got him to bed, and sent for the doctors. He had a slight stroke of apoplexy, to cure which, according to the science of the day, the physicians had recourse to the most cruel means to rouse him from the stupor into which he was falling. He endured a veritable martyrdom. But, although he felt all the pain of the red-hot irons applied to his head and to the back of his neck, though the frightful torture caused his tears to flow abundantly, yet he never made a complaint. Constant to his invariable rule of never asking for anything, never refusing anything, he let them do as they would with him and never rebelled against their terrible remedies.

The Bishop of Belley, in his "Esprit de St. François de Sales," gives us a realistic picture of Francis when stretched on a bed of pain : " He suffered sickness with a patience accompanied with so much love and sweetness that the slightest complaint never escaped his lips, nor the smallest desire that was not conformable to the Divine will. He never expressed the least regret for the services he might have rendered to God and his neighbour had he been in health. He was willing to suffer because such was God's will. ' He knows better than I do what is good for me,' he would say. ' Let us not interfere with Him. He is the Lord, let Him do what seems good in His eyes. O Lord, Thy will be done, not mine. Even so, heavenly Father, it is my will, since it is Thine. Yes, Lord, I will it. May Thy adorable will and Thy just law be engraven in my heart.' When asked if he would take some medicine or some soup, or whether he would be bled, he would reply : ' Do what you will with this poor sick man. God has placed me in the hands of the physicians.' When suffering the most acute pain, one could read in his eyes the serenity of his soul."

Francis remained quite conscious, though at times the stupor increased. To rouse him they then applied a hot iron to the nape of his neck and to his head, so that it burned the bone. In the midst of this unspeakable agony he intoned the *Te Deum*, Canticles, and the Psalms.

" My meat is to do the will of my Father Who is in Heaven. My soul hath thirsted for the strong, the living God. Show me, O Thou Whom my soul loveth, where Thou feedest, where Thou liest in the midday."

When he appeared about to faint, they effectually roused him by asking :

"Are you sure you are not a Calvinist in your secret heart ?"

"God forbid !" cried Francis, quite recovering consciousness, and coming back almost from the threshold of eternity to refute so horrible an idea. "I was never a heretic; it would be too great a treason." He made a large sign of the Cross, and said in a clear, ringing voice: " I have lived, and I desire to die, in the faith of the Holy

Roman Catholic and Apostolic Church, the only true religion."

He asked them to give him his rosary beads, with the blessed medals attached to it that he had got at Rome and Loreto. The Rector of the Jesuits placed it on his arm, and, according to his request, suggested to him constantly acts of faith, hope, and charity.

Père Forrier, S.J., his old director, arrived, and, coming over to Francis, asked him if he remembered him. The dying man looked with affection and gratitude at his old friend, and said:

"If I forget thee, may my right hand be forgotten."

"Will you not pray Our Lord to leave you with us a little longer?" Père Forrier, S.J., asked him. "Say with St. Martin, 'Lord, if I am still necessary to Thy people, I refuse not the labour.'"

Francis sighed, crying: "I necessary? Ah no! No, I am an absolutely useless servant—servus inutilis, inutilis, inutilis," he repeated thrice, very sadly.

Noticing that a Jesuit Brother was particularly attentive to him, he asked him what he could do in return.

"Monseigneur," replied the good Brother, "remember me in the Kingdom of God."

Francis promised to do so, and then, turning to his domestics, who were weeping bitterly:

"Do not cry, my children," he said kindly. "Must not the will of God be accomplished?"

The frightful remedies tried by the doctors only helped to accelerate his death. A nun in attendance, trying to comfort him, told him his brother, the Bishop of Chalcedon, had arrived.

" My sister," said Francis gravely, " you should never tell lies."

They asked him if he was not sorry to part with his Daughters of the Visitation. He replied serenely : " He Who hath begun the work will perfect it." This he repeated thrice.

In the course of the day he confessed, and asked to receive Extreme Unction. At one o'clock in the morning they administered the Last Sacraments, but, as he was constantly vomiting, he could not receive the Holy Viaticum. He continued to recite verses from the Psalms.

" My soul hath thirsted after the strong, living God ; when shall I come and appear before the face of God ?

" Hope in God, for I will yet praise Him, who is the salvation of my countenance and my God.

" In the day of my trouble I sought God with my hands *lifted up* unto Him in the night, and I was not deceived.

" The mercies of the Lord I will sing for evermore, my heart and my flesh have rejoiced in the living God.

" O Lord, the God of my salvation, I have cried in the day and the night before Thee ; let my prayer have entrance into Thy sight, incline Thine ear to my petition."

He grew gradually weaker. They could scarcely rouse him now. Even the burning iron failed. Then one of the priests asked him if he feared to be vanquished in the last combat. He opened his eyes and smiled, and said slowly, and with infinite tenderness:

"Mine eyes are ever towards the Lord, for He shall pluck my feet out from the snare.

"Bring forth the spear and stop the way against them that persecute me. Say unto my soul, I am thy salvation."

And he again repeated: "He who has begun the work will perfect it."

Turning to one of his friends, he pressed his hand, saying: "Advesperavit et inclinata est jam dies" (It is towards evening, and the day is now far spent).

Having pronounced the holy name of Jesus, he became speechless. That was his last word on earth—Jesus.

For a few minutes longer the soul lingered in its earthly tenement. The kneeling assistants recited the prayers for the dying. When they came to the invocation, "All ye Holy Innocents pray for him," they repeated it thrice, for it was the Feast of the Holy Innocents. At the third repetition, Francis de Sales, Prince-Bishop of Geneva, passed away from earth in the seraphic beauty of holiness, washed in the Precious Blood of Jesus, and radiant with the reflection of His glory.

# CHAPTER XXXIII

## *THE STONE ROLLED BACK*

THE soul of Francis de Sales had left the prison of his body and flown to its heavenly home—to the feet of his Beloved, who would " give unto him beauty for ashes, the oil of joy for mourning, the garment of praise for the spirit of heaviness." No longer would his ardent spirit groan over the heaviness and the weariness that kept him chained to earth. Now his beautiful soul was free, enjoying the Beatific Vision—" eye hath not seen, nor ear heard, neither hath it entered into the heart of man, what things God hath prepared for them that love Him." The worn-out corpse lay calm and peaceful, with no sign of struggle on the beautiful dead face; he looked, indeed, as if he had entered into his rest, as if he quietly slept.

" Dear beauteous death, the jewel of the just.
    And yet, as angels in some brighter dreams
    Call to the soul when man doth sleep,
    As some strange thoughts transcend our wonted themes,
    And into glory peep."

Francis de Sales died on December 28, 1622, in the fifty-sixth year of his age and the twentieth of his episcopate. Yet, though not an old man, he was quite worn out from suffering and privations. When his body was examined, it was found that his heart was sound ; but his liver was burnt up, one lung was wounded by a sword, part of the brain was suffused with blood, and instead of the gall, were three hundred little hard balls like the beads of a rosary. This phenomenon, the doctors explained, was caused by the extreme efforts he had made during his life to restrain his natural propensity to anger.

Yet Francis was, of all God's saints, the gentlest —the gentle saint. Of him it might truly be said, as of Our Blessed Lord : "A bruised reed he shall not break, and the smoking flax he shall not quench." All through his life he preached meekness, humility, and gentleness, and he undoubtedly practised what he preached. "The Spirit of the Visitation is to be one of humble love of God, and extreme sweetness towards our neighbour." Devoted self-sacrifice and loving sweetness were his own most remarkable characteristics ; but it is not for me even to endeavour to describe the glorious virtues and splendid character of this noblest of saints.

Some people have slightingly called Francis de Sales the Apostle of "the upper classes." Certainly the Bishop of Geneva considered that they have souls to save as well as the lowly. He was as courteous to a queen as to a washerwoman, and he treated kings and princes with as much deference as though they were artisans and labourers. He was kind, polite, courteous to everyone ; he was a perfect gentleman, a true nobleman, a holy priest, an heroic saint—

> " A man with heart, head, hand,
>     Like some of the simple great ones gone
>     For ever and ever by.
> One still, strong man in a blatant land,
>     Whatever they call him, what care I,
>     Aristocrat, democrat, autocrat—one
> Who can rule and who dare not lie."

Others have accused Francis of a too great supineness, of a sweetness so sweet that it cloyed; have reproached him with so easily giving up the original plan for the formation of the Order of the Visitation, ascribing his great renunciation to instability, and his unreserved submission to the judgment of others to weakness of will.

" The stronger will always rule, say some, with an air of confidence that is like a lawyer's flourish, forbidding exceptions or additions. But what is strength ? Is it blind wilfulness that sees no terrors, no many-linked consequences, no bruises and wounds of those whose bonds it tightens ? Is it the narrowness of a brain that sees no end differing from its own, and looks to no results beyond the bargains of to-day, that tugs with emphasis for every small purpose, and thinks it weakness to exercise the sublime power of resolved renunciation ? There is a sort of subjection that is the peculiar heritage of largeness and of love, and strength is often only another name for willing bondage to irremediable weakness."

The body of Francis de Sales was removed to Annecy, and given up to his Daughters of the Visitation, who placed it in their church. There it was preserved until the French Revolution, when it was hidden away to save it from desecration.

Peace once more being restored, the present Church and Monastery of the Visitation were built, mainly through the assistance given by Charles Félix, and his Queen, Marie Christine. It was consecrated in 1826, and then the remains of St. Francis de Sales and of St. Jeanne Françoise de Chantal were deposited there. It is a handsome church in the Italian style, small, but perfect in every detail.

In 1626 a Commission was appointed, which took the evidence of 5,000 witnesses to the heroic virtues of St. Francis de Sales and the miracles wrought by him. Even the Calvinist minister of Geneva said of him: "If we honoured any man as a saint, I know none more worthy than this man since the days of the Apostles." His cause was immediately introduced at Rome, but various obstacles arose, and it was not until 1661 that he was beatified by Alexander VII. He was canonized by the same Pope in 1665. In 1877 Pius IX. declared him a Doctor of the Church. His special title is that of Doctor of Devotion.

*If you have enjoyed this book, consider making your next selection from among the following . . .*

Prices subject to change.

The Catholic Controversy. *St. Francis de Sales.* . . . . . . . . . . . . 16.50
Introduction to the Devout Life. Unabr. *St. Francis de Sales.* . . 12.50
Introduction to the Devout Life. Abr. *St. Francis de Sales.* . . . . 13.00
Treatise/Love of God. *St. Francis de Sales. Trans., Mackey* . . . . 27.50
Sermons for Advent and Christmas. *St. Francis de Sales.* . . . . . 12.00
Sermons on Prayer. *St. Francis de Sales* . . . . . . . . . . . . . . . . . 7.00
Sermons on Our Lady. *St. Francis de Sales.* . . . . . . . . . . . . . . 15.00
Sermons for Lent. *St. Francis de Sales* . . . . . . . . . . . . . . . . . . 15.00
Catechism of the Council of Trent. *McHugh/Callan* . . . . . . . . 27.50
Spiritual Combat. *Scupoli.* . . . . . . . . . . . . . . . . . . . . . . . . . . . 12.00
Holy Eucharist—Our All. *Fr. Lukas Etlin, O.S.B.* . . . . . . . . . . 3.00
Glories of Divine Grace. *Fr. Scheeben* . . . . . . . . . . . . . . . . . . 18.00
Saint Michael and the Angels. *Approved Sources* . . . . . . . . . . 9.00
Dolorous Passion of Our Lord. *Anne C. Emmerich* . . . . . . . . . 18.00
Our Lady of Fatima's Peace Plan from Heaven. *Booklet* . . . . . . 1.00
Three Ages/Interior Life. 2 Vols. *Garrigou-Lagrange* . . . . . . . . 48.00
St. Catherine Labouré of the Mirac. Medal. *Fr. Dirvin* . . . . . . . 16.50
Manual of Practical Devotion to St. Joseph. *Patrignani.* . . . . . . 17.50
Ven. Jacinta Marto of Fatima. *Cirrincione* . . . . . . . . . . . . . . . . 3.00
Reign of Christ the King. *Davies* . . . . . . . . . . . . . . . . . . . . . . 2.00
St. Teresa of Avila. *William Thomas Walsh* . . . . . . . . . . . . . . . 24.00
Isabella of Spain—The Last Crusader. *Wm. T. Walsh* . . . . . . . . 24.00
Characters of the Inquisition. *Wm. T. Walsh* . . . . . . . . . . . . . . 16.50
Blood-Drenched Altars—Cath. Comment. Hist. Mexico . . . . . . 21.50
Self-Abandonment to Divine Providence. *de Caussade.* . . . . . . 22.50
Way of the Cross. *Liguorian.* . . . . . . . . . . . . . . . . . . . . . . . . . 1.50
Way of the Cross. *Franciscan.* . . . . . . . . . . . . . . . . . . . . . . . . . 1.50
Modern Saints—Their Lives & Faces, Bk. 1. *Ann Ball* . . . . . . . 21.00
Modern Saints—Their Lives & Faces, Bk. 2. *Ann Ball* . . . . . . . 23.00
Divine Favors Granted to St. Joseph. *Pere Binet* . . . . . . . . . . . 7.50
St. Joseph Cafasso—Priest of the Gallows. *St. J. Bosco* . . . . . . 6.00
Why Squander Illness? *Frs. Rumble & Carty* . . . . . . . . . . . . . . 4.00
Fatima—The Great Sign. *Francis Johnston.* . . . . . . . . . . . . . . . 12.00
Heliotropium—Conformity of Human Will to Divine . . . . . . . . 15.00
Charity for the Suffering Souls. *Fr. John Nageleisen.* . . . . . . . . 18.00
Devotion to the Sacred Heart of Jesus. *Verheylezoon* . . . . . . . . 16.50
Fundamentals of Catholic Dogma. *Ott* . . . . . . . . . . . . . . . . . . . 27.50
St. Anthony—The Wonder Worker of Padua. *Stoddard* . . . . . . . 7.00
The Precious Blood. *Fr. Faber* . . . . . . . . . . . . . . . . . . . . . . . . . 16.50
Clean Love in Courtship. *Fr. Lawrence Lovasik* . . . . . . . . . . . . 4.50
The Secret of the Rosary. *St. Louis De Montfort* . . . . . . . . . . . . 5.00

*At your Bookdealer or direct from the Publisher.*
*Toll-Free 1-800-437-5876*            *Fax 815-226-7770*

Prices subject to change.